Learning C# by Develo Games with Unity 2019
Fourth Edition

Code in C# and build 3D games with Unity

Harrison Ferrone

BIRMINGHAM - MUMBAI

Learning C# by Developing Games with Unity 2019
Fourth Edition

Acquisition Editor: Karan Gupta
Content Development Editor: Pranay Fereira
Technical Editor: Ralph Rosario
Copy Editor: Safis Editing
Project Coordinator: Pragati Shukla
Proofreader: Safis Editing
Indexer: Tejal Daruwale Soni
Graphics: Alishon Mendonsa
Production Coordinator: Nilesh Mohite

First published: September 2013
Second edition: March 2016
Third edition: December 2017
Fourth edition: March 2019

Production reference: 1290319

Published by Packt Publishing Ltd.
Livery Place
35 Livery Street
Birmingham
B3 2PB, UK.

ISBN 978-1-78953-205-0

www.packtpub.com

To Kelsey, my partner in crime and loving companion on this journey. To Wilbur, Merlin, Walter, and Evey for their courageous spirits and gracious hearts.

– Harrison Ferrone

`mapt.io`

Mapt is an online digital library that gives you full access to over 5,000 books and videos, as well as industry leading tools to help you plan your personal development and advance your career. For more information, please visit our website.

Why subscribe?

- Spend less time learning and more time coding with practical eBooks and Videos from over 4,000 industry professionals

- Improve your learning with Skill Plans built especially for you

- Get a free eBook or video every month

- Mapt is fully searchable

- Copy and paste, print, and bookmark content

Packt.com

Did you know that Packt offers eBook versions of every book published, with PDF and ePub files available? You can upgrade to the eBook version at `www.packt.com` and as a print book customer, you are entitled to a discount on the eBook copy. Get in touch with us at `customercare@packtpub.com` for more details.

At `www.packt.com`, you can also read a collection of free technical articles, sign up for a range of free newsletters, and receive exclusive discounts and offers on Packt books and eBooks.

Contributors

About the author

Harrison Ferrone was born in Chicago, IL, and raised all over. Most days, you can find him creating instructional content for LinkedIn Learning and Pluralsight, or tech editing for the Ray Wenderlich website.

He holds various fancy looking pieces of paper from the University of Colorado at Boulder and Columbia College Chicago. Despite being a proud alumnus, most of these are stored in a basement somewhere.

After a few years as an iOS developer at small start-ups, and one Fortune 500 company, he fell into a teaching career and never looked back. Throughout all this, he's bought many books, acquired a few cats, worked abroad, and continually wondered why Neuromancer isn't on more course syllabi.

Completing this book wouldn't have been possible without the support of my partner Kelsey, my sounding board, Basel Farag, and my family.

About the reviewer

Dr. Davide Aversa holds a Ph.D. in Artificial Intelligence and an M.Sc. in Artificial Intelligence and Robotics from the University of Rome "La Sapienza" in Italy. He has a strong interest in Artificial Intelligence for the development of Interactive Virtual Agents and Procedural Content Generation (PCG). He serves at the PC of videogame-related conferences such as the IEEE Conference on Computational Intelligence and Games (CIG) and he also is regularly participating in game-jam contests. He also writes a blog on Game Design and game development.

Luiz Henrique Bueno is a Certified ScrumMaster (CSM) and Unity Certified Developer with over 29 years of experience in software development.

In 2002, he wrote the book *Web Applications with Visual Studio.NET, ASP.NET, and C#*, at the time of the launch of Visual Studio.NET.

He's worked as a Chief Editor at *Casa Conectada*, a magazine about smart homes. For six years, he's developed projects using Crestron and Control4.

In 2017, he worked as a reviewer on the book *Unity 2017 Game Optimization, Second Edition*, published by Packt.

Since 2010, he's been developing apps and games, including VR/AR and voice applications, using Unity, C#, Xcode, Obj-C, Swift, AWS, Node.js, and Alexa Skills.

His motto is "Do not write code for QA, write code for production." You can reach him on Twitter at @hackingwithrick.

Packt is searching for authors like you

If you're interested in becoming an author for Packt, please visit authors.packtpub.com and apply today. We have worked with thousands of developers and tech professionals, just like you, to help them share their insight with the global tech community. You can make a general application, apply for a specific hot topic that we are recruiting an author for, or submit your own idea.

Table of Contents

Preface	1

Section 1: Programming Foundations and C#

Chapter 1: Getting to Know your Environment	11
Some basic prerequisites	12
Starting out with Unity 2019	12
Creating a new project	14
Navigating the editor	14
Using C# with Unity	16
Working with C# scripts	16
Time for action – creating a C# script	17
Introducing the Visual Studio editor	17
Time for action – opening a C# file	18
Beware of naming mismatches	18
Syncing C# files	19
Fixing a broken sync	19
Documentation	19
Accessing Unity's documentation	19
Time for action – opening the Reference Manual	20
Time for action – using the Scripting Reference	21
Locating C# resources	21
Time for action – looking up a C# class	22
Pop quiz – dealing with scripts	23
Summary	23
Chapter 2: The Building Blocks of Programming	25
Defining variables	26
Names are important	27
Variables act as placeholders	27
Time for action – creating a variable	28
Time for action – changing a variable's value	30
A method to the madness	30
Methods drive actions	31
Methods are placeholders too	31
Time for action – a simple method	32
Introducing classes	33
A class all along	33
Everyday blueprints	34
Commenting is key	35
Practical backslashes	35

Time for action – adding comments	36
Putting it together in Unity	36
Scripts become components	36
Variables and the Inspector panel	37
A helping hand from MonoBehavior	38
Hero's trial – MonoBehavior in the Scripting API	39
Class and component communication	39
Enter dot notation	39
Pop quiz – C# building blocks	40
Summary	40
Chapter 3: Diving into Variables, Types, and Methods	41
Writing proper C#	42
Simple debugging	43
Variable syntax	43
Type and value declarations	44
Type-only declarations	44
Access modifiers	45
Choosing a security level	45
Time for action – making a variable private	46
Working with types	46
Common built-in types	47
Time for action – playing with different types	48
Time for action – creating interpolated strings	48
Type conversions	49
Inferred declarations	50
Custom types	50
Types roundup	51
Naming variables	51
Best practices	51
Variable scope	52
Introducing operators	54
Arithmetic and assignments	54
Time for action – executing incorrect type operations	55
Pop quiz #1 – variables and types	56
Defining methods	56
Basic syntax	56
Modifiers and parameters	57
Time for action – defining a simple method	58
Naming conventions	59
Methods are logic detours	59
Specifying parameters	60
Assigning arguments	61
Time for action – adding method parameters	61
Specifying return values	62
Time for action – adding a return type	63

Using return values   63
    Time for action – capturing return values   64
      Hero's trial – methods as arguments   65

Common Unity methods   65
The Start method   65
The Update method   66

Pop quiz #2 – Understanding methods   66
Summary   67

Chapter 4: Control Flow and Collection Types   69
Selection statements   70
The if-else statement   70
    Basic Syntax   70
      Time for action – thieving prospects   72
    Using the NOT operator   73
    Nesting statements   74
    Evaluating multiple conditions   75
      Time for action – reaching the treasure   76
The switch statement   77
    Basic syntax   77
    Pattern matching   78
      Time for action – choosing an action   78
    Fall-through cases   79
      Time for action – rolling the dice   80
Pop quiz #1 – If, and, or but   81

Collections at a glance   81
Arrays   81
    Basic syntax   82
    Indexing and subscripts   83
    Range exceptions   83
Lists   84
    Basic syntax   84
      Time for action – party members   85
    Common methods   85
Dictionaries   86
    Basic syntax   87
      Time for action – setting up an inventory   87
    Working with dictionary Pairs   88
Pop quiz #2 – all about collections   89

Iteration statements   90
For loops   90
    Time for action – finding an element   92
Foreach loops   93
    Looping through key-value pairs   94
      Hero's trial – finding affordable items   95
While loops   95
    Time for action – tracking player lives   96
To infinity and beyond   97

Summary   97

Chapter 5: Working with Classes, Structs, and OOP   99
  Defining a class   100
    Basic syntax   100
      Time for action – creating a character class   100
    Instantiating class objects   101
      Time for action – creating a new character   101
    Adding class fields   102
      Time for action – fleshing out character details 102
    Using constructors   103
      Time for action – specifying starting properties 104
    Declaring class methods   105
      Time for action – printing out character data   105
  What's a struct?   107
    Basic syntax   107
      Time for action – creating a weapon struct   107
  Classes vs structs   108
    Reference types   109
      Time for action – creating a new hero   109
    Value types   110
      Time for action – copying weapons   110
  The Object-Oriented mindset   111
    Encapsulation   112
      Time for action – adding a reset   112
    Inheritance   113
      Base constructors   114
        Time for action – calling a base constructor   114
    Composition   115
    Polymorphism   116
      Time for action – functional variations   116
    OOP roundup   117
  Applying OOP in Unity   118
    Objects are a class act   118
    Accessing components   119
      Basic syntax   120
        Time for action – accessing the current transform component   120
      Finding GameObjects   121
        Time for action - finding components on different objects   122
      Drag and drop   123
        Time for action – assigning variables in Unity   123
  Pop quiz: all things OOP   124
  Summary   124

Section 2: Scripting Game Mechanics in Unity

Chapter 6: Getting Your Hands Dirty with Unity   127
  A game design primer   128

Game design documents   128
The Hero Born one-page   129
Building a level   130
Creating primitives   130
   Time for action – creating a ground plane   131
Thinking in 3D   131
Materials   133
   Time for action – changing the ground color   134
White-boxing   135
  Editor tools   136
    Hero's Trial – putting up drywall   138
  Keeping the Hierarchy clean   138
    Time for action – using empty objects   138
  Working with prefabs   139
    Time for action – creating a turret   140
    Time for action – updating the prefab   141
    Time for action – finishing the level   142
    Hero's trial – creating a health pickup   142
Lighting basics   143
Creating lights   144
Light component properties   144
Animating in Unity   145
Creating clips   146
   Time for action – creating a new clip   146
Recording keyframes   147
   Time for action – spinning animation   148
Curves and tangents   150
   Time for action – smoothing the spin   151
The particle system   152
   Time for action – adding sparkle effects   152
Pop quiz – basic Unity features   153
Summary   154
Chapter 7: Movement, Camera Controls, and Collisions   155
Moving the player   156
Player setup   156
   Time for action – creating the player capsule   157
Understanding vectors   158
Getting player input   159
   Time for action – player locomotion   161
Camera follow   163
Time for action – Scripting camera behavior   163
Working with Unity physics   166
Rigidbodies in motion   168
   Time for action – accessing the Rigidbody   169
   Time for action – moving the Rigidbody   170
Colliders and collisions   172

Time for action – picking up an item | 173
Using Collider triggers | 176
Time for action – creating an enemy | 176
Time for action – capturing trigger events | 177
Hero's trial – all the prefabs! | 179
Physics roundup | 180
Pop quiz – player controls and physics | 180
Summary | 181

Chapter 8: Scripting Game Mechanics | 183
Adding jumps | 184
Enter enumerations | 184
Underlying types | 185
Time for action – pressing the spacebar to jump! | 186
Working with layer masks | 188
Time for action – setting object layers | 188
Time for action – one jump at a time | 190
Shooting projectiles | 193
Instantiating objects | 193
Time for action – creating a projectile prefab | 193
Time for action – adding the shooting mechanic | 194
Managing GameObject buildup | 197
Time for action – destroying bullets | 197
The game manager | 198
Tracking player properties | 199
Time for action – creating a game manager | 199
The Get and Set properties | 200
Time for action – adding backing variables | 202
Time for action – updating item collection | 203
Player Polish | 205
Graphical User Interfaces | 205
Time for action – adding UI elements | 206
Win and Loss Conditions | 209
Time for action – winning the game | 210
Using directives and namespaces | 212
Time for action – pausing and restarting | 212
Pop quiz – working with mechanics | 214
Summary | 214

Chapter 9: Basic AI and Enemy Behavior | 217
Navigating in Unity | 218
Navigation components | 218
Time for action – setting up the NavMesh | 219
Time for action – setting up enemy agents | 220
Moving enemy agents | 222
Procedural programming | 222
Time for action – referencing the patrol locations | 222
Time for action – moving the enemy | 225

Time for action – patrolling continuously between locations | 227
Enemy game mechanics | 229
Seek and destroy | 230
Time for action – changing the agent's destination | 230
Time for action – lowering player health | 231
Time for action – detecting bullet collisions | 233
Time for action – updating the game manager | 235
Refactoring and keeping it DRY | 237
Time for action – creating a restart method | 237
Hero's trial – refactoring win/lose logic | 239
Pop quiz – AI and navigation | 239
Summary | 239

Section 3: Leveling Up Your C# Code

Chapter 10: Revisiting Types, Methods, and Classes | 243
Access Modifier redux | 244
Constant and read-only properties | 244
Using the static keyword | 244
Time for action – creating a static class | 245
Methods Redux | 247
Overloading methods | 247
Time for action – overloading the level restart | 248
Ref parameters | 249
Time for action – tracking player restarts | 250
Out parameters | 251
OOP redux | 252
Interfaces | 252
Time for action – creating a manager interface | 253
Time for action – adopting an interface | 254
Abstract classes | 255
Class extensions | 257
Time for action – extending the string class | 258
Time for action – using an extension method | 259
Namespace Redux | 260
Type aliasing | 261
Pop quiz – leveling up | 261
Summary | 262

Chapter 11: Exploring Generics, Delegates, and Beyond | 263
Introducing generics | 264
Generic objects | 264
Time for action – creating a generic collection | 265
Generic methods | 266
Time for action – adding a generic item | 267
Constraining type parameters | 269
Time for action – limiting generic elements | 269

Delegating actions   270
   Basic syntax   270
     Time for action – creating a debug delegate   271
   Delegates as parameter types   272
     Time for action – using a delegate argument   273
Firing events   274
   Basic syntax   275
     Time for action – creating an event   275
   Handling event subscriptions   276
     Time for action – subscribing to an event   277
Handling exceptions   279
   Throwing exceptions   279
     Time for action – checking negative scene indexes   280
   Using a try-catch   281
     Time for action – catching restart errors   282
Design pattern primer   285
   Common game patterns   285
Pop quiz – intermediate C#   286
Summary   286

Chapter 12: The Journey Continues   287
   Scratching the surface   287
     Putting the pieces together   288
   Remembering your OOP   288
   Approaching Unity projects   289
     Unity features we didn't cover   289
   Next steps   290
     C# resources   290
     Unity resources   291
     Unity certifications   291
     Hero's trial – putting something out into the world   292
   Summary   292

Appendix A: Completed Game Files   293
   Bullet behavior   293
   Camera behavior   293
   Enemy behavior   294
   Game behavior   296
   Item behavior   299
   Player behavior   300

Appendix B: Supplementary Classes   303
   Custom extensions   303
   IManager   303
   Inventory list   304
   Utilities   304

Appendix C: Pop Quiz Answers   307
    Chapter 1 – Getting to Know Your Environment   307
      Pop quiz – dealing with scripts   307
    Chapter 2 – Introducing the Building Blocks of Programming   307
      Pop quiz – C# building blocks   307
    Chapter 3 – Diving into Variables, Types, and Methods   308
      Pop quiz #1 – variables and types   308
      Pop quiz #2 – understanding methods   308
    Chapter 4 – Using Collections and Controlling Your Code   308
      Pop quiz #1 – If, and, or but   308
      Pop quiz #2 – all about collections   309
    Chapter 5 – Working with Classes, Structs, and OOP   309
      Pop quiz – all things OOP   309
    Chapter 6 – Getting Your Hands Dirty with Unity   309
      Pop quiz – basic Unity features   309
    Chapter 7 – Movement, Camera Controls, and Collisions   310
      Pop quiz – player controls and physics   310
    Chapter 8 – Scripting Game Mechanics   310
      Pop quiz – working with mechanics   310
    Chapter 9 – Basic AI and Enemy Behavior   310
      Pop quiz – AI and navigation   310
    Chapter 10 – Revisiting Types, Methods, and Classes   311
      Pop quiz – leveling up   311
    Chapter 11 – Exploring Generics, Delegates, and Beyond   311
      Pop quiz – intermediate C#   311

Other Books You May Enjoy   313

Index   317

Preface

Unity has become one of the most popular game engines in the world, catering to amateur hobbyists, professional AAA studios, and cinematic production houses. While mainly considered a 3D tool, Unity has a host of dedicated features that support everything from 2D games and virtual reality to post-production and cross-platform publishing.

While developers love its drag-and-drop interface and built-in features, it's the ability to write custom C# scripts for behaviors and game mechanics that really take Unity the extra mile. Learning to write C# code might not be a huge obstacle to a seasoned programmer that already has other languages under his or her belt, but it can be daunting for those of you who have no programming experience. That's where this book comes in, as I'll be taking you through the building blocks of programming and the C# language from scratch, all while building out a fun and playable game in Unity.

Who this book is for

This book was written primarily for those of you who don't have any experience with the basic tenants of programming or the C# language. If you're a competent novice or seasoned programmer coming from another language, or even C#, but need to get hands-on with game development in Unity, then this is where you need to be.

What this book covers

Chapter 1, *Getting to Know Your Environment*, will get you started with the Unity installation process, the editors main features, and finding documentation for both C# and Unity-specific topics. We'll also go through creating C# scripts from inside Unity and take a look at the Visual Studio application, where all our code editing will take place.

Chapter 2, *The Building Blocks of Programming*, begins by laying out the atomic-level concepts of programming, giving you an opportunity to relate variables, methods, and classes to situations in everyday life. From there we move on to simple debugging techniques, proper formatting and commenting, and a look at how Unity turns C# scripts into components.

`Chapter 3`, *Diving into Variables, Types, and Methods*, takes a deeper look at variables. This includes C# data types, naming conventions, access modifiers, and everything else you'll need for the foundation of a program. We'll also go over how to write methods, incorporate parameters, and use return types effectively, ending with an overview of standard Unity methods belonging to the `MonoBehaviour` class.

`Chapter 4`, *Control Flow and Collection Types*, introduces the common approaches to making decisions in code, consisting of the `if-else` and `switch` statements. From there we move on to working with arrays, lists, and dictionaries, and incorporating iteration statements for looping through collection types. We end the chapter with a look at conditional looping statements and a special C# data type called enumerations.

`Chapter 5`, *Working with Classes, Structs, and OOP*, details our first contact with constructing and instantiating class and struct objects in code. We'll go through the basic steps of creating constructors, adding class or struct variables and methods, and the fundamentals of subclassing and inheritance. The chapter will end with a comprehensive explanation of object-oriented programming and how it applies to C#.

`Chapter 6`, *Getting Your Hands Dirty with Unity*, will mark our departure from C# syntax into the world of game design, level building, and Unity's featured tools. We'll start by going over the basics of a game design document, then move into blocking out our level geometry and adding lighting and a simple particle system.

`Chapter 7`, *Movement, Camera Controls, and Collisions*, will explain different approaches to moving a player object and setting up a third-person camera. We'll discuss incorporating Unity physics for more realistic locomotion effects, as well as how to work with collider components and capture interactions within a scene.

`Chapter 8`, *Scripting Game Mechanics*, will introduce the concept of game mechanics and how to effectively implement them. We'll start with a simple jump action, and create a shooting mechanic, and build off the last chapter's code by adding logic to handle item collection.

`Chapter 9`, *Basic AI and Enemy Behavior*, starts with a brief overview of artificial intelligence in games and the concepts we will be applying to Hero Born. Topics covered in this chapter will include navigation in Unity using the level geometry and a navigation mesh, smart agents, and automated enemy movement.

`Chapter 10`, *Revisiting Types, Methods, and Classes*, takes a more in-depth look at data types, intermediate method features, and additional behaviors that can be used for more complex classes. This chapter will give you a deeper understanding of the versatility and breadth of the C# language.

`Chapter 11`, *Exploring Generics, Delegates, and Beyond*, will detail some of the more intermediate features of the C# language and how to apply them in practical, real-world scenarios. We'll start with an overview of generic programming and progress to concepts such as delegation, events, and exception handling. The chapter will end with a brief discussion of common design patterns and set you up for further study.

`Chapter 12`, *The Journey Continues*, reviews the main topics you've learned throughout the book and leaves you with resources for further study in both C# and Unity. Included in these resources will be online reading material, certification information, and a host of my favorite video tutorial channels.

`Appendix A`, *Completed Game Files*, contains all the necessary C# scripts that make up Hero Born.

`Appendix B`, *Supplementary Classes*, contains the intermediate code from `Chapters 10`, *Revisiting Types, Methods, and Classes* and `Chapter 11`, *Exploring Generics, Delegates, and Beyond*, that don't have any direct impact on the game mechanics of Hero Born.

`Appendix C`, *Pop Quiz Answers*, contains the answers to each chapter quiz presented throughout the book.

To get the most out of this book

The only thing you need to get the most from your upcoming C# and Unity adventure is a curious mind and a will to learn. Having said that, doing all the *Time for Action* and *Heroes Trial* sections is a must if you hope to cement the knowledge you're learning, as well as completing the chapter quizzes. Lastly, revisiting topics and entire chapters to refresh or solidify your understanding before moving on is always a good idea. There's no sense building a house on an unstable foundation.

Downloading the Example Code Files

You can download the example code files for this book from your account at `www.packt.com`. If you purchased this book elsewhere, you can visit `www.packt.com/support` and register to have the files emailed directly to you. You can download the code files by following these steps:

1. Log in or register at `www.packt.com`.
2. Select the SUPPORT tab.

3. Click on Code Downloads & Errata.
4. Enter the name of the book in the Search box and follow the onscreen instructions.

Once the file is downloaded, please make sure that you unzip or extract the folder using the latest version of:

- WinRAR/7-Zip for Windows
- Zipeg/iZip/UnRarX for Mac
- 7-Zip/PeaZip for Linux

The code bundle for the book is also hosted on GitHub at `https://github.com/PacktPublishing/Learning-C-with-Unity-2019`. In case there's an update to the code, it will be updated on the existing GitHub repository.

We also have other code bundles from our rich catalog of books and videos available at `https://github.com/PacktPublishing/`. Check them out!

Downloading the Color Images

We also provide a PDF file that has color images of the screenshots/diagrams used in this book, which you can download here: `https://www.packtpub.com/sites/default/files/downloads/9781789532050_ColorImages.pdf`.

Conventions Used

There are a number of text conventions used throughout this book.

`CodeInText`: Indicates code words in text, database table names, folder names, filenames, file extensions, pathnames, dummy URLs, user input, and Twitter handles. Here is an example: "Optionally, an `else` keyword with its own pair of curly brackets and code block"

A block of code is set as follows:

```
public
int
firstName
=
"Bilbo";
```

When we wish to draw your attention to a particular part of a code block, the relevant lines or items are set in bold:

```
accessModifier returnType UniqueName(parameterType parameterName)
{
    method body
}
```

Bold: Indicates a new term, an important word, or words that you see onscreen. For example, words in menus or dialog boxes appear in the text like this. Here is an example: "Choose **Create**, and select **C# Script**"

 Warnings or important notes appear like this.

 Tips and tricks appear like this.

Sections

In this book, you will find several headings that appear frequently (Time for action, What just happened?, Pop quiz, and Hero's trial).

To give clear instructions on how to complete a procedure or task, we use these sections as follows:

Time for Action

1. Step 1

2. Step 2

3. Step 3

Extra explanations are often required to break down instructions, so they are followed with:

What just happened?

This heading explains the working of tasks or instructions that you have just completed. You will also find some other learning aids in the book, including:

Pop Quiz – Heading

These are short multiple-choice questions intended to help you test your own understanding.

Hero's Trial – Heading

These practical challenges give you ideas for experimenting with what you have learned.

Get in Touch

Feedback from our readers is always welcome.

General feedback: If you have questions about any aspect of this book, mention the book title in the subject of your message and email us at customercare@packtpub.com.

Errata: Although we have taken every care to ensure the accuracy of our content, mistakes do happen. If you have found a mistake in this book, we would be grateful if you would report this to us. Please visit www.packt.com/submit-errata, selecting your book, clicking on the Errata Submission Form link, and entering the details.

Piracy: If you come across any illegal copies of our works in any form on the Internet, we would be grateful if you would provide us with the location address or website name. Please contact us at copyright@packt.com with a link to the material.

If you are interested in becoming an author: If there is a topic that you have expertise in and you are interested in either writing or contributing to a book, please visit authors.packtpub.com.

Reviews

Please leave a review. Once you have read and used this book, why not leave a review on the site that you purchased it from? Potential readers can then see and use your unbiased opinion to make purchase decisions, we at Packt can understand what you think about our products, and our authors can see your feedback on their book. Thank you!

For more information about Packt, please visit `packt.com`.

Section 1: Programming Foundations and C# 1

This section will introduce you to the Unity development environment, the fundamentals of programming, and the C# language from the ground up. By the end of the section, you'll know your way around Unity and have the foundation knowledge necessary to start creating a simple game.

The following chapters will be covered in this section:

- Chapter 1, *Getting to Know Your Environment*
- Chapter 2, *The Building Blocks of Programming*
- Chapter 3, *Diving into Variables, Types, and Methods*
- Chapter 4, *Control Flow and Collection Types*
- Chapter 5, *Working with Classes, Structs, and OOP*

1
Getting to Know your Environment

Pop culture has taught us that computer programmers are usually outsiders, lone wolves, or geeky hackers who possess extraordinary mental gifts for algorithmic thought, little social IQ, and the odd anarchic bent. While this is definitely not the case, in reality, there is something to the idea that learning to code fundamentally changes the way you look at the world. The good news is that your naturally curious mind will quickly adapt to this new way of thinking, and maybe even come to enjoy it.

You already use analytical skills in your everyday life that translate to programming—you're just missing the right language and syntax to map those life skills into code. You know your age, right? That's a variable. When you cross the street, I presume you look left, right, then left again like the rest of us. That's evaluating different conditions or what we call control flow. When you look at a can of pop, you instinctively identify that it has properties, such as shape, weight, and contents. That's a class object. You get the idea.

We're going to begin our adventure into C# programming by covering the following topics:

- Basic prerequisites
- Starting out with Unity
- Using C# with Unity
- Working with the Visual Studio editor
- Accessing documentation and resources

Some basic prerequisites

Sometimes it's easier to start with what a thing isn't, rather than what it is. The main goal of this book isn't to learn the vast ins and outs of Unity or all of game development. By necessity, we'll cover these topics at a basic level, and in more detail in `Chapter 6`, *Getting Your Hands Dirty with Unity*, but their purpose is to provide a fun, accessible way for us to learn the C# programming language from the ground up.

Since this book is aimed at complete beginners to programming, if you have no previous experience with either C# or Unity, you're in the right place! If you've had some experience with the Unity editor but not with programming, guess what? This is still the place to be. Even if you've dabbled in a bit of C# mixed with Unity, but want to explore some more intermediate or advanced topics, the later chapters can provide you with what you're looking for.

If you're an experienced programmer in other languages, feel free to skip the beginner theory and dive right into the parts you're interested in.

Starting out with Unity 2019

Head over to `https://store.unity.com/` and you'll see a few options. Don't get overwhelmed—you can get Unity completely free by selecting the personal option on the right. The other paid options offer more advanced functionality and services, but you can check these out on your own down the road:

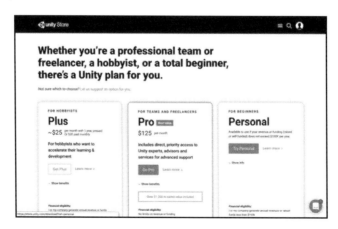

After selecting the personal plan, you'll end up on the download screen; accept the terms and conditions and hit **Download Installer for Mac OS X**:

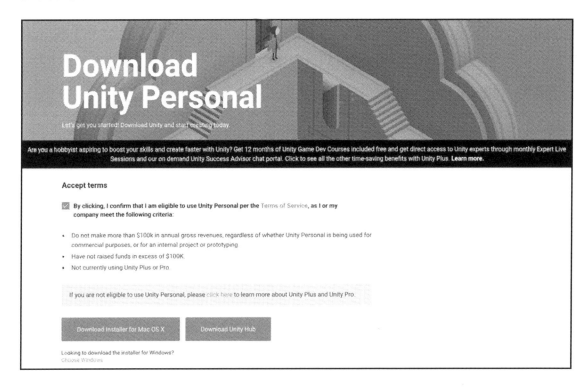

If you're using a Windows machine, select the **Choose Windows** link located underneath the installer button, accept the terms and conditions, and you're good to go!

 You can also download and manage different versions of Unity through the Unity Hub application, which can be also be downloaded from this screen.

When the download is complete, open up the package (by double-clicking it) and follow the installation instructions. When you get the green light, go ahead and fire up Unity!

 All of the examples and screenshots for this book were created and captured using Unity **2018.3.8f1** and verified with version **2019.2.0a7**. If you're using a newer version, things might look slightly different in the editor, but following along won't be a problem.

Creating a new project

The first thing you'll see when Unity finishes thinking about opening is the dashboard. If you have a Unity account, go ahead and **Sign in**. If not, you can either create one or hit **Skip** at the bottom of the screen.

Now, let's set up a new project by selecting the **New** tab at the top right and setting the following fields:

- **Project Name**: I'll be calling mine *Hero Born*
- **Location**: Wherever you'd like the project to be saved
- **Template**: Make sure this is set to **3D** and hit **Create Project**:

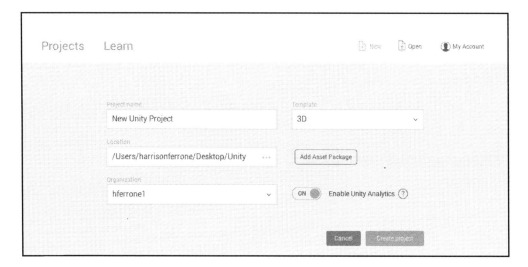

Navigating the editor

When the new project finishes initializing, you'll see the glorious Unity editor! I've marked the important tabs (or panels, if you prefer) in the following screenshot, which we can break down as follows:

- The **Toolbar** is the topmost part of the Unity editor. From here, you can manipulate objects (far-left button group), and play and pause the game (center buttons). The rightmost button group contains Unity Services, layer masks, and layout scheme features that we won't be using in this book.
- The **Hierarchy Window** shows every item currently in the game scene. In the starter project, this is just the default camera and directional light, but when we create our prototype environment, this window will start to get filled in.
- The **Game** and **Scene Views** are the most visual aspects of the editor. Think of the **Scene View** as your stage, where you can move and arrange 2D and 3D objects. When you hit *Play*, the **Game View** will take over, rendering the **Scene** and any programmed interactions.
- The **Inspector** Window is your one-stop-shop for viewing and editing the properties of your objects. In the preceding screenshot, you can see that the **Main Camera** has several parts (Unity calls them components) displayed – all of them are accessible from here.
- The **Project** window holds every asset that's currently in your project. Think of this as a representation of your project's folders and files.
- The **Console** is where any output we want our scripts to print will show up. From here on out, if we talk about the console or debug output, this panel is where it will be displayed.

You can find more in-depth breakdowns of each window's functionality in the Unity docs at `https://docs.unity3d.com/Manual/UsingTheEditor.html`.

I know that was a lot to process if you're new to Unity, but rest assured that any instructions going forward will always reference the necessary steps. I won't leave you hanging, wondering what button to push. With that out of the way, let's get a jump on creating some actual C# scripts.

Using C# with Unity

Going forward, it's important to think of Unity and C# as symbiotic entities. Unity is the engine where you will create scripts and eventually run them, but the actual programming will take place in another program, called **Visual Studio**. Don't sweat that right now—we'll get to that in a moment.

Working with C# scripts

Even though we haven't covered any basic programming concepts yet, we still need to know how to create a C# script in Unity.

There are several ways to create C# scripts in the editor:

- From the menu bar, navigate to **Assets | Create | C# Script**
- In the **Project** tab, select **Create | C# Script**
- Right-click in the **Project** tab (on the right-hand side) and select **Create | C# Script** from the popup menu

Going forward, whenever you're instructed to create a C# script, please use whichever method you prefer.

Resources and objects other than C# scripts can be created in the editor using the preceding methods. I'm not going to call out each of these variations every time we create something new, so just keep the options in the back of your mind.

Time for action – creating a C# script

For the sake of organization, we're going to store our various assets and scripts inside their own clearly marked folders. This isn't just a Unity-related task—it's something you should always do (your coworkers will thank you, I promise):

1. Click **Create** | **Folder** (or whichever method you like best) from the **Project** tab and name it **Scripts**.
2. Double-click on the **Scripts** folder and create a new C# script. By default, the script will be named `NewBehaviourScript`, so immediately rename it to `LearningCurve`.

What just happened?

We've just created a subfolder named **Scripts**, which is pictured in the following screenshot. Inside that parent folder, we've created a C# script named `LearningCurve.cs` (the `cs` file type stands for C-Sharp, in case you were wondering), which is now saved as part of our *Hero Born* project assets:

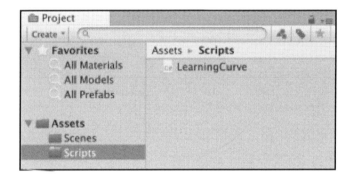

Introducing the Visual Studio editor

While Unity can create and store C# scripts, they need to be edited using an application called Visual Studio. A copy of Visual Studio comes pre-packaged with Unity and will open up automatically when you double-click any C# script from inside the editor.

Time for action – opening a C# file

Unity will synchronize with Visual Studio the first time you open a file. The simplest way to do this is to select a script from the **Project** tab:

- In Unity's **Project** tab, double-click on `LearningCurve.cs` and watch it open up in Visual Studio:

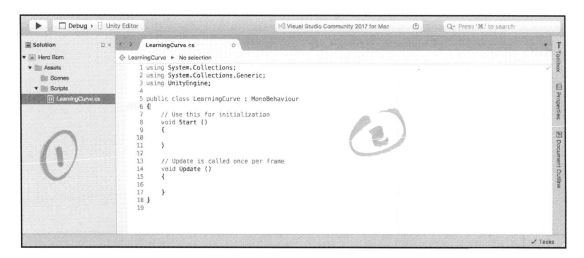

On the left-hand side of the interface, you'll see a folder structure that mirrors the one in Unity, which you can access like any other. On the right-hand side is the actual code editor where the magic happens. There are, of course, more features to Visual Studio, but this is all we need to keep moving forward.

Beware of naming mismatches

One common pitfall that trips up new programmers is file naming, more specifically naming mismatches, which we can illustrate using line number 5 from the previous screenshot:

```
public class LearningCurve : MonoBehaviour
```

The `LearningCurve` **class name is the same** as the `LearningCurve.cs` filename. **This is essential and an absolute requirement**. It's OK if you don't know what a class is yet; just remember that the filename and the class name must be the same.

When you create a C# script file in Unity, the filename in the **Project** tab is already in Edit mode, ready to be renamed. It's a good habit to rename it then and there. If you rename the script later, the filename and the class name won't match. The filename would change, but line five would be as follows:

```
public class NewBehaviourScript : MonoBehaviour
```

If you accidentally do this, it's not the end of the world. Go into Visual Studio and change `NewBehaviourScript` to the name of your C# script.

Syncing C# files

As part of their symbiotic relationship, Unity and Visual Studio keep in touch with each other to synchronize their content. This means that if you add, delete, or change a script file in one application, the other application will see the changes automatically.

Fixing a broken sync

So, what happens when Murphy's Law strikes and syncing just doesn't seem to be working correctly? If you run into this situation, take a deep breath and do the following:

- Right-click on Unity's **Project** window and select **Sync Visual Studio Project**.

Documentation

The last topic we'll touch on in this first foray into Unity and C# scripts is documentation. Not sexy, I know, but it's important to form good habits early when dealing with new programming languages or development environments.

Accessing Unity's documentation

Once you start writing scripts in earnest, you'll probably be using Unity's documentation quite often, so it's beneficial to know how to access it early on. The *Reference Manual* will give you an overview of a component or topic, while specific programming examples can be found in the *Scripting Reference*.

Time for action – opening the Reference Manual

Every *GameObject* (item in the **Hierarchy** panel) in a Scene has a **Transform** component that controls its placement, **Rotation**, and **Scale**. To keep things simple, we'll just look up the camera's **Transform** component in the *Reference Manual*:

1. In the **Hierarchy** tab, select the **Main Camera** object.
2. Click on the book icon at the top-right of the **Transform** component:

What just happened?

Now, you should see a web browser open on the **Transform** page of the *Reference Manual*. All of the components in Unity have this feature, so if you ever want to know more about how something works, you know what to do:

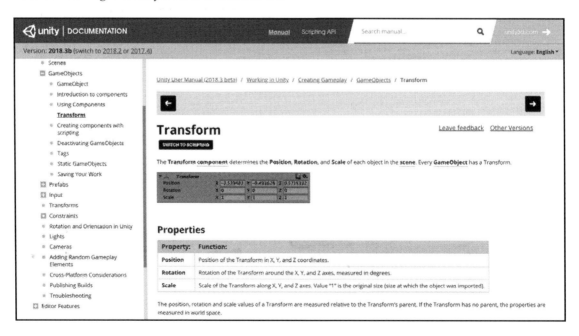

Time for action – using the Scripting Reference

So, we've got the *Reference Manual* open, but what if we wanted concrete coding examples related to the **Transform** component? It's pretty simple—all we need to do is ask the *Scripting Reference*:

- Click the **Switch to Scripting** link underneath the component or class name (**Transform**, in this case)

What just happened?

The *Reference Manual* automatically switched to the *Scripting Reference* for the **Transform** component:

 The *Scripting Reference* is a large document because it has to be. However, this doesn't mean you have to memorize or even be familiar with all of its information to start writing scripts. As the name suggests, it's a reference, not a test.

Locating C# resources

Now that we've got our Unity resources taken care of, let's take a look at some of Microsoft's C# docs at https://docs.microsoft.com/en-us/dotnet/csharp/programming-guide/index.

> There's a ton of other C# resources, ranging from tutorials and quickstart guides to version specifications (if you're into that), available at https://docs.microsoft.com/en-us/dotnet/csharp.

Time for action – looking up a C# class

Load up the programming guide link and let's look up the C# `String` class:

1. Either enter **Strings** in the search bar in the top-left corner of the web page or scroll down to the *Language Sections* and click on the **Strings** link directly:

What just happened?

You should see something like the following screenshot of the class description page. Unlike Unity's documentation, the C# reference and scripting information is all bundled up into one, but its saving grace is the subtopic list on the right-hand side. Use it well:

Pop quiz – dealing with scripts

1. What type of relationship do Unity and Visual Studio share?
2. The *Scripting Reference* supplies example code in regards to using a particular Unity component or feature. Where could you find more detailed (non-code-related) information about Unity components?
3. The *Scripting Reference* is a large document. How much of it do you have memorized before attempting to write a scripts?
4. When is the best time to name a C# script?

Summary

We covered quite a bit of logistical information in this chapter, so I can understand if you're itching to write some code. Starting new projects, creating folders and scripts, and accessing documentation are topics that are easily forgotten in the excitement of a new adventure. Just remember that this chapter has a lot of resources you might need in the coming pages, so don't be afraid to come back and visit. Thinking like a programmer is a muscle: the more you work it, the stronger it gets.

In the next chapter, we'll start laying out the theory, vocabulary, and main concepts you'll need to prime your coding brain. Even though the material is conceptual, we'll still be writing our first lines of code in the `LearningCurve` script. Get ready!

2
The Building Blocks of Programming

Any programming language starts off looking like ancient Greek to inexperienced eyes, and C# is no exception. The good news is that underneath the mystery and occasional incomprehensibility, all programming languages are made up of the same essential building blocks. Variables, methods, and classes (or objects) make up the DNA of conventional programming; understanding these simple concepts opens up an entire world of diverse and complex applications. After all, there are only four different DNA molecules in every person on earth; yet, here we are, unique organisms to the last.

If you're new to programming, there's going to be a lot of information coming at you in this chapter, and will possibly mark the first lines of code that you've written. The point is not to overload your brain with facts and figures; it's to give you a holistic look into the building blocks of programming using examples from everyday life.

Ramblings aside, we're going to focus on the following topics over the course of this chapter:

- Defining what variables are and how to use them
- Understanding the purpose of methods
- Classes and their role as objects
- Turning C# scripts into Unity components
- Component communication and dot notation

Defining variables

Let's start off with a simple question: what is a variable? Depending on your point of view, there are a few different ways of answering that question, as follows:

- **Conceptually**, a variable is the most basic unit of programming, such as an atom. Everything starts with variables, and programs can't exist without them.
- **Technically**, a variable is a tiny section of your computer's memory that holds an assigned value. Every variable keeps track of where its information is stored (this is called a memory address), its value, and its type (for instance, numbers, words, or lists).
- **Practically**, a variable is a container. You can create new ones at will, fill them with stuff, move them around, and reference them as needed. They can even be empty and still be useful:

A useful real-life example of a variable is a mailbox; remember those? They can hold letters, bills, a picture from your aunt Mabel – anything really. The point is that what's in a mailbox can vary.

Names are important

Referring to the preceding photo, if I asked you to go over and open the mailbox, the first thing you'd probably ask is: which one? If I said the Smith family mailbox, or the brown mailbox, or the round mailbox, then you'd know the exact mailbox I was referencing. Similarly, when you are creating variables, you have to give them unique names that you can reference later. We'll get into the specifics of proper formatting and descriptive naming in the next chapter.

Variables act as placeholders

When you create and name a variable, you're actually creating a placeholder for the value that you want to store. Let's take the following simple math equation as an example:

```
2 + 9 = 11
```

Okay, there is no mystery there, but what if we wanted the number 9 to be its own variable? Consider the following code block:

```
myVariable = 9
```

Now we can use the variable name, myVariable, as a reference or substitute for 9 anywhere:

```
2 + myVariable = 11
```

Even though this example isn't real C# code, it illustrates the power of variables and their use as placeholder references.

 If you're wondering whether variables have other rules or regulations, you'd be right. We'll get to those in the next chapter, so sit tight.

Time for action – creating a variable

Alright, enough theory; let's create a real variable in our `LearningCurve` script. Don't worry about the syntax right now, just make sure your script is the same as the script that is shown in the following screenshot:

1. Double-click on `LearningCurve` to open it in Visual Studio and add lines **7**, **12**, and **14** from the following screenshot.
2. Save the file using *command + S* on a macOS keyboard, or *Ctrl + S* on a Windows keyboard:

```
LearningCurve.cs                    x
LearningCurve  ▶  Update()

 1 using System.Collections;
 2 using System.Collections.Generic;
 3 using UnityEngine;
 4
 5 public class LearningCurve : MonoBehaviour
 6 {
 7     public int carDoors = 4;
 8
 9     // Use this for initialization
10     void Start ()
11     {
12         Debug.Log(2 + 4);
13
14         Debug.Log(carDoors - 2);
15     }
16
17     // Update is called once per frame
18     void Update ()
19     {
20
21     }
22 }
```

In order for scripts to run in Unity, they have to be attached to objects (referred to as GameObjects in Unity) in the scene. *HeroBorn* only has a camera and directional light right now, so let's attach `LearningCurve` to the camera to keep things simple:

1. Drag and drop `LearningCurve` onto **Main Camera.**
2. Select **Main Camera** so that it appears in the **Inspector** panel, and verify that the `LearningCurve` **(Script)** component is attached properly (this is highlighted in the following screenshot).

3. Click Play and watch for the output in the **Console** panel:

What just happened?

The `Debug.Log()` statements printed out the result of the simple math equations we put in between the parentheses. As you can see in the following **Console** screenshot, the equation that used our variable worked exactly the same as if it was a real number:

We'll get into how Unity converts C# scripts into components at the end of this chapter.

Time for action – changing a variable's value

Since `carDoors` was declared as a variable on line **7**, the value it stores can be changed. The updated value will then trickle down to wherever the variable is used in code; let's see this in action:

1. Stop the game by clicking the **Play** button if the scene is still running.
2. Change **Car Doors** to 3 in the **Inspector** panel and play the scene again, looking at the new output in the **Console** panel:

What just happened?

The first output will still be **6**, but the second output is now **1** because we changed the value of our variable.

 The goal here wasn't to go over variable syntax, but to show how variables act as containers that can be created once and referenced elsewhere. We'll go into more detail in `Chapter 3`, *Diving into Variables, Types, and Methods*.

A method to the madness

On their own, variables can't do much more than keep track of their assigned values. While this is vital, they are not very useful on their own in terms of creating meaningful applications. So, how do we go about creating actions and driving behavior in our code? The short answer is by using methods.

Before we get to what methods are and how to use them, we should clarify a small point of terminology. In the world of programming, you'll commonly see the terms *method* and *function* used interchangeably, especially in regards to Unity. Since C# is an object-oriented language (this is something that we'll cover in `Chapter 5`, *Working with Classes and Object-Oriented Programming)*, we'll be using the term *method* for the rest of the book to conform to standard C# guidelines.

> When you come across the word *function* in the *Scripting Reference* or any other documentation, think *method*.

Methods drive actions

Similarly to variables, defining programming methods can be tediously long-winded or dangerously brief; here's another three-pronged approach to consider:

- **Conceptually**, methods are how work gets done in an application.
- **Technically**, a method is a block of code containing executable statements that run when the method is called by name. Methods can take in arguments (also called parameters), which can be used inside the method's scope.
- **Practically**, a method is a container for a set of instructions that run every time it's executed. These containers can also take in variables as inputs, which can only be referenced inside the method itself.

Methods are placeholders too

Let's take an oversimplified example of adding two numbers together to drive the concept home. When writing a script, you're essentially laying down lines of code for the computer to execute in sequential order. The first time you need to add two numbers together, you could just brute-force it like in the following code block:

```
someNumber + anotherNumber
```

But then you come to the conclusion that these numbers need to be added together somewhere else. Instead of copying and pasting the same line of code (which is generally something you want to avoid at all costs), you can create a named method that will take care of this action:

```
AddNumbers
{
```

```
            someNumber + anotherNumber
   }
```

Now `AddNumbers` is holding a place in memory, just like a variable; however, instead of a value, it holds a block of instructions. Using the name of the method (or calling it) anywhere in a script puts the stored instructions at your fingertips without having to repeat any code.

If you find yourself writing the same lines of code over and over, you're likely missing a chance to simplify or condense frequent actions into common methods. You'll hear this referred to as *spaghetti code* because it's all over the place and hard to untangle.

Time for action – a simple method

Let's open up `LearningCurve` again and see how a method actually works in C#. Just like with the variables example you'll want to copy the code into your script exactly as they appear in the following screenshot. I've deleted the previous example code to make things neater, but you can, of course, keep them in your script for reference:

1. Open up `LearningCurve` in Visual Studio and add in lines **7**, **8**, **13**, and **16** to **19**.

2. Save the file, and then go back and hit **Play** in Unity to see the new **Console** output:

```
◈ LearningCurve ▸ ▣ AddNumbers()
 1 using System.Collections;
 2 using System.Collections.Generic;
 3 using UnityEngine;
 4
 5 public class LearningCurve : MonoBehaviour
 6 {
 7     public int firstNumber = 2;
 8     public int secondNumber = 3;
 9
10     // Use this for initialization
11     void Start ()
12     {
13         AddNumbers();          ◀——— Calling the method
14     }
15
16     void AddNumbers()
17     {
18         Debug.Log(firstNumber + secondNumber);    ◀——— The method
19     }
20 }
21
```

What just happened?

You just defined your first method on lines **16** to **19** and called it on line **13**. Now wherever `AddNumbers()` is called, the two variables will be added together and printed to the console, even if their values change:

Go ahead and try out different variable values in the **Inspector** panel to see this in action! More details on the actual code syntax of what you just wrote is coming up in the next chapter.

Introducing classes

We've seen how variables store information and how methods perform actions, but our programming toolkit is still somewhat limited. We need a way of creating a sort of super container that has its own variables and methods that can be referenced from the container itself; enter classes:

- **Conceptually**, a class holds related information, actions, and behaviors inside a single container. They can even communicate with each other.
- **Technically**, classes are data structures. They can contain variables, methods, and other programmatic information, all of which can be referenced when an object of the class is created.
- **Practically**, a class is a blueprint. It sets out the rules and regulations for any object (called an instance) created using the class blueprint.

A class all along

Before you wonder what a class actually looks like in C#, you should know that you've been working with a class this whole chapter. By default, every script created in Unity is a class, which you can see from the `class` keyword on line **5**:

```
public class LearningCurve: MonoBehavior
```

`MonoBehavior` just means that this class can be attached to a GameObject in the Unity scene. In C#, classes can exist on their own, which we'll see when we create standalone classes in `Chapter 5`, *Working with Classes and Object-Oriented Programming.*

 The terms *script* and *class* are sometimes used interchangeably in Unity resources. For consistency, I'll be referring to C# files as scripts if they're attached to GameObjects, and as classes if they are standalone.

Everyday blueprints

For our last example, go ahead and think about your local post office. It's a separate, self-contained environment that has properties, such as a physical address (a variable), and the ability to execute actions, such as sending in your secret decoder ring voucher (methods).

This makes a post office a great example of a potential class that we can outline in the following code block:

```
PostOffice
{
    // Variables
    Address = "1234 Letter Opener Dr."

    // Methods
    DeliverMail()
    SendMail()
}
```

The main takeaway here is that when information and behaviors follow a predefined blueprint, complex actions and inter-class communication becomes possible.

For instance, if we had another class that wanted to send a letter through our `PostOffice` class, it wouldn't have to wonder where to go to fire this action. It could simply call the `SendMail` function from the `PostOffice` class, as follows:

```
PostOffice.SendMail()
```

Or, you can even use it to look up its address, as follows:

```
PostOffice.Address
```

If you're wondering about the use of periods (called dot notation) between words, we'll be diving into that at the end of the chapter, hold tight.

Your basic programming toolkit is now complete (well, the theory drawer, at least). We'll spend the rest of this section taking you deeper into the syntax and practical uses of variables, methods, and classes.

Commenting is key

You might have noticed that LearningCurve has two odd lines of grey text (**9 and 17**) starting with two backslashes, which were created by default with the script. These are code comments, a very powerful, if simple, tool for programmers.

In C#, there are a few ways that you can use to create comments, and Visual Studio (and other code editing applications) will often make it even easier with built-in shortcuts.

Some professionals would not call commenting an essential building block of programming, but I'll have to respectfully disagree. Correctly commenting out your code with meaningful information is one of the most fundamental habits a new programmer should have.

Practical backslashes

The single-line comment is exactly what's already in LearningCurve: any line starting with two backslashes (without empty space) is ignored by Visual Studio:

```
// This is a single-line comment
```

Since it's in the name, you'd be right to assume that single-line comments only apply to one line of code. If you want multiple-line comments, you'll need to use a backslash and an asterisk as opening and closing characters around the comment text:

```
/* this is a
      multi-line comment */
```

You can also comment and uncomment blocks of code by highlighting them and using the *command + ?* shortcut.

Time for action – adding comments

Visual Studio also provides a handy auto-generated commenting feature; type in three backslashes on the line preceding any line of code (variables, methods, classes, and more) and a summary comment block will appear:

1. Open up `LearningCurve` and add in three backslashes above the `AddNumbers()` method.

```
19    /// <summary>
20    /// Adds the numbers.
21    /// </summary>
22    void AddNumbers()
23    {
24        Debug.Log(firstNumber + secondNumber);
25    }
```

What just happened?

You should see a three-line comment with a description of the method generated by Visual Studio from the method's name, sandwiched between two `<summary>` tags. You can, of course, change the text, or add new lines by hitting *Enter* just as you would in a text document; just make sure not to touch the tags.

Putting it together in Unity

With the building blocks squared away, it's time to do a little Unity-specific housekeeping before wrapping up this chapter. Specifically, we need to know more about how Unity handles C# scripts attached to GameObjects like how we've done with `LearningCurve` and **Main Camera**.

Scripts become components

All GameObject components are scripts, whether you or the good people at Unity wrote them. Unity-specific components such as **Transform**, and their respective scripts, just aren't supposed to be edited by us.

The moment a script that you have created is dropped onto a GameObject, it becomes another component of that object, which is why it appears in the **Inspector** panel. To Unity, it walks, talks, and acts like any other component, complete with public variables underneath the component that can be changed at any time. Even though we aren't supposed to edit the components provided by Unity, we can still access their properties and methods, making them powerful development tools.

Unity also makes some automatic readability adjustments when a script becomes a component. You might have noticed that when we added `LearningCurve` to **Main Camera**, Unity displayed it as `Learning Curve`, with `firstNumber` changing to `First Number`.

Variables and the Inspector panel

Part of a previous *Time for Action* section already had you update a variable in the **Inspector** panel, but it's important to touch on how this works in more detail. There are two situations in which you can modify a property value:

- In **Play** mode
- In development mode

Changes made in **Play** mode take effect immediately in real time, which is great for testing and fine-tuning gameplay. However, it's important to note that any changes made while in **Play** mode will be lost when you stop the game and return to development mode.

When you're in development mode, any changes that you make to the variables will be saved by Unity. This means that if you were to quit Unity and then restart it, the changes would be retained.

The changes that you make to variable values in the **Inspector** panel do not modify your script. The only way these variables can be changed is for you to edit the values themselves in Visual Studio. The values that are shown in the **Inspector** panel override any values you had assigned in your script.

If you need to undo any changes made in the **Inspector** panel, you can reset the script to its default (sometimes called initial) values. Click on the cog icon (the gear) to the far right of any component, and then select **Reset**, as shown in the following screenshot:

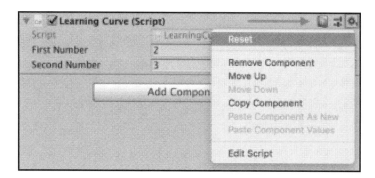

A helping hand from MonoBehavior

Since C# scripts are classes, how does Unity know to make some scripts components and not others? The short answer is that LearningCurve (and any script created in Unity) inherits from MonoBehavior (another class). This let's Unity know that the C# class can be transformed into a component.

The topic of class inheritance is a bit advanced for this point of your programming journey; think of it as the MonoBehaviour class lending a few of its variables and methods to LearningCurve. Chapter 5, *Working with Classes, Struct, and OOP*, will cover class inheritance in practical detail.

The Start() and Update() methods that we've used belong to MonoBehavior, which Unity runs automatically on any script attached to a GameObject. The Start() method runs once when the scene starts playing, while the Update() method runs once per frame (depending on the frame rate of your machine).

Hero's trial – MonoBehavior in the Scripting API

Now it's time for you to get comfortable using the Unity documentation on your own, and what better way than to look up some of the common `MonoBehavior` methods:

- Try searching for the `Start()` and `Update()` methods in the Scripting API to gain a better understanding of what they do in Unity, and when.
- If you're feeling brave, go the extra step and have a look at the `MonoBehavior` class in the manual for a more detailed explanation.

Class and component communication

Up until now, we've described classes and by extension, Unity components, as separate standalone entities; in reality, they are deeply intertwined. In fact, you'd be hard pressed to create any kind of meaningful software application without invoking some kind of interaction or communication between classes.

Enter dot notation

If you remember the post office example from earlier, the example code made use of periods (or dots) to reference classes, variables, and methods. If you think of classes as directories of information, then dot notation is the indexing tool:

```
PostOffice.Address
```

Any variables, methods, or other data types within a class can be accessed with dot notation. This applies to nested, or subclass information as well, but we'll tackle all those subjects when we get to `Chapter 5`, *Working with Classes and Object-Oriented Programming*.

Dot notation is also what drives communication between classes. Whenever a class needs information about another class or wants to execute one of its methods, dot notation is used:

```
PostOffice.DeliverMail()
```

Dot notation is sometimes referred to as `(.)` `Operator`, so don't be thrown off if you see it mentioned this way in the documentation.

Pop quiz – C# building blocks

1. What is the main purpose of a variable?
2. What role do methods play in scripts?
3. How does a script become a component?
4. What's the purpose of dot notation?

Summary

We've come a long way in a few short pages, but understanding the overarching theory of fundamental concepts such as variables, methods, and classes will give you a strong foundation to build on. Bear in mind that these building blocks have very real counterparts in the real world. Variables hold values like mailboxes hold letters; methods store instructions like recipes, to be followed for a predefined result; and classes are blueprints just like real blueprints. You can't build a house without a well-thought-out design to follow if you expect it to stay standing.

The rest of this book will take you on a deep dive into C# syntax from scratch, starting with more detail in the next chapter on how to create variables, manage value types, and work with simple and complex methods.

3
Diving into Variables, Types, and Methods

The initial steps into any programming language are plagued with a basic disconnect—you understand the words, but not the meaning or context behind them. Normally, this would be cause for a paradox, but programming is a special case.

C# is not really its own language; it's written in English. The discrepancy between recognizing words you use every day and the code in Visual Studio comes from missing context, which is something that has to be learned all over again. You know how to say the words and you know how to spell the words, but what you don't know is where, when, why, and, most importantly, how they make up the syntax of the C# language.

This chapter marks our departure from programming theory and the beginning of our journey into actual coding. There's a lot of ground to cover, but by the time you reach the last quiz you'll be comfortable with the following high-level topics:

- Writing proper C#
- Simple debugging techniques
- Declaring variables
- Common C# types
- Access modifiers
- Working with operators
- Working with methods

Writing proper C#

Lines of code function like sentences, meaning they need to have some sort of separating, or ending, character. In C#, all lines of code, which are called statements, end with a semicolon to separate them for the code editor to process.

Unlike the written word in normal circumstances, a C# statement doesn't technically have to be on a single line; whitespace and newlines are ignored by the code editor. For example, a simple variable could be written in different ways. It could be written like this:

```
public int firstName = "Bilbo";
```

Alternatively, it could also be written as follows:

```
public
int
firstName
=
"Bilbo";
```

These two code snippets are perfectly acceptable to Visual Studio, but the second option is highly discouraged as it makes code extremely hard to read. The idea is to write your programs as efficiently and clearly as possible.

There will be times when a statement will be too long to reasonably fit on a single line, but those are few and far between. Just make sure that it's formatted in a way someone else could understand, and don't forget the semicolon.

The standard formatting for curly brackets after methods or classes is to include each one on a new line, as follows:

```
public void MethodName()
{

}
```

However, when you create a new script or go online to the Unity documentation, you'll see the first curly bracket located on the same line as the declaration:

```
public void MethodName() {

}
```

While this isn't something to tear out your hair over, it is important to understand these subtle differences early on. The choice is up to you; the important thing is to be consistent.

Simple debugging

While we're working through practical examples, we'll need a way to print out information and feedback to the **console**. The term for this is debugging, and C# and Unity provide helper methods to make this process easy. Whenever I ask you to debug or print something out, please use one of the following methods:

- For simple text or individual variables, use a standard `Debug.Log()`. Text needs to be inside a set of parentheses, and variables can be used directly with no added characters:

  ```
  Debug.Log("Text goes here.");
  Debug.Log(yourVariable);
  ```

- For more complex debugging, use `Debug.LogFormat()`. This will let you place variables inside the printed text by using placeholders marked with a pair of curly brackets. Each set of brackets contains an index, starting from 0, corresponding to a sequential variable.

In the following example, the `{0}` placeholder is replaced with the `variable1` value, `{1}` with `variable2`, and so on:

```
Debug.LogFormat("Text goes here, add {0} and {1} as variable placeholders",
variable1, variable2);
```

Variable syntax

We've seen how variables are created, and touched on the high-level functionality that they provide, but we're still missing the syntax that makes all of that possible. Variables don't just appear at the top of a C# script; they have to be declared according to certain rules and requirements. At its most basic level, a variable statement needs to satisfy the following requirements:

- The type of data the variable will store needs to be specified
- The variable has to have a unique name
- If there is an assigned value, it must match the specified type
- The variable declaration needs to end with a semicolon

The result of adhering to these rules is the following syntax:

```
dataType uniqueName = value;
```

Variables need unique names to avoid conflicts with words that are already taken by C#, which are called **keywords**. You can find the full list of protected keywords at https://docs.microsoft.com/en-us/dotnet/csharp/language-reference/keywords/index.

This is simple, neat, and efficient. However, a programming language wouldn't be useful in the long run if there was only one way of creating something as pervasive as variables. Complex applications and games have different use cases and scenarios, all of which have unique C# syntax.

Type and value declarations

The most common scenario for creating variables is one that has all of the pieces available. For instance, if we knew a player's age, storing it would be as easy as this:

```
int currentAge = 32;
```

All of the basic requirements are met:

- A data type is specified, which is `int` (short for integer)
- A unique name is used, which is `currentAge`
- `32` is an integer, which matches the specified data type
- The statement ends with a semicolon

Type-only declarations

Consider another scenario: you know the type of data you want a variable to store, and its name, but not its value. The value will be computed and assigned somewhere else, but you still need to declare the variable at the top of the script.

This situation is perfect for a type-only declaration:

```
int currentAge;
```

Only the type (`int`) and unique name (`currentAge`) are defined, but the statement is still valid because we've followed the rules. With no assigned value, default values will be assigned according to the variable's type. In this case, `currentAge` will be set to `0`, which matches the `int` type. Whenever the actual value is available, it can easily be set in a separate statement:

```
currentAge = 32;
```

Access modifiers

Now that the basic syntax is no longer a mystery, let's get into the finer details of variable statements. Since we read code from left to right, it makes sense to begin our variable deep-dive with a topic we haven't discussed yet: access modifiers.

Take a quick look back at the variables we used in `LearningCurve` and you'll see they had an extra keyword at the front of their statements: `public`. This is the variables access modifier. Think of it as a security setting, determining who and what can access the variable's information.

> Any variable that isn't marked **public** won't show up in the Unity **Inspector** panel.

If you include a modifier, the updated syntax recipe looks like this:

```
accessModifier dataType uniqueName = value;
```

While access modifiers aren't necessary to declare a variable, it's a good habit to get into as a new programmer. That extra word goes a long way toward readability and professionalism in your code.

Choosing a security level

There are four main access modifiers available in C#, but the two you'll be working with most often as a beginner are the following:

- **Public**: This is available to any script without restriction.
- **Private**: This is only available in the class they're created in (which is called the containing class). Any variable without an access modifier defaults to private.

The two advanced modifiers have the following characteristics:

- **Protected**: Accessible from their containing class or types derived from it
- **Internal**: Only available in the current assembly

There are specific use cases for each of these modifiers, but until we get to the advanced chapters, don't worry about **protected** and **internal**.

Two combined modifiers also exist, but we won't be using them in this book. You can find more information about them at `https://docs.` `microsoft.com/en-us/dotnet/csharp/language-reference/keywords/` `access-modifiers`.

Time for action – making a variable private

Just like information in real life, some data needs to be protected or shared with specific people. If there's no need for a variable to be changed in the **Inspector** or accessed from other scripts, it's a good candidate for a private access modifier.

Perform the following steps to update `LearningCurve`:

1. Change the access modifier in front of `firstNumber` from `public` to `private` and save the file.
2. Go back into Unity, select **Main Camera**, and take a look at what changed in the `LearningCurve` section.

What just happened?

Since `firstNumber` is now private, it's no longer visible in the Inspector and can only be accessed within **Learning Curve**. If we click **Play,** the script will still work exactly as it did before:

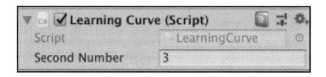

Working with types

Assigning a specific type to a variable is an important choice, one that trickles down into every interaction the variable is involved in. C# is what's called a strongly-typed or type-safe language, meaning that every variable has to have a data type without exception. This also means that there are specific rules when it comes to performing operations, and regulations when converting a given variable into another type.

Common built-in types

All data types in C# trickle down (derive) from a common ancestor: `System.Object`. This hierarchy, called the **Common Type System** (**CTS**), means that different types have a lot of shared functionality. The following table lays out some of the most common data type options and the values they store:

Type	Contents of the variable
int	A simple integer, such as the number 3
float	A number with a decimal, such as the number 3.14
string	Characters in double quotes, such as, "Watch me go now"
bool	A boolean, either **true** or **false**

In addition to specifying the kind of value a variable can store, types contain added information about themselves, including the following:

- Required storage space
- Minimum and maximum values
- Allowed operations
- Location in memory
- Accessible methods
- Base (derived) type

If this seems overwhelming, take a deep breath. Working with all of the types C# offers is a perfect example of using documentation over memorization. Pretty soon using even the most complex custom types will feel like second-nature.

 You can find a complete list of all of the C# built-in types and their specifications at `https://docs.microsoft.com/en-us/dotnet/csharp/programming-guide/types/index`.

Time for action – playing with different types

Go ahead and open up LearningCurve and add a new variable for each type in the preceding chart from the *Common built-in types* section. The names and values are your choice, just make sure they're marked as public so we can see them in the Inspector. If you need inspiration take a look at my code in the following screenshot:

```
5 public class LearningCurve : MonoBehaviour
6 {
7     private int firstNumber = 2;
8     public int secondNumber = 3;
9     public float pi = 3.14f;
10    public string firstName = "Bilbo";
11    public bool allGood = true;
```

 When dealing with string types, the actual text value needs to be inside a pair of double quotes, while float values need to end with a lowercase *f*, as you can see with pi and firstName.

What just happened?

All, our different variable types are now visible. Take note of the bool variable that Unity displays as a checkbox (true is checked and false is unchecked):

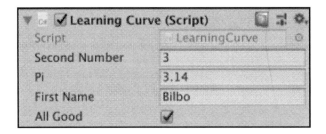

Time for action – creating interpolated strings

While number types behave as you'd expect from grade school math, strings are a different story. It's possible to insert variables and literal values directly into text by starting with a $ character, which is called string interpolation. The interpolated values are added inside curly brackets, just like using the LogFormat() method. Let's create a simple interpolated string of our own inside the LearningCurve to see this in action:

Print out the interpolated string inside the `Start()` method pictured here and hit **Play**:

```
15      // Use this for initialization
16      void Start()
17      {
18          Debug.Log($"A string can have variables like {firstName} inserted directly!");
19      }
```

What just happened?

Thanks to the curly brackets, the value of `firstName` is treated as a value and prints out inside the interpolated string. It's also possible to create interpolated strings using the + operator, which we'll get to in a few minutes:

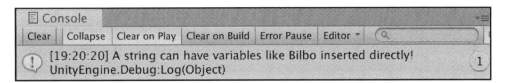

Type conversions

We've already seen that variables can only hold values of their declared types, but there will be situations where you need to combine or assign different variable types. In programming terminology, these are called conversions and come in two main flavors:

- **Implicit** conversions take place automatically, usually when a smaller value will fit into another variable type without any rounding. For example, any integer can be implicitly converted into a `double` or `float` without additional code:

  ```
  float implicitConversion = 3;
  ```

- **Explicit** conversions are needed when there is a risk of losing a variable's information during a conversion. For example, if we wanted to convert `double` into `int`, we would have to explicitly cast (convert) it by adding the destination type in parentheses before the value we want to convert. This tells the compiler that we are aware data (or precision) might be lost.

In this explicit conversion, `3.14` would be rounded down to `3`, losing the decimal values:

```
int explicitConversion = (int)3.14;
```

C# provides built-in methods for explicitly converting values to common types. For example, any type can be converted into a string value with the `ToString()` method, while the `Convert` class can handle more complicated conversions. You can find more info about these features under the Methods section at `https://docs.microsoft.com/en-us/dotnet/api/system.convert?view=netframework-4.7.2`.

Inferred declarations

So far, we've learned that types have rules regarding their interactions, operations, and conversion, but how do we handle a situation where you need to store a variable of an unknown type? This might sound crazy, but think about a data-download scenario—you know the information is coming into your game, but you're not sure what form it will take.

Luckily, C# has the ability to infer a variable's type from its assigned value. The `var` keyword lets the program know that the type of `currentAge` needs to be determined by its value of `32`, which is an integer:

```
var currentAge = 32;
```

While this is handy in certain situations, don't be suckered into the lazy programming habit of using inferred variable declarations for everything. This adds a lot of guesswork into your code, where it should be crystal clear.

Custom types

When we're talking about data types, it's important to understand early on that numbers and words (referred to as *literal values*) are not the only kinds of values a variable can store. For instance, a class, struct, or enumeration can be stored as variables, topics we will introduce in `Chapter 5`, *Working with Classes and OOP*, and in greater detail in `Chapter 10`, *Revisiting Types Methods and Classes*.

Types roundup

Types are complicated, and the only way to get comfortable with them is by using them. However, here are some important things to keep in mind:

- All variables need to have a specified type (be it explicit or inferred).
- Variables can only hold values of their assigned type (`string` can't be assigned to `int`).
- Each type has a set of operations that it can and can't apply (`bool` can't be subtracted from another value).
- If a variable needs to be assigned or combined with a variable of a different type, a conversion needs to take place (either implicit or explicit).
- The C# compiler can infer a variable's type from its value using the `var` keyword, but should only be used when the type isn't known when it's created.

Naming variables

Picking names for your variables might seem like an afterthought in light of everything we've learned about access modifiers and types, but it shouldn't be a trivial choice. Clear and consistent naming conventions in your code will not only make it more readable, but will also ensure that other developers on your team understand your intentions without having to ask.

Best practices

The first rule of a variable name is that it be meaningful; the second, that you use camel case. Let's take a common example from games and declare a variable to store a player's health:

```
public int health = 100;
```

If you find yourself declaring a variable like this, alarm bells should be going off in your head. Whose health? Is it storing the maximum or minimum value? What other code will be affected when this value changes? These are all questions that should be easily answered by a meaningful variable name; you don't want to find yourself confused by your own code in a week or a month's time.

With that said, let's try to make this a bit better using a camel case name:

```
public int maxCharacterHealth = 100;
```

 Remember, camel casing starts a variable name with a lowercase letter, then capitalizes the first letter in each word thereafter. It also makes a clear distinction between variable and class names, which start with an uppercase letter.

That's much better. With a little thought, we've updated the variable name with meaning and context. Since there is no technical limit on how long a variable name can be, you might find yourself going overboard and writing out ridiculously descriptive names, which will give you problems just as surely as a short, non-descriptive name.

As a general rule, make a variable name as descriptive as it needs to be—no more, no less. Find your own style and stick to it.

Variable scope

We're getting to the end of our shallow dive into variables, but there's still one more important topic we need to cover: scope. Similar to access modifiers determining which outside classes can grab a variable's information, variable scope is the term used to describe where a given variable exists and can be accessed within its containing class.

There are three main levels of variable scope in C#:

- **Global** scope refers to a variable that can be accessed by an entire program, in this case, a game. C# doesn't directly support global variables, but the concept is useful in certain cases, which we'll cover in `Chapter 10`, *Revisiting Types, Methods, and Classes*
- **Class** or **member** scope refers to a variable that is accessible anywhere in its containing class.
- **Local** scope refers to a variable that is only accessible inside the specific block of code it's created in:

```
 4
 5 public class LearningCurve : MonoBehaviour
 6 {
 7     public string characterClass = "Ranger";        ◄────────  Class scope
 8
 9     // Use this for initialization
10     void Start ()
11     {
12         int characterHealth = 100;      ◄──────────  Local scope 1
13         Debug.Log(characterClass + " - HP: " + characterHealth);
14     }
15
16     void CreateCharacter()
17     {
18         int characterName = "Aragorn";      ◄────────  Local scope 2
19         Debug.Log(characterName + " - " + characterClass);
20     }
21 }
22
```

When we talk about code blocks, we're referring to the area inside any set of curly brackets. These brackets serve as a kind of visual hierarchy in programming; the farther right-indented they are, the deeper they are nested in the class.

Let's break down the class and local scope variables in the preceding screenshot:

- characterClass is declared at the very top of the class, which means we can reference it by name anywhere inside LearningCurve. You might hear this concept referred to as variable visibility, which is a good way of thinking about it.
- characterHealth is declared inside the Start() method, which means it is only visible inside that block of code. We can still access characterClass from Start() with no issue, but if we attempted to access characterHealth from anywhere but Start(), we would get an error.
- characterName is in the same boat as characterHealth; it can only be accessed from the CreateCharacter() method. This was just to illustrate that there can be multiple, even nested, local scopes in a single class.

If you're around programmers enough, you'll hear discussions (or arguments, depending on the time of day) about the best place to declare a variable. The answer is simpler than you might think: variables should be declared with their use in mind. If you have a variable that needs to be accessed throughout a class, make it a class variable. If you only need a variable in a specific section of code, declare it as a local variable.

Note that only class variables can be viewed in the Inspector, which isn't an option for local or global variables.

Introducing operators

Operator symbols in programming languages represent the *arithmetic, assignment, relational,* and *logical* functionality that types can perform. Arithmetic operators represent basic math functions, while assignment operators perform math and assignment functions together on a given value. Relational and logical operators evaluate conditions between multiple values, such as greater than, lesser than, or equal to. At this point, it only makes sense to cover arithmetic and assignment operators, but we'll get to relational and logical functionality when it becomes relevant in the next chapter.

C# also offers bitwise and miscellaneous operators, but these won't come into play for you until you're well on your way to creating more complex applications.

Arithmetic and assignments

You're already familiar with the arithmetic operator symbols from school:

- + for addition
- − for subtraction
- / for division
- * for multiplication

C# operators follow the conventional order of operations, evaluating parentheses first, then exponents, multiplication, division, addition, and finally subtraction (BEDMAS). For instance, the following equations would have different results even though they contain the same values and operators:

```
5 + 4 - 3 / 2 * 1 = 8
5 + (4 - 3) / 2 * 1 = 5
```

Operators work exactly the same when applied to variables as they do with literal values.

Assignment operators are used as a shorthand replacement for any math operation by using any arithmetic and equals symbol together. For example, if we wanted to multiply a variable, both of the following options would produce the same result:

```
int currentAge = 32;
currentAge = currentAge * 2;
```

Or the alternative way would be as follows:

```
int currentAge = 32;
currentAge *= 2;
```

 The equals symbol is also considered an assignment operator in C#. The other assignment symbols follow the same syntax pattern as our preceding multiplication example: +=, -=, and /= for add and assign, subtract and assign, and divide and assign, respectively.

Strings are a special case when it comes to operators, as they can use the addition symbol to create patchwork text, as follows:

```
string fullName = "Joe" + "Smith";
```

 This approach tends to produce clunky code, making string interpolation the preferred method for putting together different bits of text in most cases.

Time for action – executing incorrect type operations

We've learned that types have rules that govern what kind of operations and interactions they can have, but we haven't seen that in practice. Let's do a little experiment: try to add our `float` and `bool` variables together like we did earlier with our numbers:

```
13    // Use this for initialization
14    void Start ()
15    {
16        Debug.Log(firstName + allGood);
17    }
```

What just happened?

If you look in the **Console**, you'll see that we've got an error message letting us know that a float and a bool can't be added. Whenever you see this type of error, go back and inspect your variable types for incompatibilities:

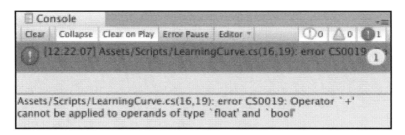

Pop quiz #1 – variables and types

1. What is the proper way to write a variable name in C#?
2. How do you make a variable appear in Unity's Inspector panel?
3. What are the four access modifiers available in C#?
4. When are explicit conversions needed between types?

Defining methods

In the last chapter, we briefly touched on the role methods play in our programs, namely, that they store and execute instructions, just like variables store values. Now we need to understand the syntax of method declarations and how they drive action and behavior in our classes.

Basic syntax

As with variables, method declarations have their own basic requirements, which are as follows:

- The type of data that will be returned by the method
- A unique name starting with a capital letter

- A pair of parentheses following the method name
- A pair of curly brackets marking the method body (where instructions are stored)

Putting all of these rules together, we get a simple method blueprint:

```
returnType UniqueName()
{
    method body
}
```

Let's break down the default `Start()` method in `LearningCurve` as a practical example:

```
13    // Use this for initialization
14    void Start ()
15    {
16        |
17    }
```

- The method starts out with the `void` keyword, which is used as the method's return type if it doesn't return any data.
- The method has a unique name.
- The method has a pair of parentheses after its name to hold any potential parameters.
- The method body is defined by a set of curly brackets.

In general, if you have a method that has an empty method body, it's good practice to delete it from the class. You always want to be pruning your scripts of unused code.

Modifiers and parameters

Methods can also have the same four access modifiers that are available to variables, as well as input parameters. Parameters are variable placeholders, which can be passed into methods and accessed inside them. The number of input parameters isn't limited, but each one needs to be separated by a comma, have its own data type, and a unique name.

Think of method parameters like variable placeholders whose values can be used inside the method body.

If we apply these options, our updated blueprint looks like this:

```
accessModifier returnType UniqueName(parameterType parameterName)
{
    method body
}
```

 If there is no explicit access modifier, the method defaults to private. A private method, like a private variable, cannot be called from other scripts.

To call a method (meaning to run or execute its instructions), we simply use its name followed by a pair of parentheses, with or without parameters, and cap it off with a semicolon:

```
// Without parameters
UniqueName();

// With parameters
UniqueName(parameterVariable);
```

 Like variables, every method has its own fingerprint that describes its access level, return type, and parameters. This is called its *method signature*. Essentially, a method's signature marks it as unique to the compiler so Visual Studio knows what to do with it.

Time for action – defining a simple method

One of the *Time for action* segments in the last chapter had you blindly copy a method called `AddNumbers` into `LearningCurve` without knowing what you were getting into. This time, let's purposefully create a method:

1. Declare a `public` method with a void return type called `GenerateCharacter()`
2. Add a simple `Debug.Log()` that prints out a character name from your favorite game or movie
3. Call `GenerateCharacter()` inside the `Start()` method and hit **Play**:

```
// Use this for initialization
void Start ()
{
    GenerateCharacter();
}

public void GenerateCharacter()
{
    Debug.Log("Character: Spike");
}
```

What just happened?

When the game starts up, Unity automatically calls `Start()`, which in turn calls our `GenerateCharacter()` method and prints to the **Console**.

 If you read enough documentation, you'll see different terminology relating to methods. Throughout the rest of this book, when a method is created or declared, I'll refer to this as **defining** a method. Similarly, I'll refer to running or executing a method as **calling** that method.

Naming conventions

Like variables, methods need unique, meaningful names to distinguish them in code. Methods drive actions, so it's a good practice to name them with that in mind. For example, `GenerateCharacter()` sounds like a command, which reads well when you call it in a script, whereas a name such as `Summary()` is bland and doesn't paint a very clear picture of what the method will accomplish.

Methods always start with an uppercase letter, followed by capitalizing the first letter in any subsequent words. This is called *PascalCase* (a step-sibling of the *CamelCase* format we used with variables).

Methods are logic detours

We've seen that lines of code execute sequentially in the order they're written, but bringing methods into the picture introduces a unique situation. Calling a method tells the program to take a detour into the method instructions, run them one by one, then resume sequential execution where the method was called.

Take a look at the following screenshot and see whether you can figure out in what order the debug logs will be printed out to the console:

```
13      // Use this for initialization
14      void Start ()
15      {
16          Debug.Log("Choose a character.");
17          GenerateCharacter();
18          Debug.Log("A fine choice.");|
19      }
20
21      public void GenerateCharacter()
22      {
23          Debug.Log("Character: Spike");
24      }
```

1. `Choose a character` prints out first because it's the first line of code.
2. When `GenerateCharacter()` is called, the program jumps to line 23, prints out `Character: Spike`, then resumes execution at line 17.
3. `A fine choice` prints out last, after all lines in `GenerateCharacter()` are finished running. You can see the final debug log in the screenshot below for reference:

Specifying parameters

Chances are your methods aren't always going to be as simple as `GenerateCharacter()`. In order to pass in additional information, we'll need to define parameters that our method can accept and work with. Every method parameter is an instruction and needs to have two things:

- An explicit type
- A unique name

Does this sound familiar? Method parameters are essentially stripped-down variable declarations and perform the same function. Each parameter acts like a local variable, only accessible inside their specific method.

 You can have as many parameters as you need. Whether writing your own custom methods or using built-in ones, the parameters that are defined are what the method requires to perform its specified task.

Assigning arguments

If parameters are the blueprint for the types of values a method can accept, then arguments are the values themselves. To break this down further, consider the following:

- The argument passed into a method always needs to match the parameters types, just like a variable and its value.
- Arguments can be literal values (for instance, the number 2) or variables declared elsewhere in the class.

 Argument names and parameter names don't need to match in order to compile.

Time for action – adding method parameters

Let's update `GenerateCharacter()` to take in two parameters:

1. Add two method parameters, one for a character's name of the `string` type, and one for a character's level of the `int` type.
2. Update `Debug.Log()` to use the new parameters.

3. Update the `GenerateCharacter()` method call in `Start()` with your own arguments, either literal values or declared variables:

```
13    // Use this for initialization
14    void Start ()
15    {
16        int characterLevel = 32;
17        GenerateCharacter("Spike", characterLevel);
18    }
19
20    public void GenerateCharacter(string name, int level)
21    {
22        Debug.LogFormat("Character: {0} - Level: {1}", name, level);
23    }
```

Arguments

Parameters

What just happened?

We defined two parameters, `name` (string) and `level` (int), and used them inside the `GenerateCharacter()` method just like local variables. When we called the method inside `Start()`, we added argument values for each parameter with corresponding types. In the preceding screenshot, you can see that using the literal string value in quotations produced the same result as using `characterLevel`:

Specifying return values

Aside from accepting parameters, methods can return values of any C# type. All of our previous examples have used the `void` type, which doesn't return anything, but being able to write instructions and pass back computed results is where methods really shine.

According to our blueprints, method return types are specified after the access modifier. In addition to the type, the method needs to contain the `return` keyword followed by the return value. A return value can be a variable, a literal value, or even an expression, as long as it matches the declared return type.

Methods that have a return type of void can still use the return keyword with no value or expression assigned. Once the line with the return keyword is reached, the method will stop executing. This is useful in cases where you want to avoid certain behaviors or guard against program crashes.

Time for action – adding a return type

Let's update the `GenerateCharacter` method to return an integer:

1. Change the return type in the method declaration from `void` to `int`.
2. Set the return value to `level + 5` using the `return` keyword:

```
20    public int GenerateCharacter(string name, int level)
21    {
22        Debug.LogFormat("Character: {0} – Level: {1}", name, level);
23        return level + 5;
24    }
```

What just happened?

`GenerateCharacter()` will now return an integer, computed from adding 5 to the level argument. We haven't specified how, or if, we want to use this return value, which means that right now the script won't do anything new.

Using return values

When it comes to using return values, there are two approaches available:

- Create a local variable to capture (store) the returned value.
- Use the calling method itself as a stand-in for the returned value, using it just like a variable. The calling method is the actual line of code that fires the instructions, which in our example would be `GenerateCharacter("Spike", characterLevel)`. You can even pass a calling method into another method as an argument if need be.

 The first option is preferred in most programming circles for its readability. Throwing around method calls as variables can get messy fast, especially when using them as arguments in other methods.

Time for action – capturing return values

We're going to use both ways of capturing and using return variables with two simple debug logs:

1. Create a new local variable of the int type, called nextSkillLevel, and assign it to the return value of the GenerateCharacter() method call we already had in place.
2. Add two debug logs: the first printing out nextSkillLevel, and the second printing out a new calling method with argument values of your choice.
3. Comment out the debug log inside GenerateCharacter() with two backslashes (//) to make the console output less cluttered.
4. Save the file and hit **Play** in Unity:

```
13      // Use this for initialization
14      void Start ()
15      {
16          int characterLevel = 32;
17
18          int nextSkillLevel = GenerateCharacter("Spike", characterLevel);
19          Debug.Log(nextSkillLevel);
20          Debug.Log(GenerateCharacter("Faye", characterLevel));
21      }
22
23      public int GenerateCharacter(string name, int level)
24      {
25          //Debug.LogFormat("Character: {0} – Level: {1}", name, level);
26          return level + 5;
27      }
```

What just happened?

To the compiler, nextSkillLevel and the GenerateCharacter() method caller represent the same information, namely an integer, which is why both logs show the number 37:

Hero's trial – methods as arguments

If you're feeling brave, why not try creating a new method that takes in an `int` parameter and simply prints it out to the console—no return type necessary. When you've got that, call the method in `Start`, pass in a `GenerateCharacter` method call as its argument, and take a look at the output.

Common Unity methods

We're now at a point where we can realistically discuss the most common default methods that come with any new Unity C# script: `Start()` and `Update()`. Unlike the methods we define ourselves, methods belonging to the `MonoBehaviour` class are called automatically by the Unity engine according to their respective rules. It's important in most cases to have at least one `MonoBehaviour` method in a script to kick off your own code.

> You can find a complete list of all available `MonoBehaviour` methods and their descriptions here: `https://docs.unity3d.com/ScriptReference/MonoBehaviour.html`.

The Start method

Unity calls this method on the first frame where a script is enabled. Since `MonoBehaviour` scripts are almost always attached to *GameObjects* in a scene, their attached scripts are enabled at the same time they are loaded when you hit play. In our project, `LearningCurve` is attached to the **Main Camera** *GameObject*, which means that its `Start()` method runs when the **Main Camera** is loaded in the scene. `Start()` is primarily used to set up variables or perform logic that needs to happen before `Update()` runs for the first time.

> The examples we've worked on so far have all used `Start()` even though they weren't performing setup actions, which isn't normally the way it would be used. However, it only fires once, making it an excellent tool to use for displaying one-time-only information to the console.

The Update method

If you spend enough time looking at sample code in the *Scripting Reference*, you'll notice that a vast majority of the code is executed using the `Update()` method. As your game runs, the **Scene** is displayed many times per second, which is called the frame rate or **Frames Per Second** (**FPS**). After each frame is displayed, the `Update()` method is called by Unity, making it one of the most executed methods in your game. This makes it ideal for detecting mouse and keyboard input or running gameplay logic.

If you're curious about the **FPS** on your machine, hit **Play** in Unity and click the **Stats** tab in the upper-right corner of the **Game** view:

Pop quiz #2 – Understanding methods

1. What are the minimum requirements for defining a method?
2. What is the purpose of the parentheses at the end of the method name?
3. What does a return type of `void` mean in a method definition?
4. How often is the `Update()` method called by Unity?

Summary

This chapter has been a fast descent from the basic theory of programming and its building blocks into the strata of real code and C# syntax. We've seen good and bad forms of code formatting, learned how to debug information to the Unity console, and created our first variables. C# types, access modifiers, and variable scope weren't far behind, as we worked with member variables in the Inspector and started venturing into the realm of methods and actions.

Methods helped us to understand written instructions in code, but more importantly how to properly harness their power into useful behaviors. Input parameters, return types, and method signatures are all important topics, but the real gift is the potential for new kinds of actions. You're now armed with the two fundamental building blocks of programming; almost everything you'll do from now on is an extension or application of these two concepts.

In the next chapter, we'll take a look at a special subset of C# types called collections, which can store groups of related data, and how to write decision-based code.

Control Flow and Collection Types

One of a computer's central duties is controlling what happens when certain conditions are met. When you click on a folder, you expect it to open; when you type on the keyboard, you expect the text to mirror your keystrokes. Writing code for applications or games is no different, they both need to behave in a certain way in one state, and in another when conditions change. In programming terms, this is called control flow, which is apt because it's literally controlling the flow of code execution across different scenarios.

In addition to working with control statements, we'll be taking a hands-on look at collection data types. Collections are a category of types that allow multiple values, and groupings of values, to be stored in a single variable. These go hand in hand with many of the control-flow scenarios you'll commonly run into, so it's natural that we discuss them together.

In this chapter, we'll be focusing on the following topics:

- Selection statements
- Working with **Array**, **Dictionary**, and **List** collections
- Iteration with `for`, `foreach`, and `do-while` loops
- Execution control with the `break`, `continue`, and `return` keywords
- Understanding C# **Enumerations**

Selection statements

The most complex programming problems can often be boiled down to sets of simple choices that a game or program evaluates and acts on. Since Visual Studio and Unity can't make those choices by themselves, writing out those decisions is up to us. The `if-else` and `switch` selection statements let you specify branching paths, based on one or more conditions, and the actions you want taken in each case. Traditionally, these conditions include the following:

- Detecting user input
- Evaluating expressions and Boolean logic
- Comparing variables or literal values

The if-else statement

`if-else` statements are the most common way of making decisions in code. Stripped of all its syntax the basic idea is *if my condition is met, execute this block of code. If it's not, execute this other block of code.* Think of these statements as gates, or doors, with the conditions as their keys. In order to pass through, the key needs to be valid. Otherwise, entry will be denied and the code will be sent to the next possible gate.

Basic Syntax

A valid `if-else` statement needs the following:

- The `if` keyword at the beginning of the line
- A pair of parentheses to hold the condition
- A pair of curly brackets to hold the code block
- Optionally, an `else` keyword with its own pair of curly brackets and code block

In blueprint form, the syntax almost reads like a sentence:

```
if(condition is true)
{
    Execute this code block
}
else
{
    Execute this code block
}
```

Since these are great introductions to logical thinking, at least in programming, we'll break down the three different `if-else` variations in more detail:

1. A single `if` statement can exist by itself in cases where you don't care about what happens if the condition isn't met. In the following example, if `hasDungeonKey` is set to `true` a debug log will print out, if set to `false` no code will execute:

```
5 public class LearningCurve : MonoBehaviour
6 {
7     public bool hasDungeonKey = true;
8
9     // Use this for initialization
10    void Start()
11    {
12        if(hasDungeonKey)
13        {
14            Debug.Log("You possess the sacred key - enter.");
15        }
16    }
17 }
```

When referring to a condition as being met, I mean that it evaluates to true, or passes.

2. Add an `else` statement in cases where action needs to be taken whether the condition is true or false. If `hasDungeonKey` were `false`, the if statement would fail and the code execution would jump to the `else` statement:

```
5 public class LearningCurve : MonoBehaviour
6 {
7     public bool hasDungeonKcy = true;
8
9     // Use this for initialization
10    void Start()
11    {
12        if(hasDungeonKey)
13        {
14            Debug.Log("You possess the sacred key - enter.");
15        }
16        else
17        {
18            Debug.Log("You have not proved yourself worthy, warrior.");
19        }
20    }
21 }
```

3. For cases where you need to have more than two possible outcomes, add an `else-if` statement with its own parentheses, conditions, and curly brackets. This is best shown rather than explained, which we'll see next.

 Keep in mind that `if` statements can be used by themselves, but the other statements cannot exist on their own.

Time for action – thieving prospects

Let's write out an `if-else` statement that checks the amount of money in a character's pocket, returning different debug logs for three different cases: more than 50, less than 15, and anything else:

1. Open up `LearningCurve` and add a new `int` variable named `currentGold`, setting its value between 1 and 100.
2. Declare an `if` statement to check whether `currentGold` is greater than 50 and print a message to the console if it's true.
3. Add an `else-if` statement to check whether `currentGold` is less than 15 with a different debug log.
4. Add an `else` statement with no condition and a final default log.
5. Save the file and hit **Play**:

```
5 public class LearningCurve : MonoBehaviour
6 {
7     public int currentGold = 32;
8
9     // Use this for initialization
10    void Start()
11    {
12        if(currentGold > 50)
13        {
14            Debug.Log("You're rolling in it - beware of pickpockets.");
15        }
16        else if (currentGold < 15)
17        {
18            Debug.Log("Not much there to steal.");
19        }
20        else
21        {
22            Debug.Log("Looks like your purse is in the sweet spot.");
23        }
24    }
25 }
```

What just happened?

With `currentGold` set to `32` in my example, we can break down the code sequence as follows:

1. The `if` statement and debug log is skipped because `currentGold` is not greater than `50`.
2. The `else-if` statement and debug log is also skipped because `currentGold` is not less than `15`.
3. Since neither previous conditions was met, the `else` statement executes and the third debug log is displayed:

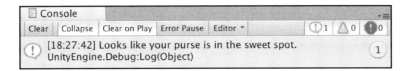

Using the NOT operator

Use cases won't always require checking for a positive, or `true`, condition, which is where the NOT operator comes in. Written with a single exclamation point, the NOT operator allows for negative, or false, conditions to be met by `if` or `else-if` statements. As we've seen, we can check for Boolean values, literal values, or expressions in an if condition, so naturally the NOT operator has to be adaptable. Take a look at the following example of two different negative values used in an if statement:

```
5 public class LearningCurve : MonoBehaviour
6 {
7     public bool hasDungeonKey = false;
8     public string weaponType = "Arcane Staff";
9
10    // Use this for initialization
11    void Start()
12    {
13        if(!hasDungeonKey)
14        {
15            Debug.Log("You may not enter without the sacred key.");
16        }
17
18        if(weaponType != "Longsword")
19        {
20            Debug.Log("You don't appear to have the right type of weapon...");
21        }
22    }
23 }
```

- The first statement can be translated to, "If `hasDungeonKey` is `false`, the if statement evaluates to0 true and executes its code block."

 If you're asking yourself how a false value can evaluate to true, think of it this way: the **if** statement is not checking whether the value is true, but that the expression itself is true. `hasDungeonKey` might be set to false, but that's what we're checking for, so it's true in the context of the if condition.

- The second statement can be translated to, "If the string value of `weaponType` is `not equal` to `Longsword`, execute this code block."

You can see the debug results in the following screenshot, but if you're still fuzzy, copy the preceding code into *LearningCurve* and play around with the variable values until it clicks:

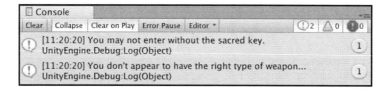

Nesting statements

One of the most valuable functions of an `if-else` statement is that they can be nested inside each other, creating complex logic routes through your code. In programming, we call these decision trees. Just like a real hallway, there can be doors behind other doors, creating a labyrinth of possibilities:

```
5 public class LearningCurve : MonoBehaviour
6 {
7      public bool weaponEquipped = true;
8      public string weaponType = "Longsword";
9
10     // Use this for initialization
11     void Start()
12     {
13         if(weaponEquipped)
14         {
15             if(weaponType == "Longsword")
16             {
17                 Debug.Log("For the Queen!");
18             }
19         }
20         else
21         {
22             Debug.Log("Fists aren't going to work against armor...");
23         }
24     }
25 }
```

Let's break down the preceding example:

- First, an `if` statement checks whether we have `weaponEquipped`. At this point, the code only cares whether it's `true`, not what type of weapon it is.
- The second `if` statement checks the `weaponType` and prints out the associated debug log.
- If the first `if` evaluates to `false`, the code would jump to the `else` statement and its debug log. If the second if evaluates to `false`, nothing is printed because there is no `else` statement.

> The responsibility of handling logic outcomes is 100% on the programmer. It's up to you to determine the possible branches or outcomes your code can take.

Evaluating multiple conditions

In addition to nesting statements, it's also possible to combine multiple condition checks into a single if or `else-if` statement with AND and OR logic operators:

- AND is written with two ampersand characters, `&&`. Any condition using the AND operator means that all conditions need to evaluate to true for the if statement to execute.
- OR is written with two pipe character, `||`. An if statement using the OR operator will execute if one or more of its conditions is true.

In the following example, the `if` statement has been updated to check for both `weaponEquipped` and `weaponType`, both of which need to be true for the code block to execute:

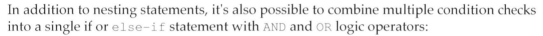

```
13        if(weaponEquipped && weaponType == "Longsword")
14        {
15            Debug.Log("For the Queen!");
16        }
```

> AND and OR operators can be combined to check multiple conditions in any order or number. Just be careful when using them together that you don't create logic conditions that will never execute.

Time for action – reaching the treasure

Let's cement this topic with a little treasure chest experiment:

1. Declare three variables at the top of LearningCurve: pureOfHeart is a bool and should be true; hasSecretIncantation is also a bool and should be false; rareItem is a string and the value is up to you.

2. Create a public method with no return value called OpenTreasureChamber and call it inside Start.

3. Inside OpenTreasureChamber, declare an if-else statement to check whether pureOfHeart is true *and* rareItem matches the string value you assigned to it.

4. Create a nested if-else statement inside the first, checking whether hasSecretIncantation is false.

5. Add debug logs for each if-else case, save, and hit Play:

```
 5 public class LearningCurve : MonoBehaviour
 6 {
 7     public bool pureOfHeart = true;
 8     public bool hasSecretIncantation = false;
 9     public string rareItem = "Relic Stone";
10
11     // Use this for initialization
12     void Start()
13     {
14         OpenTreasureChamber();
15     }
16
17     public void OpenTreasureChamber()
18     {
19         if (pureOfHeart && rareItem == "Relic Stone")
20         {
21             if(!hasSecretIncantation)
22             {
23                 Debug.Log("You have the spirit, but not the knowledge.");
24             }
25             else
26             {
27                 Debug.Log("The treasure is yours, worthy hero!");
28             }
29         }
30         else
31         {
32             Debug.Log("Come back when you have what it takes.");
33         }
34     }
35 }
```

What just happened?

If you matched the variable values to the preceding screenshot, the nested if statement debug log will be printed out. This means that our code got past the first if checking for two conditions, but failed the third:

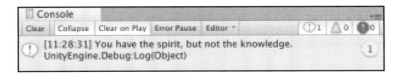

The switch statement

`if-else` statements are a great way to write decision logic, but when you have more than three or four branching actions, they just aren't feasible. Before you know it, your code can end up looking like a tangled knot that's hard to follow, and a headache to update. `switch` statements take in expressions and let us write out actions for each possible outcome, but in a much more concise format than `if-else`.

Basic syntax

Switch statements need the following elements:

- The `switch` keyword followed by a pair of parentheses holding its condition
- A pair of curly brackets
- A `case` statement for each possible path ending with a colon:
    - Individual lines of code or methods, followed by the `break` keyword and a semicolon
- A default case statement ending with a colon:
    - Individual lines of code or methods, followed by the `break` keyword and a semicolon

In blueprint form, it looks as follows:

```
switch(matchExpression)
{
    case matchValue1:
        Executing code block
        break;
    case matchValue2:
```

```
        Executing code block
        break;
    default:
        Executing code block
        break;
}
```

The highlighted keywords in the blueprint are the important bits. When a `case` is defined, anything between its colon and `break` keyword acts like the code block of an if-else. The `break` keyword just tells the program to exit the `switch` statement entirely after the selected case fires.

Pattern matching

In switch statements, pattern matching is how a match expression is validated against multiple case statements. Match expressions can be of any type that isn't null or nothing; all case statement values need to match the type of the match expression. For example, if we had a switch that was evaluating an integer variable, each case statement would need to specify an integer value for it to check against. The case statement with a value that matches the expression is the one that is executed. If no case is matched, the default case fires.

Time for action – choosing an action

That was a lot of new syntax and information, but it helps to see it in action. Let's create a simple switch statement for different actions a character could take:

1. Create a new string variable (member or local) named `characterAction` and set it to `Attack`.
2. Declare a `switch` statement and use `characterAction` as the match expression.
3. Create two case statements for `Heal` and `Attack` with different debug logs, and don't forget to include the `break` keyword at the end of each.
4. Add a default case with a debug log and break.
5. Save the file and hit Play in Unity:

```
 5 public class LearningCurve : MonoBehaviour
 6 {
 7     // Use this for initialization
 8     void Start()
 9     {
10         string characterAction = "Attack";
11
12         switch(characterAction)
13         {
14             case "Heal":
15                 Debug.Log("Potion sent.");
16                 break;
17             case "Attack":
18                 Debug.Log("To arms!");
19                 break;
20             default:
21                 Debug.Log("Shields up.");
22                 break;
23         }
24     }
25 }
```

What just happened?

Since `characterAction` is set to `Attack`, the switch executes the second case and prints out its debug log. Change `characterAction` to either `Heal` or an undefined action to see the first and default cases in action:

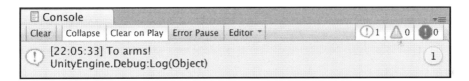

Fall-through cases

Switch statements are able to execute the same action for multiple cases, similar to how we specified several conditions in a single if statement. The term for this is called fall-through, or sometimes fall-through cases. If a case block is left empty and without a `break` keyword, it will fall through to the case directly beneath it.

Cases can be written in any order, even the default, so creating fall-through cases greatly increases code readability and efficiency.

Time for action – rolling the dice

Let's simulate a tabletop game situation with a switch statement and fall-through case, where a dice roll determines the outcome of a specific action:

1. Create an `int` variable named `diceRoll` and assign it a value of `7`.

2. Declare a switch statement with `diceRoll` as the match expression.

3. Add three cases for possible dice rolls: `7`, `15`, and `20`.

4. Case `15` and `20` should have their own debug logs and break statements, case `7` should fall through to case `15`.

5. Save the file and run it in Unity:

```
7    // Use this for initialization
8    void Start()
9    {
10       int diceRoll = 7;
11
12       switch(diceRoll)
13       {
14           case 7:
15           case 15:
16               Debug.Log("Mediocre damage, not bad.");
17               break;
18           case 20:
19               Debug.Log("Critical hit, the creature goes down!");
20               break;
21           default:
22               Debug.Log("You completely missed and fell on your face.");
23               break;
24       }
25    }
```

What just happened?

With `diceRoll` set to `7`, the switch will match with the first case, which will fall through and execute case `15` because it lacks a code block and break statement. If you change `diceRoll` to `15` or `20`, the console will show their respective messages, and any other value will fire off the default case at the end of the statement:

Switch statements are extremely powerful and can simplify even the most complex decision logic. If you want to dig deeper into switch pattern matching, check out this link: `https://docs.microsoft.com/en-us/dotnet/csharp/language-reference/keywords/switch`.

Pop quiz #1 – If, and, or but

1. What values are used to evaluate if statements?
2. Which operator can turn a true condition false or a false condition true?
3. If two conditions need to be true in order for an if statement's code to execute, what logical operator would you use to join the conditions?
4. If only one of two conditions needs to be true in order to make an if statement's code executes, what logical operator would you use to join the two conditions?

Collections at a glance

So far we've only needed variables to store a single value, but there are many conditions where a group of values will be required. Collection types in C# include Arrays, Dictionaries, and Lists, each with its own strengths and weaknesses, which we'll discuss in the following sections.

Arrays

Arrays are the most basic collection C# offers. Think of them as containers for a group of values, called *elements* in programming terminology, each of which can be accessed or modified individually:

- Arrays can store any type of value; all the elements need to be of the same type.
- The length, or number of elements, an array can have is set when it's created, and can't be modified afterward.
- If no initial values assigned when it's created, each element will be given a default value. Arrays storing number types default to zero, while any other type gets set to null or nothing.

Arrays are the least flexible collection type in C#, mainly because elements can't be added or removed after creation. However, they are particularly useful when storing information that isn't likely to change.

Basic syntax

Declaring an array is similar to other variable types we've worked with, but has a few modifications:

- Array variables need a specified element type, a pair of square brackets, and a unique name
- The **new** keyword is used to create the array in memory, followed by the value type and another pair of square brackets
- The number of elements the array will store goes inside the second pair of square brackets

In blueprint form, it looks like this:

```
elementType[] name = new elementType[numberOfElements];
```

Let's take an example were we need to store the top three high scores in our game:

```
int[] topPlayerScores = new int[3];
```

Broken down, `topPlayerScores` is an array of integers that will store three integer elements. Since we didn't add any initial values, each of the three values in `topPlayerScores` is 0.

You can assign values directly to an array when it's created by adding them inside a pair of curly brackets at the end of the variable declaration. C# has a longhand and shorthand way of doing this, but both are equally valid:

```
// Longhand initializer
int[] topPlayerScores = new int[] {713, 549, 984};

// Shortcut initializer
int[] topPlayerScores = { 713, 549, 984 };
```

 Initializing arrays with the shorthand syntax is very common, so I'll be using it for the rest of the book. However, if you want to remind yourself of the details, feel free to use the explicit wording.

Indexing and subscripts

Each array element is stored in the order it's assigned, which is referred to as its index. Arrays are zero-indexed, meaning that the element order starts at 0 instead of one. Think of an element's index as its reference, or location. In `topPlayerScores`, the first integer, `452`, is located at index **0**, `713` at index **1**, and `984` at index **2**:

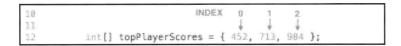

Individual values are located by their index by using the subscript operator, which is a pair of square brackets that contains the index of the elements. For example, to retrieve and store the second array element in `topPlayerScores`, we would use the array name followed by subscript brackets and index `1`:

```
// The value of score is set to 713
int score = topPlayerScores[1];
```

The subscript operator can also be used to directly modify an array value just like any other variable, or even passed around as an expression by itself:

```
topPlayerScores[1] = 1001;
Debug.Log(topPlayerScores[1]);
```

The values in `topPlayerScores` are now `452`, `1001`, and `984`.

Range exceptions

When arrays are created, the number of elements is set and unchangeable, which means we can't access an element that doesn't exist. In the `topPlayerScores` example, the array length is 3, so the range of valid indexes is from `0` – `2`. Any index of 3 or higher is out of the array's range and will generate an aptly-named `IndexOutOfRangeException` in the console:

Good programming habits dictate that we avoid range exceptions by checking whether the value we want is within an arrays index range, which we'll cover in the *Iteration statements* section.

Lists

Lists are closely related to arrays, collecting multiple values of the same type into a single variable. However, they're much more flexible when it comes to adding, removing, and updating elements, making them the preferred choice of the two in most situations.

Basic syntax

A list-type variable needs to meet the following requirements:

- The List keyword, its element type between a left and right arrow character, and a unique name.
- The new keyword to initialize the list in memory, with the List keyword and element type between arrow characters.
- A pair of parentheses capped off by a semicolon.

In blueprint form, it reads as follows:

```
List<elementType> name = new List<elementType>();
```

 List length can always be modified, so there is no need to specify how many elements it will eventually hold when created.

Like arrays, lists can be initialized in the variable declaration by adding element values inside a pair of curly brackets:

```
List<elementType> name = new List<elementType>() { value1, value2 };
```

Elements are stored in the order they are added, zero-indexed, and can be accessed using the subscript operator.

Time for action – party members

Let's do a warm-up exercise by creating a list of party members in a fictional role-playing game:

1. Create a new `List` of the `string` type called `questPartyMembers` and initialize it with the names of three characters.
2. Add a debug log to print out the number of party members in the list using the `Count` method.
3. Save the file and **Play** it in Unity:

```
 7      // Use this for initialization
 8      void Start()
 9      {
10          List<string> questPartyMembers = new List<string>()
11          { "Grim the Barbarian", "Merlin the Wise", "Sterling the Knight"};
12
13          Debug.LogFormat("Party Members: {0}", questPartyMembers.Count);
14      }
15 }
```

What just happened?

We initialized a new list called `questPartyMembers`, which now holds three string values, and used the Count method from the List class to print out the number of elements:

Common methods

List elements can be accessed and modified like arrays with a subscript operator and index, as long as the index is within the list range. However, the list class has a variety of methods that extend its functionality, such as adding, inserting, and removing elements.

Sticking with the `questPartyMembers` list, let's add a new member to the team:

```
questPartyMembers.Add("Craven the Necromancer");
```

The `Add` method appends the new element at the end of the list, which brings the `questPartyMembers` count to 4 and element order to the following:

```
{ "Grim the Barbarian", "Merlin the Wise", "Sterling the Knight", "Craven
the Necromancer"};
```

To add an element in a specific spot in a list, we can pass the `Insert` method the index and value we want to add:

```
questPartyMembers.Insert(1, "Tanis the Thief");
```

When an element is inserted at a previously-occupied index, all the elements in the list have their indexes increased by 1. In our example, `"Tanis the Thief"` is now at index 1, meaning that `"Merlin the Wise"` is now at index 2 instead of 1, and so on:

```
{ "Grim the Barbarian", "Tanis the Thief", "Merlin the Wise", "Sterling the
Knight", "Craven the Necromancer"};
```

Removing an element is just as simple, all we need is the index or literal value and the `List` class does the work:

```
// Both of these methods would remove the required element
questPartyMembers.RemoveAt(0);
questPartyMembers.Remove("Grim the Barbarian");
```

At the end of our edits, `questPartyMembers` now contains the following elements indexed from `0 - 3`:

```
{ "Tanis the Thief", "Merlin the Wise", "Sterling the Knight", "Craven the
Necromancer"};
```

There are many more `List` class methods that allow for value checks, finding and sorting elements, and working with ranges. A full method list with descriptions can be found here: `https://docs.microsoft.com/en-us/dotnet/api/system.collections.generic.list-1?view=netframework-4.7.2`.

Dictionaries

The Dictionary type steps away from arrays and lists by storing value pairs in each element, instead of single values. These elements are referred to as key-value pairs: the key acting as the index, or lookup value, for its corresponding value. Unlike arrays and lists, dictionaries are unordered. However, they can be sorted and ordered in various configurations after they are created.

Basic syntax

Declaring a dictionary is almost the same as declaring a List, but with one added detail – both the key and value type need to be specified inside the arrow symbols:

```
Dictionary<keyType, valueType> name = new Dictionary<keyType, valueType>();
```

To initialize a dictionary with key-value pairs, do the following:

- Use a pair of curly brackets at the end of the declaration.
- Add each element within its own pair of curly brackets, with the key and value separated by a comma.
- Separate elements with a comma, except the last element where the comma is optional.

```
Dictionary<keyType, valueType> name = new Dictionary<keyType, valueType>()
{
    {key1, value1},
    {key2, value2}
};
```

An important note when picking key values: each key must be unique, and they cannot be changed. If you need to update a key, either change its value in the variable declaration or remove it and add another in code.

Just like with Arrays and Lists, Dictionaries can be initialized on a single line with no problems from Visual Studio. However, writing out each key-value pair on its own line, like the preceding example, is a good habit to get into, both for readability and your own sanity.

Time for action – setting up an inventory

Let's create a dictionary to store items that a character might carry:

1. Declare a `Dictionary` with a `key` type of `string` and a `value` type of int called `itemInventory`.
2. Initialize it to a `new Dictionary<string; int>()` and add three key-value pairs of your choice. Make sure each element is in its own pair of curly brackets.
3. Add a debug log to print out the `itemInventory.Count` property so we can see how items are stored.

4. Save the file and Play:

```
7     // Use this for initialization
8     void Start()
9     {
10        Dictionary<string, int> itemInventory = new Dictionary<string, int>()
11        {
12            { "Potion", 5 },
13            { "Antidote", 7 },
14            { "Aspirin", 1 }
15        };
16
17        Debug.LogFormat("Items: {0}", itemInventory.Count);|
18    }
19 }
```

What just happened?

A new Dictionary, called `itemInventory`, was created and initialized with three key-value pairs. We specified the keys as strings, with corresponding values as integers, and printed out how many elements itemInventory currently holds:

Working with dictionary Pairs

Key-value pairs can be added, removed, and accessed from dictionaries using both subscript and class methods. To retrieve an element's value, use the subscript operator with the elements key—in the following example, numberOfPotions would be assigned a value of 5:

```
int numberOfPotions = itemInventory["Potion"];
```

An elements value can be updated using the same method—the value associated with "Potion" would now be 10:

```
itemInventory["Potion"] = 10;
```

Elements can be added to dictionaries in two ways: with the `Add` method, and with the subscript operator. The `Add` method takes in a key and value and creates a new key-value element, as long as their types correspond to the dictionary declaration:

```
itemInventory.Add("Throwing Knife", 3);
```

If the subscript operator is used to assign a value to a key that doesn't exist in a dictionary, the compiler will automatically add it as a new key-value pair. For example, if we wanted to add a new element for "Bandages", we could do so with the following code:

```
itemInventory["Bandage"] = 5;
```

This brings up a crucial point about referencing key-value pairs: it's better to be certain that an element exists before trying to access it, in order to avoid mistakenly adding new key-value pairs. Pairing the `ContainsKey` method with an `if` statement is the simple solution since `ContainsKey` returns a Boolean value based on whether the key exists. In the following example, we're sure that the "`Aspirin`" key exists before modifying its value:

```
if(itemInventory.ContainsKey("Aspirin"))
{
    itemInventory["Aspirin"] = 3;
}
```

Finally, a key-value pair can be deleted from a dictionary using the `Remove` method, which takes in a key parameter:

```
itemInventory.Remove("Antidote");
```

Like Lists, Dictionaries offer a variety of methods and functionality to make development easier, but we can't cover them all here. If you're curious, the documentation can be found at `https://docs.microsoft.com/en-us/dotnet/api/system.collections.generic.dictionary-2?view=netframework-1.7.2`.

Pop quiz #2 – all about collections

1. What is an element in an array or list?
2. What is the index number of the first element in an array or list?
3. Can a single array or list store different types of data?
4. How can you add more elements to an array to make room for more data?

Iteration statements

We've accessed individual collection elements through the subscript operator, and collection type methods, but what do we do when we need to go through the entire collection element by element? In programming, this is called iteration, and C# provides several statement types that let us loop through (or iterate over, if you want to be technical) collection elements. Iteration statements are like methods, in that they store a block of code to be executed; unlike methods, they can repeatedly execute their code blocks as long as their conditions are met.

For loops

The `for` loop is most commonly used when a block of code needs to be executed a certain number of times before the program continues. The statement itself takes in three expressions, each with a specific function to perform before the loop executes. Since `for` loops keep track of what iteration they're on, they are best suited to Arrays and Lists.

Take a look at the following looping statement blueprint:

```
for (initializer; condition; iterator)
{
    code block;
}
```

Let's break this down:

- The `for` keyword starts the statement, followed by a pair of parenthesis.
- Inside the parenthesis are the gatekeepers: the `initializer`, `condition`, and `iterator`.
- The loop starts with the `initializer`, a local variable created to keep track of how many times the loop has executed – usually set to 0 because collection types are zero-indexed.
- Next, the `condition` expression is checked, and if true proceeds to the iterator.
- The `iterator` is used to either increase or decrease (increment or decrement) the initializer, meaning the next time the loop evaluates its condition the initializer will be different.

That all sounds like a lot, so let's look at a practical example with the `questPartyMembers` list we created earlier:

```
List<string> questPartyMembers = new List<string>()
{ "Grim the Barbarian", "Merlin the Wise", "Sterling the Knight"};

for (int i = 0; i < questPartyMembers.Count; i++)
{
    Debug.LogFormat("Index: {0} - {1}", i, questPartyMembers[i]);
}
```

Let's go through the loop again and see how it's working:

- First, the `initializer` is set as a local `int` named i set to 0.
- To make sure we never get an out-of-range exception, the `condition` makes sure that the loop only runs another time if **i** is less than the number of elements in `questPartyMembers`.
- Finally, i is increased by 1 each time the loop runs with the **++** operator.
- Inside the `for` loop, we've just printed out the index and the list element at that index using i. Notice that **i** is in step with the index of the collection elements, since both start at 0:

 Traditionally, the letter i is typically used as the initializer variable name. If you happen to have nested `for` loops, the variable names used will be the letters j, k, l, and so on.

Time for action – finding an element

While we loop through questPartyMembers, let's see whether we can identify when a certain element is iterated over and add a special debug log just for that case:

1. Add an if statement below the debug log in the for loop.
2. In the if statements condition, check whether the current questPartyMember matches "Merlin the Wise".
3. If it does, add a debug log of your choice:

```
7      // Use this for initialization
8      void Start()
9      {
10         List<string> questPartyMembers = new List<string>()
11         { "Grim the Barbarian", "Merlin the Wise", "Sterling the Knight"};
12
13         for (int i = 0; i < questPartyMembers.Count; i++)
14         {
15             Debug.LogFormat("Index: {0} - {1}", i, questPartyMembers[i]);
16
17             if(questPartyMembers[i] == "Merlin the Wise")
18             {
19                 Debug.Log("Glad you're here Merlin!");
20             }
21         }
22     }
```

What just happened?

The console output should look almost the same, except that there is now an extra debug log, one that only printed once, when it was Merlin's turn to go through the loop. More specifically, when i was equal to 1 on the second loop, the if statement fired and two logs were printed out instead of just one:

Foreach loops

Foreach loops take each element in a collection and store it in a local variable, making it accessible inside the statement. The local variable type must match the collection element type to work properly. Foreach loops can be used with Arrays and Lists, but they are especially useful with Dictionaries, as they are not based on a numeric index.

In blueprint form, a foreach loop looks as follows:

```
foreach(elementType localName in collectionVariable)
{
    code block;
}
```

Let's stick with the questPartyMembers example and do a roll-call for each of its elements:

```
List<string> questPartyMembers = new List<string>()
{ "Grim the Barbarian", "Merlin the Wise", "Sterling the Knight"};

foreach(string partyMember in questPartyMembers)
{
    Debug.LogFormat("{0} - Here!", partyMember);
}
```

We can break this down as follows:

- The element type is declared as a string, which matches the values in questPartyMembers.
- A local variable called partyMember is created to hold each element as the loop repeats.
- The in keyword followed by the collection we want to loop through, in this case, questPartyMembers, finishes things off:

This is a good deal simpler than the `for` loop, but when dealing with dictionaries, there are a few important differences we need to mention—namely how to deal with key-value pairs as local variables.

Looping through key-value pairs

In order to capture a key-value pair in a local variable, we need to use the aptly-named `KeyValuePair` type, assigning both the key and value types to match the dictionary's corresponding types. Since `KeyValuePair` is its own type, it acts just like any other element type as a local variable.

For example, let's loop through the `itemInventory` dictionary we created earlier in the *Dictionaries* section and debug each key-value like a shop item description:

```
Dictionary<string, int> itemInventory = new Dictionary<string, int>()
{
    { "Potion", 5},
    { "Antidote", 7},
    { "Aspirin", 1}
};

foreach(KeyValuePair<string, int> kvp in itemInventory)
{
 Debug.LogFormat("Item: {0} - {1}g", kvp.Key, kvp.Value);
}
```

We've specified a local variable of `KeyValuePair` called `kvp`, which is tradition like calling the `for` loop initializer `i`, and set the `key` and `value` types as `string` and `int` to match `itemInventory`.

To access the key and value of the local `kvp` variable, we use the `KeyValuePair` properties of `Key` and `Value`, respectively.

In this example, the keys are `strings` and the `values` are integers, which we can print out as the item name and item price:

Hero's trial – finding affordable items

Create a variable to store how much gold your fictional character has and see whether you can add an if statement inside the for each loop to check for items that you can afford. Hint: use `kvp.Value` to compare prices with what's in your wallet.

While loops

`while` loops are similar to `if` statements in that they run as long as a single expression or condition is true. Value comparison and Boolean variables can be used as `while` conditions, and can be modified with the `NOT` operator.

The `while` loop syntax says *while my condition is true, keep running my code block indefinitely*:

```
initializer
while (condition)
{
    code block;
    iterator;
}
```

With `while` loops, it's common to declare an initializer variable, like in a `for` loop, and manually increment or decrement it at the end of the loop's code block. Depending on your situation, the initializer is usually part of the loop's condition.

Time for action – tracking player lives

Let's take a common use case where we need to execute code while the player is alive, and debug when that's no longer the case:

1. Create an initializer variable called `playerLives`, of the `int` type, and set it to `3`.
2. Declare a `while` loop with the condition checking whether `playerLives` is greater than `0` (the player is still alive).
3. Inside the `while` loop, debug something to let us know the character is still kicking, then decrement `playerLives` by 1 using the -- operator.
4. Add a debug log after the `while` loop curly brackets to print something when our lives run out:

```
7     // Use this for initialization
8     void Start()
9     {
10        int playerLives = 3;
11
12        while(playerLives >| 0)
13        {
14            Debug.Log("Still alive!");
15            playerLives--;
16        }
17
18        Debug.Log("Player KO'd...");
19    }
20 }
```

What just happened?

With `playerLives` starting out at `3`, the `while` loop will execute three times. During each loop the debug log "Still alive!" fires, and a life is subtracted from `playerLives`. When the `while` loop goes to run a fourth time, our condition fails because `playerLives` is 0, so the code block is skipped and the final debug log prints out:

To infinity and beyond

Before closing out the chapter, we need to understand one extremely vital concept when it comes to iteration statements: *infinite loops*. These are exactly what they sound like: when a loop's conditions make it impossible for it to stop running and move on in the program. Infinite loops usually happen in `for` and `while` loops when the iterator is not increased or decreased; if the `playerLives` line of code was left out of the `while` loop example, Unity would freeze and/or crash, recognizing that `playerLives` would always be 3 and execute the loop forever.

Iterators are not the only culprits to be aware of; setting conditions in a `for` loop that will never fail, or evaluate to false, can also cause infinite loops. In the party members example from the *Looping through key-value pairs* section, if we had set the `for` loop condition to `i < 0` instead of `i < questPartyMembers.Count`, `i` would always be less than 0, looping until Unity crashed.

Summary

As we bring the chapter to a close, we should reflect on how much we've accomplished and what we can build with that new knowledge. We know how to make decisions in code using simple if-else checks and more complex switch statements. We can create variables that hold collections of values with arrays, lists, or key-value pairs with dictionaries. We can even choose the right looping statement for each collection type, while carefully avoiding infinite-loop crashes. If you're feeling overloaded, that's perfectly OK – logical, sequential thinking is all part of exercising your programming brain.

The next chapter will close out the basics of C# programming with a look into classes, structs, and object-oriented programming (more commonly known as OOP). We'll be putting everything we've learned so far into these topics, preparing for our first real dive into understanding and controlling objects in the Unity engine.

Working with Classes, Structs, and OOP

5

Obviously, the goal of this book isn't to give you a nervous breakdown, but these next topics will definitely take you out of the beginner's cubicle and into the open air of **object-oriented programming (OOP)**. Up to this point, we've been relying exclusively on predefined variable types that are part of the C# language; under-the-hood strings, lists, and dictionaries that are classes, which is why we can create them and use their properties through dot notation. However, relying on built-in types has one glaring weakness—the inability to deviate from the blueprints that C# has already set.

Creating your own classes gives you the freedom to define and configure blueprints of your own design, capturing information and driving action that is specific to your game or application. In essence, custom classes and OOP are the keys to the programming kingdom; without them, unique programs will be few and far between.

In this chapter, we will get hands-on with the following topics:

- Creating classes and instantiating class objects
- Adding class variables, constructors, and methods
- Declaring and using structs
- Understanding reference and value types
- Exploring the basics of OOP

Defining a class

Back in Chapter 2, *The Building Blocks of Programming,* we briefly talked about how classes are blueprints for objects, and mentioned that they can be treated as custom variable types. We also learned that the LearningCurve script is a class, but one that Unity recognizes as being attachable to objects in the scene. The main thing to remember with classes is that they are *reference types*—when they are assigned or passed to another variable, the original object is referenced, not a new copy. We'll get into this after we talk about structs, but before any of that, we need to understand how to create classes.

Basic syntax

For now, we're going to set aside how classes and scripts work in Unity and bring the focus back to the basics of how they are created, and used, strictly in C#. If you remember the blueprint we roughed out, classes are created using the class keyword, as follows:

```
accessModifier class UniqueName
{
    Variables
    Constructors
    Methods
}
```

To make the examples as cohesive as possible throughout this chapter, we'll be creating and modifying a simplified Character class that a typical game will have. We'll also be moving away from code screenshots almost entirely to get you accustomed to reading and interpreting code as you'll see it in the programming wild.

Time for action – creating a character class

We'll need a class to practice with before we can understand their inner workings, so let's create a new C# script and start from scratch:

1. Right-click in the Scripts folder, choose **Create**, and select **C# Script**
2. Name it Character, open it up in Visual Studio, and delete all the generated code after using UnityEngine
3. Declare a public class called Character followed by a set of curly braces, and then save the file, as follows:

```
using System.Collections;
using System.Collections.Generic;
```

```
using UnityEngine;
public class Character
{

}
```

What just happened?

`Character` is now registered as a public blueprint, meaning that any class in the project can use it to create characters. However, these are just the instructions—to actually create a character takes an additional step, which is called *instantiation*.

Instantiating class objects

Instantiation is the act of creating an object from a specific set of instructions, which is called an instance. If classes are blueprints, instances are the houses built from their instructions; every new instance of `Character` is its own object, just like two houses built from the same instructions are still two different physical structures.

In the last chapter, we created lists and dictionaries, which are classes, using their types and the `new` keyword. We can do the exact same thing for custom classes such as `Character`.

Time for action – creating a new character

We declared the `Character` class as public, which means that a `Character` instance can be created in any other class. Since we have `LearningCurve` already working, let's declare a new character in the `Start()` method:

1. Declare a new `Character` type variable called `hero` in the `Start()` method of `LearningCurve`:

```
Character hero = new Character();
```

So, what just happened?

Let's break this down one step at a time:

- The variable type is specified as `Character`, meaning that the variable is an instance of that class.
- The variable is named `hero`, and is created using the `new` keyword, followed by the `Character` class name and two parentheses. This is where the actual instance is created in the programs memory, even if the class is empty right now.

We can use the `hero` variable just like any other object we've worked with so far. When the `Character` class gets variables and methods of its own, we can access them from hero using dot notation.

Adding class fields

Adding variables, or fields, to a custom class is no different than what we've already been doing with `LearningCurve`. The same concepts apply, including access modifiers, variable scope, and value assignments. However, any variables belonging to a class are created with the class instance, meaning that if there are no values assigned, they will default to zero or null. In general, choosing to set initial values comes down to what information they will store:

- If a variable needs to have the same starting value whenever a class instance is created, setting an initial value is a solid idea
- If a variable needs to be customized in every class instance, leave its value unassigned and use a class constructor (a topic that we'll get to later on)

Time for action – fleshing out character details

The `Character` class doesn't do much right now, so let's change that by incorporating two variables to hold the character's name and the number of starting experience points:

1. Add two `public` variables inside the `Character` class's curly braces—a `string` variable for the name, and an `integer` variable for the experience points

2. Leave the `name` value empty, but assign the experience points to `0` so that every character starts from the bottom:

```
public class Character
{
    public string name;
    public int exp = 0;
}
```

3. Add a debug log in `LearningCurve` underneath where the `Character` variable was initialized, and print out the new character's `name` and `exp` variables using DOT notation:

```
Character hero = new Character();
Debug.LogFormat("Hero: {0} - {1} EXP", hero.name, hero.exp);
```

What just happened?

When `hero` is initialized, `name` is assigned a null value that shows up as an empty space in the debug log, with `exp` printing out `0`. At this point, our class is working, but it's not very practical with an empty value, which we can fix with a class constructor:

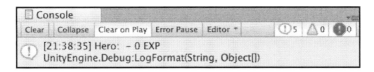

Using constructors

Class constructors are special methods that fire automatically when a class instance is created, similar to how the `Start` method runs in `LearningCurve`. Constructors literally build the class according to its blueprint:

- If a constructor is not specified, C# generates a default one. The default constructor sets any variables to their default type values—that is, numeric values to zero, other types to null.
- Custom constructors can be defined with parameters, just like any other method, which are used to set class variable values at initialization.
- A class can have multiple constructors.

Constructors are written like regular methods, but with a few differences; for instance, they need to be public, have no return type, and the method name is always the class name. As an example, let's add a basic constructor with no parameters to the `Character` class that will set the name field to something other than null. Put this new code directly underneath the class variables, as follows:

```
public string name;
public int exp;

public Character()
{
    name = "Not assigned";
}
```

Now, if we run the project in Unity, the `hero` instance will use this new constructor, and the debug log will show the hero's name as **Not assigned** instead of a null value:

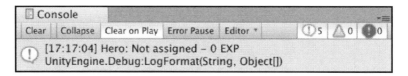

Time for action – specifying starting properties

Now, the `Character` class is starting to behave more like a real object, but we can make this even better by adding a second constructor to take in a name at initialization and set it to the name field:

1. Add another constructor to `Character` that takes in a `string` parameter called `name`.

2. Assign the parameter to the class's `name` variable using the `this` keyword:

```
public Character(string name)
{
    this.name = name;
}
```

3. For convenience, constructors will often have parameters that share a name with a class variable. In these cases, use the `this` keyword to specify which variable belongs to the class. In the example here, `this.name` refers to the classes variable, while `name` is the parameter; without the `this` keyword, the compiler will throw an error because it won't be able to tell them apart.

4. Create a new `Character` instance in `LearningCurve` called `heroine`, use the custom constructor to pass in a name when it's initialized, and log out the details:

```
Character heroine = new Character("Agatha");
Debug.LogFormat("Hero: {0} - {1} EXP", heroine.name, heroine.exp);
```

When a class has multiple constructors or a method has multiple variations, Visual Studio will show a set of arrows in the autocomplete popup that can be scrolled through using the arrow keys:

What just happened?

We can now choose between the basic and custom constructor when we initialize a new `Character` class. The `Character` class itself is now much more flexible when it comes to configuring different instances for different situations:

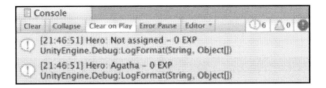

Declaring class methods

Adding methods to custom classes is no different from adding them to `LearningCurve`. However, this is a good opportunity to talk about a staple of good programming—**Don't Repeat Yourself** (**DRY**). DRY is a benchmark of all well-written code. Essentially, if you find yourself writing the same line, or lines, over and over, it's time to rethink and reorganize. This usually takes the form of a new method to hold the repeated code, making it easier to modify and call that functionality elsewhere.

In programming terms, you'll hear this referred to as *abstracting* out a method or feature.

Time for action – printing out character data

Our repeated debug logs are a perfect opportunity to abstract out some code directly into the `Character` class:

1. Add a new `public` method with a `void` return type to the `Character` class, called `PrintStatsInfo`
2. Copy and paste the debug log from `LearningCurve` into the method body, changing the variables to `name` and `exp`, since they can now be referenced from the class directly:

```
public void PrintStatsInfo()
{
    Debug.LogFormat("Hero: {0} - {1} EXP", name, exp);
}
```

3. Replace the debug logs in `LearningCurve` with method calls to `PrintStatsInfo`, and hit **Play**:

```
Character hero = new Character();
hero.PrintStatsInfo();

Character heroine = new Character("Agatha");
heroine.PrintStatsInfo();
```

What just happened?

Now that the `Character` class has a method, any instance can freely access it using DOT notation. Since `hero` and `heroine` are both separate objects, `PrintStatsInfo` debugs their respective `name` and `exp` values to the **Console**.

> This behavior is better than having the debug logs directly in `LearningCurve`; it's always a good idea to group functionality into a class and drive action through methods. This makes the code more readable – as our `Character` objects are giving a command when printing out the debug logs, instead of repeating code.

The entire `Character` class can be seen in the following screenshot for reference:

```
5 public class Character
6 {
7       public string name;
8       public int exp = 0;
9
10      public Character()
11      {
12          name = "Not assigned";
13      }
14
15      public Character(string name)
16      {
17          this.name = name;
18      }
19
20      public void PrintStatsInfo()
21      {
22          Debug.LogFormat("Hero: {0} - {1} EXP", name, exp);
23      }
24 }
```

What's a struct?

Structs are similar to classes in that they are also blueprints for objects you want to create in your programs. The main difference is that they are *value types*—meaning they are passed by value instead of reference, such as classes. We'll go into this in detail in the next section.First, we need to understand how structs work and the specific rules that apply when creating them.

Basic syntax

Structs are declared the same way as classes, and can hold fields, methods, and constructors:

```
accessModifier struct UniqueName
{
    Variables
    Constructors
    Methods
}
```

However, structs have a few limitations:

- Variables cannot be initialized with values inside the struct declaration, unless they're marked with the `static` or `const` modifier—you can read more about this in `Chapter 10`, *Revisiting Types, Methods, and Classes*.
- Constructors without parameters aren't permitted.
- Structs come with a default constructor that will automatically set all variables to their default values according to their type.

Time for action – creating a weapon struct

Our characters are going to need good weapons to see them through quests, which are good candidates for a simple struct:

1. Create a `public struct` called `Weapon` in the `Character` script, making sure it is outside the class curly braces
2. Add two fields, one for `name` of type `string`, and the other for `damage` of type `int`

3. Declare a constructor with the `name` and `damage` parameters and set the struct fields using the `this` keyword:

```
public struct Weapon
{
    public string name;
    public int damage;
    public Weapon(string name, int damage)
    {
        this.name = name;
        this.damage = damage;
    }
}
```

4. In `LearningCurve`, create a new `Weapon` struct using the custom constructor and the `new` keyword:

```
Weapon huntingBow = new Weapon("Hunting Bow", 105);
```

What just happened?

Even though the `Weapon` struct was created in the `Character` script, since it is outside of the actual class declaration (curly braces), it is not part of the class itself. Our new `huntingBow` object uses the custom constructor and provides values for both fields on initialization.

 It's a good idea to limit scripts to a single class; it's fairly common to see structs that are used exclusively by a class included in the file, such as in the `Character` script and `Weapon` struct example.

Classes vs structs

Other than keywords and initial field values, we haven't seen much difference between classes and structs so far. Classes are best suited for grouping together complex actions and data that will change throughout a program; structs are a better choice for simple objects and data that will remain constant for the most part. Besides their uses, they are fundamentally different in one key area—that is, how they are passed, or assigned, between variables. Classes are *reference types*, meaning that they are passed by value; structs are *value types*, meaning that they are passed by value.

Reference types

When the instances of our `Character` class are initialized, the `hero` and `heroine` variables don't actually hold their class information—instead, they hold a reference to where the object is located in the program's memory. If we assigned `hero` or `heroine` to another variable, the memory reference is actually assigned, not the character data. This has several implications, the most important being that if we have multiple variables storing the same memory reference, a change to one affects them all.

Time for action – creating a new hero

Let's take a look at the following practical example:

1. Declare a new `Character` variable in `LearningCurve` called `hero2`, assign it `hero`, and use the `PrintStatsInfo` method to print out both sets of information.

2. Hit **Play** and take a look at the two debug logs that show up in **Console**:

```
Character hero = new Character();
Character hero2 = hero;

hero.PrintStatsInfo();
hero2.PrintStatsInfo();
```

3. The two debug logs will be identical because `hero2` was assigned the `hero` variable when it was created. At this point, both `hero2` and `hero` point to where `hero` is located in memory:

4. Now, change the name of `hero2` to something fun and hit **Play** again:

```
Character hero2 = hero;
hero2.name = "Sir Krane the Brave";
```

What just happened?

You'll see that both `hero` and `hero2` now have the same name, even though only one of our character's data was supposed to change. The lesson here is that reference types need to be treated carefully, and that they are not copied when assigned to new variables. Any change to one reference trickles up and down to all other variables holding the same reference:

If you're trying to copy a class, either create a new, separate instance of it, or reconsider if a struct might be a better choice for your object blueprint.

Value types

When a struct object is created, all its data is stored in its corresponding variable with no references or connections to its memory location. This makes structs useful for creating objects that need to be copied quickly and efficiently, while still retaining their separate identities.

Time for action – copying weapons

Let's create a new weapon object by copying `huntingBow` into a new variable, and updating its data to see whether the changes affect both structs:

1. Declare a new `Weapon` in `LearningCurve` and assign it `huntingBow` to start.
2. Print out each weapon's data using the debug method that you hopefully added during the last *Heroes Trial*. If you didn't get around to that, then take a minute to revisit the *What's a struct?* section and add that in:

```
Weapon huntingBow = new Weapon("Hunting Bow", 105);
Weapon warBow = huntingBow;

huntingBow.PrintWeaponStats();
warBow.PrintWeaponStats();
```

3. The way they're set up now, both `huntingBow` and `warBow` will have the same debug logs, just like our two characters did before we changed any data:

4. Change the `warBow.name` and `damage` fields to values of your choice and hit play again:

```
Weapon warBow = huntingBow;

warBow.name = "War Bow";
warBow.damage = 155;
```

What just happened?

The console will show that only the data relating to `warBow` was changed, and that `huntingBow` retains its original data. The take away from this example is that structs are easily copied and modified as their own separate objects, unlike classes that retain references to an original object. Now that we understand a little more about how structs and classes work under the hood, we're in a good place to start talking about OOP and how it fits into the programming landscape:

The Object-Oriented mindset

If class and struct instances are the blueprints of our programs, then OOP is the architecture that holds everything together. When we refer to OOP as a programming paradigm, we are saying that it has specific principles for how the overall program should work and communicate. Essentially, OOP focuses on objects rather than pure sequential logic—the data they hold, how they drive action, and, most importantly, how they communicate with each other.

Things in the physical world operate on a similar level; when you want to buy a soft drink, you grab a can of soda, not the liquid itself. The can is an object, grouping related information and actions together in a self-contained package. However, there are rules when dealing with objects, both in programming and the grocery store. Who can access them, different variations, and generic actions all play into the objects that are all around us. In programming terms, these rules are the main tenants of OOP – *encapsulation*, *inheritance*, and *polymorphism*.

Encapsulation

One of the best things about OOP is that it supports encapsulation—defining how accessible an object's variables and methods are to outside code (this is sometimes referred to as *calling code*). Take our soda can as an example—in a vending machine, the possible interactions are limited. Since the machine is locked, not just anyone can come up and grab one; if you happen to have the right change, you'll be allowed provisional access to it, but in a specified quantity. If the machine itself is locked inside a room, only someone with the door key will even know the soda can exists.

The question you're asking yourself now is—how do we set these limitations? The simple answer is that we've been using encapsulation this entire time by specifying access modifiers for our object variables and methods. If you need a refresher, go back and visit the *Access Modifiers* section in `Chapter 3`, *Diving into Variables, Types, and Methods*.

Time for action – adding a reset

Our `Character` class is public, as are its fields and method. However, what if we wanted a method that reset a character's data back to their initial values? This could come in handy, but can prove disastrous if it was accidentally called, making it a perfect candidate for a private object member:

1. Create a `private` method called `Reset` with no return value inside the `Character` class
2. Inside `Reset`, set the `name` and `exp` variables back to `"Not assigned"` and `0`, respectively

3. Try and call `Reset` from `LearningCurve` after printing out the `hero2` data:

```
private void Reset()
{
    this.name = "Not assigned";
    this.exp = 0;
}
```

What just happened?

If you're wondering if Visual Studio is broken, it's not. Marking a method or variable as private will make it inaccessible using DOT notation; if you manually type it in and hover over `Reset()`, you'll see an **Error** message regarding the method being protected:

```
14
15          hero.PrintStatsInfo();
16          hero2.PrintStatsInfo();
17          hero2.Reset();
```
Error: 'Character.Reset()' is inaccessible due to its protection level

 Encapsulation does allow for more complex accessibility setups with objects, but for now, we're going to stick with `public` and `private` members. As we begin to flesh out our game prototype in the next chapter, we'll add in different modifiers as needed.

Inheritance

Just as in life, a C# class can be created in the image of another class, sharing its member variables and methods, but able to define its own unique data. In OOP, we refer to this as *inheritance*, and it's a powerful way of creating related classes without having to repeat code. Take the soda example again—there are generic sodas on the market that have all the same basic properties, and then there are special sodas. The special sodas share the same basic properties, but have different branding, or packaging that sets them apart. When you look at both side by side, it's obvious that they're both cans of soda but they're also obviously not the same.

The original class is usually called the base or parent class; the inheriting class is called the derived or child class. Any base class members marked with the `public`, `protected`, or `internal` access modifiers are automatically part of the derived class—that is, except for constructors. Class constructors always belong to their containing class, but they can be used from derived classes to keep repeated code to a minimum.

Most games have more than one type of character, so let's create a new class called `Paladin` that inherits from the `Character` class. You can add this new class into the `Character` script, or create a new one, whichever you prefer:

```
public class Paladin: Character
{

}
```

Just as `LearningCurve` inherits from `Monobehavior`, all we need to do is add a colon and the base class we want to inherit from and C# does the rest. Now any `Paladin` instances will have access to a `name` and `exp` property, as well as a `PrintStatsInfo` method.

Base constructors

When a class inherits from another class, they form a pyramid of sorts with member variables flowing down from the parent class to any of its derived children. The parent class isn't aware of any of its children, but all children are aware of their parent. However, parent classes constructors can be called directly from child constructors with a simple syntax modification:

```
public class ChildClass: ParentClass
{
    public ChildClass(): base()
    {

    }
}
```

The `base` keyword stands in for the parent constructor—in this case, the default constructor. However, since `base` is standing in for a constructor, and a constructor is a method, a child class can pass parameters up the pyramid to its parent constructor.

Time for action – calling a base constructor

Since we want all `Paladin` objects to have a name, and `Character` already has a constructor that handles this, we can call the `base` constructor directly from the `Paladin` class and save ourselves the trouble of rewriting a constructor:

1. Add a constructor to the `Paladin` class that takes in a `string` parameter called `name`.

2. Use a `colon` and the `base` keyword to call the parent constructor, passing the `name` parameter into `base`:

```
public class Paladin: Character
{
    public Paladin(string name): base(name)
    {
    }
}
```

3. Create a new `Paladin` instance called `knight` in `LearningCurve` and use the name constructor to assign a value.
4. Call `PrintStatsInfo` from `knight` and take a look at the console:

```
Paladin knight = new Paladin("Sir Arthur");
knight.PrintStatsInfo();
```

What just happened?

The debug log will be the same as our other `Character` instances, but with the name that we assigned to the `Paladin` constructor. When the `Paladin` constructor fires, it passes the `name` parameter to the `Character` constructor, which sets the `name` value. Essentially, we used the `Character` constructor to do the initialization work for the `Paladin` class, making the `Paladin` constructor only responsible for initializing its unique properties, which it doesn't have at this point:

Composition

Aside from inheritance, classes can be composed of other classes. Take our `Weapon` struct, for example, `Paladin` can easily contain a `Weapon` variable inside itself, and have access to all its properties and methods. Let's do that by updating `Paladin` to take in a starting weapon and assign its value in the constructor:

```
public class Paladin: Character
{
    public Weapon weapon;

    public Paladin(string name, Weapon weapon): base(name)
```

```
    {
        this.weapon = weapon;
    }
}
```

Since `weapon` is unique to `Paladin` and not `Character`, we need to set its initial value in the constructor. We also need to update the `knight` instance to include a `Weapon` variable, so let's use `huntingBow`:

```
Paladin knight = new Paladin("Sir Arthur", huntingBow);
```

If you run the game now you won't see anything different because we're using the `PrintStatsInfo` method from the `Character` class, which doesn't know about the Paladin's weapon property. To tackle this problem, we need to talk about polymorphism.

Polymorphism

Polymorphism is the Greek word for *many-shaped* and applies to OOP in two distinct ways:

- Derived class objects are treated the same as parent class objects. For example, an array of `Character` objects could also store `Paladin`'s, as they derive from `Character`.
- Parent classes can mark methods as `virtual`, meaning that their instructions can be modified by derived classes using the `override` keyword. In the case of `Character` and `Paladin`, it will be useful if we could debug different messages from `PrintStatsInfo` for each one.

Polymorphism allows derived classes to keep the structure of their parent class, while having the freedom to tailor actions to fit their specific needs.

Time for action – functional variations

Let's modify `Character` and `Paladin` to print out different debug logs using `PrintStatsInfo`:

1. Change `PrintStatsInfo` in the `Character` class by adding the `virtual` keyword between `public` and `void`:

```
public virtual void PrintStatsInfo()
{
    Debug.LogFormat("Hero: {0} - {1} EXP", name, exp);
}
```

2. Declare the `PrintStatsInfo` method in the `Paladin` class, but instead of virtual, use the `override` keyword

3. Add a debug log to print out the `Paladin` properties in whatever way you like:

```
public override void PrintStatsInfo()
{
    Debug.LogFormat("Hail {0} - take up your {1}!", name,
    weapon.name);
}
```

What just happened?

This might look like repeated code, which we already said is bad form, but this is a special case. What we've done by marking `PrintStatsInfo` as `virtual` in the `Character` class is tell the compiler that this method can have many shapes according to the calling class. When we declared the overridden version of `PrintStatsInfo` in `Paladin`, we added the custom behavior that only applies to that class. Thanks to polymorphism, we don't have to choose which version of `PrintStatsInfo` we want to call from a `Character` or `Paladin` object—the compiler already knows:

OOP roundup

This was a lot to take in, I know, so let's review some of the main points of OOP as we approach the finish line:

- OOP is all about grouping related data and actions into objects—objects that can communicate and act independently from each other
- Access to class members can be set using access modifiers, just like variables
- Classes can inherit from other classes, creating trickle-down hierarchies of parent/child relationships
- Classes can have members of other class or struct types
- Classes can override any parent methods marked as virtual, allowing them to perform custom actions while retaining the same blueprint

OOP is not the only programming paradigm that can be used with C# – you can find practical explanations of the other main approaches here: http://cs.lmu.edu/~ray/notes/paradigms.

Applying OOP in Unity

If you're around OOP languages enough you'll eventually hear the phrase *everything is an object* whispered like a secret prayer between developers. Following OOP principles, everything in a program should be an object, but **GameObjects** in Unity can literal represent your classes and structs. However, that's not to say all objects in Unity have to be in the physical scene, so we can still use our new-found programmed classes behind the scenes.

Objects are a class act

Back in Chapter 2, *The Building Blocks of Programming*, we discussed how a script is transformed into a component when it's added to a GameObject in Unity. Think of this in terms of the OOP principle of composition—GameObjects are the parent containers, and can be made up of multiple components. This might sound contradictory to the idea of one C# class per script, but, in truth, that's more of a guideline for better readability than an actual requirement. Classes can absolutely be nested inside one another, it just gets messy fast. However, having multiple script components attached to a single GameObject can be very useful, especially when dealing with manager classes or behaviors.

Always try to boil down objects to their most basic elements, then use composition to build bigger, more complex objects out of those smaller classes. It's easier to modify a GameObject made out of small, interchangeable components than one large, clunky one.

Let's take a look at **Main Camera** to see this in action:

Each component in the above screenshot (that is, **Transform**, **Camera**, **Audio Listener**, and, of course, **Learning Curve (Script)**) started off as a class in Unity. Like instances of **Character** or **Weapon**, these components become objects in computer memory when we hit **Play**, complete with their own member variables and methods. We can even create our own instances of these components using their component name as the data type; like classes, Unity component classes are reference types:

```
Transform objectTransform;
```

If we were to attach LearningCurve (or any script or component) to 1,000 GameObjects and click **Play**, 1,000 separate instances of LearningCurve will be created and stored in memory.

Accessing components

Now that we know how components act on GameObjects, how do we go about accessing their specific instances? Lucky for us, all GameObjects in Unity inherit from the GameObject class, which means we can use their member methods to find anything we need in a scene. There are two ways to assign or retrieve GameObjects that are active in the current scene:

1. Through the GetComponent or Find methods in the GameObject class, which work with public and private variables.

2. By dragging and dropping the GameObjects themselves from the `Project` panel directly into variable slots in **Inspector**. This option only works with public variables, since those are the only ones that will appear in **Inspector**.

Basic syntax

Using `GetComponent` is fairly simple, but its method signature is a bit different than other methods that we've seen so far:

```
GameObject.GetComponent<ComponentType>();
```

All we need is the component type that we're looking for and the `GameObject` class will return the component if it exists and null if it doesn't. There are other variations of the `GetComponent` method, but this one is the simplest because we don't need to know specifics about the `GameObject` class that we're looking for. This is called a `generic` method, which we'll talk about more in `Chapter 11`, *Exploring Generics, Delegates, and Beyond*.

Time for action – accessing the current transform component

Since `LearningCurve` is already attached to `Main Camera`, let's grab the `Transform` component from `Main Camera` and store it in a public variable:

1. Add a new public `Transform` type variable called `camTransform` to `LearningCurve`:

   ```
   private Transform camTransform;
   ```

2. Initialize `camTransform` in `Start` using the `GetComponent` method from the `GameObject` class—use the `this` keyword, since `LearningCurve` is attached to the same `GameObject` component as the `Transform` component that we're looking for

3. Access and debug the `localPosition` property of `camTransform` using DOT notation:

   ```
   void Start()
   {
       camTransform = this.GetComponent<Transform>();
       Debug.Log(camTransform.localPosition);
   ```

What just happened?

We've added an uninitialized `public Transform` variable at the top of `LearningCurve` and initialized it using the `GetComponent` method inside `Start`. `GetComponent` finds the `Transform` component attached to this `GameObject` component and returns it to `camTransform`. With `camTransform` now storing a `Transform` object, we have access to all its class properties and methods—including `localPosition` in the following screenshot:

Finding GameObjects

The `GetComponent` method is fantastic for quickly retrieving components, but it only has access to components on the GameObject that the calling script is attached to. For instance, if we use `GetComponent` from the `LearningCurve` script attached to the **Main Camera**, we'll only be able to access the `Transform`, `Camera`, and `Audio Listener` components. If we want to reference a component on a separate GameObject like the **Directional Light**, we would need get a reference to the object first using the `Find` method. All it takes is a `GameObject`'s name, and Unity will kick back the appropriate `GameObject` type object for us to store or manipulate.

For reference, the name of each GameObject can be found at the top of the **Inspector** tab with the object selected:

Time for action - finding components on different objects

Let's take the `Find` method out for a spin and retrieve the `Directional Light` object from `LearningCurve`:

1. Add two public variables to `LearningCurve` underneath `camTransform`, one of type `GameObject`, and one of type `Transform`:

    ```
    public GameObject directionLight;
    private Transform lightTransform;
    ```

2. Find the `Directional Light` component by name and use it to initialize `directionLight` inside the `Start()` method:

    ```
    void Start()
    {
        directionLight = GameObject.Find("Directional Light");
    }
    ```

3. Set the value of `lightTransform` to the `Transform` component attached to `directionLight` and debug its `localPosition`. Since `directionLight` is its own `GameObject` now, `GetComponent` works perfectly:

    ```
    void Start()
    {
        directionLight = GameObject.Find("Directional Light");

        lightTransform = directionLight.GetComponent<Transform>();
        Debug.Log(lightTransform.localPosition);
    }
    ```

Before running the game, it's important to understand that method calls can be chained together to cut down the number of code steps. For instance, we could initialize `lightTransform` in a single line by combining `Find` and `GetComponent`, without having to go through `directionLight`:

```
GameObject.Find("Directional Light").GetComponent<Transform>();
```

 A word of warning—long lines of chained code can lead to poor readability and confusion when working on complex applications. It's a good rule of thumb to avoid lines longer than this example.

Drag and drop

Now that we've covered the code intensive way of doing things, let's take a quick look at Unity's drag and drop functionality. Although drag and drop is much faster than using the `GameObject` class in code, Unity sometimes loses the connections between objects and variables made this way when saving or exporting projects. When you need to assign a few variables quickly, by all means, take advantage of this feature. For most cases, I'd advise sticking with code.

Time for action – assigning variables in Unity

Let's change `LearningCurve` to show how to assign a `GameObject` component using drag and drop:

1. Comment out the following line of code where we used `GameObject.Find()` to retrieve and assign the `Directional Light` object to the `directionLight` variable:

   `//directionLight = GameObject.Find("Directional Light");`

2. Select the **Main Camera** GameObject, drag **Directional Light** onto the **Direction Light** field in the **LearningCurve** component, and click **Play**:

What just happened?

The **Directional Light** GameObject is now assigned to the **directionLight** variable. No code was involved because Unity assigned the variable internally, with no change to the `LearningCurve` class.

It is important to understand a few things when deciding whether to assign variables using drag-and-drop or `GameObject.Find()`. First, the `Find()` method is marginally slower, leaving your game open to performance issues if you are calling the method multiple times in multiple scripts. Second, you need to be sure your GameObjects all have unique names in the scene hierarchy; if they don't it may lead to some nasty bugs in situations where you have several objects of the same name or change the object names themselves.

Pop quiz: all things OOP

1. What method handles the initialization logic inside a class?
2. Being value types, how are structs passed?
3. What are the main tenants of object-oriented programming?
4. Which GameObject class method would you use to find a component on the same object as the calling class?

Summary

Our journey into classes, structs, and OOP marks the end of the first section on the fundamentals of C#. Identifying related data and actions, creating blueprints to give them shape, and using instances to build interactions are a strong foundation for approaching any program or game. Add the ability to access components to the mix, and you've got the makings of a Unity developer.

The next chapter will segue into the basics of game development and scripting object behavior directly in Unity. We'll start fleshing out the requirements of a simple open-world adventure game, work with game objects in the scene, and finish off with a white-boxed environment ready for our characters.

Section 2: Scripting Game Mechanics in Unity

The following section will cover topics in game design, intermediate C# features, and interactions in Unity 2019 through the following chapters:

- Chapter 6, *Getting Your Hands Dirty with Unity*
- Chapter 7, *Movement, Camera Controls, and Collisions*
- Chapter 8, *Scripting Game Mechanics*
- Chapter 9, *Basic AI and Enemy Behavior*

By the end of the section, you will have developed a fully playable first-person game with movement controls, animations, and enemy interactions, putting you in the perfect position to level up your C# skills in the final section.

Getting Your Hands Dirty with Unity

6

Creating a game is much more than simulating actions in code. Things such as design, story, environment, lighting, and animation all play an important part in setting the stage for your players; games are experiences first and foremost, which code alone can't deliver.

Unity has placed itself at the forefront of game development over the past decade by bringing advanced tools to programmers and non-programmers alike. Animation and effects, audio, environment design, and much more are all available directly from the Unity Editor without a single line of code. We'll discuss these topics as we define the requirements, environment, and game mechanics of *Hero Born*, but first we'll need an introduction to game design and working with GameObjects.

This chapter will set us up for the rest of the book, and we'll cover the following topics:

- Game design theory
- Building a level
- GameObjects and Prefabs
- Lighting basics
- Animating in Unity
- The Particle System

A game design primer

Before jumping into any game project, it's important to have a blueprint of what you want to build. Sometimes ideas will start out crystal clear in your mind, but the minute you start creating character classes or environments, things seem to drift away from your original intention. This is where the game design allows you to plan out the following things:

- **Concept**: The big-picture idea and design of a game, including its genre and play style.
- **Core mechanics**: The playable features or interactions that a character can take in-game. Common gameplay mechanics include jumping, shooting, puzzle-solving, or driving.
- **Control schemes**: A map of the buttons and/or keys that give players control over their character, environment interactions, and other executable actions.
- **Story**: The underlying narrative that fuels a game, creating empathy and a connection between players and the game world they play in.
- **Art style**: The game's overarching look and feel, consistent across everything from characters and menu art to the levels and environment.
- **Win and lose conditions**: The rules that govern how the game is won or lost, usually consisting of objectives or goals that carry the weight of potential failure.

These topics are by no means an exhaustive list of what goes into designing a game, but they're a good place to start fleshing out something called a game design document.

Game design documents

Googling game design documents will result in a literal flood of templates, formatting rules, and content guidelines that can leave a new programmer ready to give it all up. The truth is, design documents are tailored to the team or company that creates them, making them much easier to draft than the internet would have you think.

In general, there are three types of design documentation, as follows:

- **Game Design Document (GDD)**: The GDD houses everything from how the game is played to its atmosphere, story, and the experience it's trying to create. Depending on the game, this document can be a few pages or several hundred.
- **Technical Design Document**: This document focuses on all the technical aspects of the game, from the hardware it will run on to how the classes and program architecture need to be built out. Like a GDD, the length will vary based on the project.

- **One-Page**: Usually used for marketing or promotional situations, a One-Page is essentially a snapshot of your game. As the name suggests, it should only take up a single page.

The game we'll be working on throughout the rest of this book is fairly simple and won't require anything as detailed as a GDD or TDD. Instead, we'll create our own One-Page to keep track of our project objectives and some background information.

 There's no right or wrong way to format a GDD, so it's a good place to let your personal brand of creativity thrive. Throw in pictures of reference material that inspires you; get creative with the layout—this is your place to define your vision.

The Hero Born one-page

To keep us on track going forward, I've put together a simple document that lays out the basics of the game prototype. Read through it before moving on, and try to start imagining some of the programming concepts we've learned so far being put into practice:

Concept
Game prototype focused on stealthily avoiding enemies and collecting health items - with a little FPS on the side.

Gameplay
Main mechanic centers around using line-of-sight to stay one step ahead of patrolling enemies and collecting required items.

Combat will consist of shooting projectiles at enemies, which will automatically trigger an attack response.

Interface
Control scheme for movement will be the WASD or arrow keys using the mouse for camera control. Shooting mechanic will use the Space bar, and item collection will work off of object collisions.

Simple HUD will show items collected and remaining ammo, as well as a standard health bar.

Art Style
Level and character art style will be all primitive GameObjects for fast and efficient, no-frills development. These can be swapped out at a later date with 3D models or terrain environments if needed.

Building a level

When building your game levels, it's always a good idea to try to see things from the perspective of your players. How do you want them to see the environment, interact with it, feel while walking around in it? You're literally building the world your game exists in, so be consistent.

With Unity, you have the option of creating outdoor environments using the **Terrain Tool**, blocking out something set indoors with basic shapes and geometry, or a mixture of the two. You can even import 3D models from other programs, such as **Blender**, to use as objects in your scenes. For *Hero Born*, we'll stick with a simple indoor arena-like setting that's easy to get around, but with a few corners to hide in.

 Unity has a great introduction to the Terrain Tool here: `https://docs.unity3d.com/Manual/script-Terrain.html`. If you're going that route, there's also a wonderful free asset on the Unity Asset Store called Terrain Toolkit 2017: `https://assetstore.unity.com/packages/tools/terrain/terrain-toolkit-2017-83490`.

Creating primitives

Looking at games you might play on a regular basis, you're probably wondering how you'll ever create models and objects that look so realistic you could reach through the screen and grab them. Fortunately, Unity has a set of primitive GameObjects that you can select from to prototype faster. These won't be super fancy or high-definition, but they are a lifesaver when you're learning the ropes or don't have a 3D artist on your development team.

If you go into the **Hierarchy** panel and hit **Create** | **3D Object**, you'll see all the available options, but only about half of these are primitives or common shapes:

Other 3D object options, such as **Terrains**, **Wind Zones**, and **Trees**, are a bit too advanced for what we need, but feel free to experiment with them if you're interested.

Time for action – creating a ground plane

It's usually easier to walk around when you've got a floor underneath you, so let's start by creating a ground plane using the following steps:

1. In the **Hierarchy** panel, hit **Create** | **3D Object** | **Plane**.
2. Rename the GameObject to Ground in the **Inspector** and change the **Scale** to 3 in the **x**, **y**, and **z** axes:

What just happened?

We created a plane GameObject and increased its size to make more room for our future character to walk around. This plane will act like a 3D object bound by real-life physics, meaning other objects can't just fall through it at will. We'll talk more about the Unity Physics system and how it works in Chapter 7, *Movement, Camera Controls, and Collisions*.

Thinking in 3D

Now that we have our first object in the scene, we can talk about 3D space—specifically, how an object's position, rotation, and scale behave in three dimensions. If you think back to high school geometry, a graph with an x and y coordinate system should be familiar. In order to put a point on the graph, you had to have an x and y value.

Unity supports both 2D and 3D game development, and if we were making a 2D game, we could leave our explanation there. However, when dealing with 3D space in the Unity editor, we have an extra axis, called the z axis. The z axis maps depth, or perspective, giving our space and the objects in it their three-dimensional quality.

This might be confusing at first, but Unity has some nice visual aids to help you get your head on straight. In the top-right of the **Scene** panel, you'll see a geometric-looking icon with the **x**, **y**, and **z** axes marked in red, green, and blue, respectively. All GameObjects in the scene will also show corresponding axes arrows when they're selected:

This will always show the current orientation of the scene and the objects placed inside it. Clicking on any of these colored axes will switch the scene orientation to the selected axis. Give this a go by yourself to get comfortable with switching perspectives.

If you take a look at the Ground object's Transform component in the following screenshot, you'll see that the position, rotation, and scale are all determined by these three axes. The position determines where the object is placed in the scene, its rotation governs how it's angled, and its scale takes care of its size:

This leads to an interesting question: what is the reference, or origin point, of these positions, rotations, and scales that we're setting? The answer is that they depend on what relative space we're using, which in Unity is either **World** or **Local**:

- **World Space** uses a set origin point in the scene as a constant reference for all GameObjects. In Unity, this origin point is (0, 0, 0), or 0 on the x, y, and z, which you can see in the preceding **Ground** object's **Transform**.
- **Local Space** uses the object in question as it origin, essentially changing the perspective of the scene to revolve around it.

Both of these orientations are useful in different situations, which we'll talk about later on in this chapter when we start laying out the rest of the arena level.

Materials

Our ground plane isn't very interesting right now, but we can use **Materials** to breathe a little life into the level. **Materials** control how GameObjects are rendered in the scene, which is determined by the material's shader. Think of **Shaders** as being responsible for combining lighting and texture data into a representation of how the material looks.

Each GameObject starts out with a default **Material** and **Shader** (pictured here from the **Inspector**), setting its color to a standard white:

In order to change an object's color, we need to create a material and drag it onto the object we want to modify. Remember, everything is an object in Unity—materials are no different. Materials can be reused on as many GameObjects as needed, but any change to a **Material** will also carry through to any objects the material is attached to. If we had several enemy objects in the scene with a material that set them all to red, and we changed that base material color to blue, all our enemies would then be blue.

Time for action – changing the ground color

Let's create a new material to turn the ground plane from a dull white to a dark, vibrant blue:

1. Create a new folder in the **Project** panel and name it Materials.
2. Inside the **Materials** folder, hit **Create** | **Material** and name it Ground_Mat.
3. Click on the color box next to the **Albedo** property and select your color from the **Color Picker** window that pops up, then close it.
4. Drag the **Ground_Mat** object and drop it onto the **Ground** GameObject in the **Hierarchy** panel:

What just happened?

The new material you created is now a project asset. Dragging and dropping **Ground_Mat** onto the **Ground** GameObject changed the color of the plane, which means any changes to **Ground_Mat** will be reflected in the **Ground**:

White-boxing

White-boxing is a design term for laying out ideas using placeholders, usually with the intent of replacing them with finished assets at a later date. In level design, the practice of white-boxing is to block out an environment with primitive GameObjects to get a sense of how you want it to look. This is a great way to start things off, especially during the prototyping stages of your game.

Before diving into Unity, I'd like to start with a simple sketch of the basic layout and position of my level. This gives us a bit of direction and will help get our environment laid out quicker. In the following drawing, you'll see that the arena I have in mind, with a raised platform in the middle accessible by ramps, complete with small turrets in each corner:

Don't worry if you're not an artist—neither am I. The important thing is to have your ideas down on paper to solidify them in your mind and work out any kinks before getting busy in Unity.

Editor tools

When we discussed the Unity interface in `Chapter 1`, *Getting to Know Your Environment*, we skimmed over some of the Toolbar functionality, which we need to revisit so we know how to efficiently manipulate GameObjects.

Let's break down the different tools available to us from the Toolbar in the preceding screenshot:

- **Hand**: Allows you to pan and change position in the scene.
- **Move**: Lets you move objects along the x, y, and z axes by dragging their respective arrows.
- **Rotate**: Lets you adjust an object's rotation by turning or dragging their respective markers.
- **Scale**: Lets you modify an object's scale by dragging on specific axes.
- **Rect Transform**: Combines the move, rotate, and scale tool functionality into one package.
- **Transform Gizmos**: Combines the positioning, rotation, and scaling functionality into one package, but uses different visual aids (called handles) than the **Rect Transform** tool.

 You can find more information on navigating and positioning GameObjects in the **Scene** panel here: `https://docs.unity3d.com/Manual/PositioningGameObjects.html`.

Panning and navigating the **Scene** can be done with similar tools, although not from the Unity editor itself:

- To look around, hold down the right mouse button to pan the camera around.
- To move around while using the camera, continue to hold the right mouse button and use the W, A, S, and D keys to move forward, back, left, and right, respectively.
- Hit the F key to zoom in and focus on a selected GameObject.

 This kind of scene navigation is more commonly called fly-through mode, so when I ask you to focus on or navigate to a particular object or viewpoint, use a combination of these features.

 Getting around the **Scene** view can be a task in itself sometimes, but it all comes down to repeated practice. For a more detailed list of scene navigation features, visit `https://docs.unity3d.com/Manual/SceneViewNavigation.html`.

Hero's Trial – putting up drywall

Using primitive cubes and the Toolbar, scale and position four walls around the level to section off the main arena area (the following screenshot is for reference):

Keeping the Hierarchy clean

Normally, I would put this sort of advice in a blurb at the end of a section, but making sure your project Hierarchy is as organized as possible is so important it needed its own subsection. Ideally, you want all related GameObjects to be under a single parent object. Right now, it's not a risk because we only have a few objects in the scene, but when that gets into the hundreds on a big project you'll be hurting.

Time for action – using empty objects

Our level has a few objects that could use some organization, and Unity makes this easy by letting us create empty GameObjects. An empty object is a perfect container for holding related groups of objects because it doesn't come with any components attached—it's literally a shell.

Let's take our ground plane and four walls and group them all under a common empty GameObject:

1. Select **Create** | **Create Empty** in the Hierarchy panel and name the new object `Environment`.
2. Drag and drop the ground plane and the four walls onto **Environment,** making them child objects.

3. Select the **Environment** empty object and check that its **x**, **y**, and **z** positions are all set to **0**:

What just happened?

Environment exists in the Hierarchy as a parent object, with the arena objects as its children. Now we're able to expand or close the **Environment** object dropdown with the arrow icon, making the **Hierarchy** panel less cluttered.

Working with prefabs

Prefabs are one of the most powerful tools you'll come across in Unity, and come in handy not only in level-building but in scripting as well. Think of prefabs as GameObjects that can be saved and reused with every child object, component, C# script, and property setting intact. Once created, a prefab is like a class blueprint; each copy used in a scene is a separate instance of that prefab. Consequently, any change to the base prefab will also change all active instances in the scene.

Time for action – creating a turret

Since we want four identical turrets in each corner of the arena, they're a perfect case for a prefab, which we can create with the following steps:

1. Create an empty parent object in the Hierarchy by selecting **Create | Create Empty** and name it `Barrier_01`.

2. Create two **Cube** primitives from the **Create** menu, positioning and scaling them as a V-shaped base.

3. Create two more **Cube** primitives and place them on the ends of the turret base.

4. Create a new folder in the **Project** panel and name it `Prefabs`, then drag **Barrier_01** into it:

What just happened?

Barrier_01 and all its child objects is now a prefab, meaning that we can reuse it by dragging copies from the **Prefabs** folder or duplicating the one in the scene. **Barrier_01** turned blue in the **Hierarchy** to signify its status change, and also added a row of prefab function buttons in the **Inspector** underneath its name.

Time for action – updating the prefab

Now our turret has a huge gap in the middle, which isn't ideal for covering our character, so let's update the **Barrier_01** prefab by adding another cube and applying the change:

1. Create a **Cube** primitive and place it at the intersection of the turret base.
2. The **Prefab** label in the **Inspector** will turn yellow to show that the prefab has been updated in the **Scene.**
   - Unity will mark the new cube in white in the Hierarchy to let you know it's not part of the prefab.
3. Hit **Apply** to save the change and update the prefab:

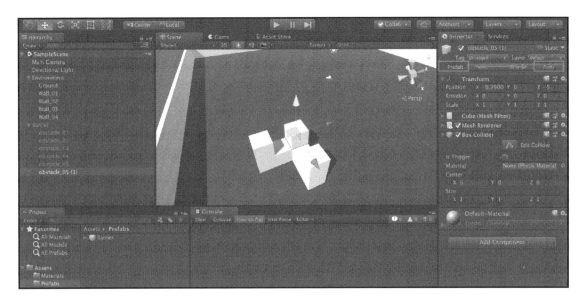

What just happened?

The **Barrier_01** prefab is now updated to include the new **Cube**, and the entire prefab hierarchy should be blue again. You should now have a turret prefab that looks like the preceding screenshot, or if you're feeling adventurous, something more creative.

Getting Your Hands Dirty with Unity

Time for action – finishing the level

Now that we've got a reusable barrier prefab, let's build out the rest of the level to match the rough sketch we had at the beginning of the section:

1. Duplicate the **Barrier_01** prefab three times and place each one in a different corner of the arena.
2. Create a new empty GameObject and name it `Raised_Platform`.
3. Create a **Cube** and scale it to form a platform.
4. Create a **Plane** and scale it into a ramp, then rotate and position it so that it connects the platform to the ground.
5. Duplicate the ramp object by using *Cmd + D* on a Mac, or *Ctrl + D* on Windows, then repeat the rotation and positioning steps.
6. Repeat the previous step twice more, until you have four ramps in total leading to the platform:

What just happened?

You've now successfully white-boxed your first game level!

Hero's trial – creating a health pickup

Putting everything we've learned so far in this chapter might take you a few minutes, but it's well worth the time. Your task, should you choose to accept it, has three steps:

1. Create, position, and scale a **Capsule** GameObject.
2. Create and attach a new **Material** to the **Capsule**.
3. Make the **Capsule** a **Prefab** and rename it `Health_Pickup`.

See the following screenshot for what the finished product should look like:

Lighting basics

Lighting in Unity is a broad topic, but it can be boiled down into two categories: realtime and precomputed. Both types of lights take into account properties such as the color and intensity of the light, as well as the direction it is facing in the scene; the difference is how the Unity engine computes how the lights act.

Realtime lighting is computed every frame, meaning that any object that passes in its path will cast realistic shadows and generally behave like a real-world light source. However, this can significantly slow down your game and cost an exponential amount of computing power, depending on the number of lights in your scene. *Precomputed lighting*, on the other hand, stores the scene's lighting in a texture called a **lightmap**, which is then applied, or baked, into the scene. While this saves computing power, baked lighting is static, meaning it doesn't react realistically or change when objects move in the scene.

> There is also a mixed type of lighting called *Precomputed Realtime Global Illumination*, which bridges the gap between the realtime and precomputed processes. This is an advanced Unity-specific topic so we won't cover it in this book, but feel free to check out the documentation: https://docs.unity3d.com/Manual/GIIntro.html.

Creating lights

By default, every scene comes with a **Directional Light** to act as a main source of illumination, but lights can be created in the Hierarchy like any other GameObject. Even though the idea of controlling light sources might be new to you, they are objects in Unity, meaning they can be positioned, scaled, and rotated to fit your needs:

Let's take a look at some examples of realtime light objects and their performance:

- **Directional** lights are great for simulating natural light, such as sunshine. They don't have an actual position in the scene, but their light hits everything as if it's always pointed in the same direction.
- **Point** lights are essentially floating globes, sending light rays out from a central point in all directions. These have defined positions and intensities in the scene.
- **Spotlights** send light out in a given direction, but locked in by their angle. Think of these like spotlights or floodlights in the real world.

 Reflection Probes and Light Probe Groups are beyond what we need for *Hero Born*, but if you're interested, you can check them out at `https://docs.unity3d.com/Manual/ReflectionProbes.html` and `https://docs.unity3d.com/Manual/LightProbes.html`.

Light component properties

The following screenshot shows the **Light** component on the Directional light in our scene. All these properties can be configured to create immersive environments, but the basic ones we need to be aware of are the **Color**, **Mode**, and **Intensity**. These govern the light's tint, realtime or computed effects, and general strength:

Like other Unity components, these properties can be accessed through scripts and the `Light` class, which can be found here: `https://docs.unity3d.com/ScriptReference/Light.html`.

Animating in Unity

Animating objects in Unity can range from a simple rotation effect all the way to complex character movements and actions, all of which are controlled through the **Animation** and **Animator** windows:

- The **Animation** window is where animation segments, called clips, are created and managed using a timeline. Object properties are recorded along this timeline and played back to create an animated effect.

- The **Animator** window manages these clips and their transitions using objects called animation controllers.

You can find more information on the **Animator** window and controllers here: `https://docs.unity3d.com/Manual/AnimatorControllers.html`.

Creating clips

Any GameObject that you want to apply an animation clip to needs to have an **Animator** component attached with an **Animation Controller** set. If there is no controller in the project when a new clip is created, Unity will create one and save it at the location of the clips, which you can then use to manage your clips.

Time for action – creating a new clip

We're going to start animating the **Health_Pickup** prefab by creating a new animation clip, which will spin the object around in an infinite loop. To create a new animation clip we need to perform the following steps:

1. Go to **Window** | **Animation** | **Animation** to open up the **Animation** panel and pin it next to the **Console**.
2. Make sure the **Health_Pickup** is selected, then click **Create** in the **Animation** panel.
3. Create a new folder from the dropdown pictured below, name it **Animations**, and name the new clip **Pickup_Spin**:

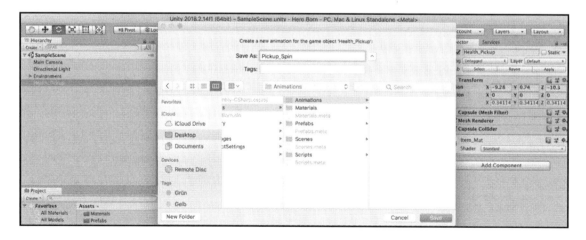

What just happened?

Since we didn't have any **Animator** Controllers, Unity created one for us in the **Animation** folder called **Health_Pickup**. With **Health_Pickup** selected, when we created the clip, an **Animator** component was also added to the prefab for us with the **Health_Pickup** Controller set:

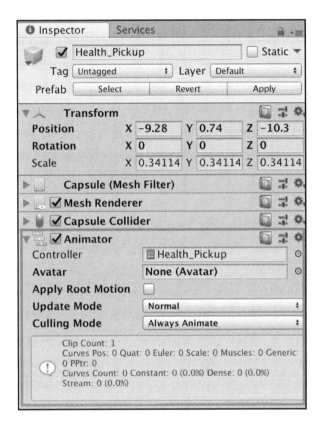

Recording keyframes

Now that we have a clip to work with, you'll see a blank timeline in the **Animation** window. Essentially, when we modify our **Health_Pickup's z** rotation, or any other property that can be animated, the timeline will record those changes as keyframes. Unity then assembles those keyframes together into your complete animation, similar to how individual frames on analog film play together into a moving picture.

Take a look at the following screenshot and remember the locations of the record button and the timeline:

Time for action – spinning animation

For the spinning animation, we want the **Health_Pickup** prefab to make a complete 360-degree rotation on its z axis every second, which can be done by setting three keyframes and letting Unity take care of the rest:

1. Hit the **Record** button to start the animation.
2. Place your cursor at **0:00** on the timeline but leave the **Health_Pickup's z** rotation at **0**.
3. Place your cursor at **0:30** on the timeline and set the **z** rotation to **180**.
4. Place your cursor at **1:00** on the timeline and set the **z** rotation to **360**.
5. Hit the **Record** button to finish the animation.
6. Click the **Play** button to the right of the record button to see the animation loop:

What just happened?

The **Health_Pickup** object now rotates on the z axis between **0**, **180**, and **360** degrees every second, creating the looping spin animation. If you play the game now, the animation will run indefinitely until the game is stopped:

Curves and tangents

In addition to animating an object property, Unity lets us manage how the animation plays out over time with animation curves. So far, we've been in the **Dopesheet** mode, which you can change at the bottom of the **Animation** window. If you click into the **Curves** view (pictured in the following screenshot) you'll see a different graph with accent points in place of our recorded keyframes. We want the spinning animation to be smooth—what we call linear—so we'll leave everything as is. However, speeding up, slowing down, or altering the animation at any point in its run can be done by dragging or adjusting the points on the curve graph:

With animation curves handling how properties act over time, we still need a way to fix the stutter that happens every time the **Health_Pickup** animation repeats. For that, we need to change the animation's **tangent**, which manages how keyframes blend from one into another. These options can be accessed by right-clicking on any keyframe on the timeline in **Dopesheet** mode, which you can see here:

Both of these topics are intermediate to advanced, so we won't be delving too deeply into them. If you're interested, you can take a look at the documentation on animation curves and tangent options here: `https://docs.unity3d.com/Manual/animeditor-AnimationCurves.html`.

Time for action – smoothing the spin

Let's adjust the tangents on the first and last frames of the animation so the spinning animation blends seamlessly together when it repeats:

1. **Right-click** on the first and last keyframe diamond icons on the animation timeline and select **Auto**.
2. Move the **Main Camera** so that you can see the **Health_Pickup** and hit **Play**:

What just happened?

Changing the first and last keyframe tangents to **Auto** tells Unity to make their transitions smooth, which eliminates the jerky stop/start motion when the animation loops.

 Objects can also be animated using C# by manipulating specific properties, such as position or rotation. Even though we won't be going into that specific topic in this book, it's important to know that programmed animations are an option in Unity.

The particle system

When it comes to creating motion effects, such as explosions or the jet stream of an alien spaceship, Unity particle effects is the way to go. Particle Systems emit sprites or meshes, which we call particles, which then create a combined effect. Particle properties can be configured from its color and size to how long it stays onscreen and how fast it's moving in a given direction. These can be created as single objects or combined together to create more realistic effects.

 Particle System effects can be extremely complex, and can be used to create almost anything you can imagine. However, getting good at creating realistic effects takes practice—take a look at these instruction for a place to start: `https://docs.unity3d.com/Manual/ParticleSystemHowTo.html`.

Time for action – adding sparkle effects

We want to draw the player's eye to the collectable items that we'll place around the level, so let's add a simple particle effect to the **Health_Pickup**:

1. Click **Create | Effects | Particle System** in the **Hierarchy** panel.
2. Position the **Particle System** object in the middle of the **Health_Pickup**.
3. Select the new Particle System and update the following properties in the **Inspector**:
    - **Start Lifetime** to **2**
    - **Start Speed** to **0.25**
    - **Start Size** to **0.75**
    - **Start Color** to orange or a color of your choice

4. Open the **Emissions** tab and change the **Rate Over Time** to **5**.
5. Open the **Shape** tab and change the **Shape** to **Sphere**:

What just happened?

The **Particle System** object we created will now render and emit particles every frame based on the properties we set in the **Inspector**.

Pop quiz – basic Unity features

1. Cubes, Capsules, and Spheres are examples of what kind of GameObject?
2. What axis does Unity use to represent depth, which gives scenes their 3D appearance?
3. How do you turn a GameObject into a reusable Prefab?
4. What unit of measurement does the Unity Animation system use to record object animations?

Summary

We made it to the end of another chapter that had a lot of moving parts, especially for those of you new to Unity. Even though this book is focused on the C# language, it's important that we took this time to get an overview of game development, documentation, and the non-scripting features of the engine. While we didn't have time for in-depth coverage of the Lighting, Animation, and Particle Systems tools, it's worth getting to know them if you're thinking about continuing to create Unity projects.

In this next chapter, we'll be switching our focus back to programming *Hero Born*'s core mechanics, starting with setting up a moveable player object, controlling the camera, and understanding how Unity Physics governs the game world.

Movement, Camera Controls, and Collisions

One of the first things players do when starting a new game is familiarize themselves with character movement and camera controls. Not only is this exciting, but it also lets your players know what kind of gameplay they can expect. *Hero Born's* character will be a capsule primitive that can be moved and rotated using the *W*, *A*, *S*, *D*, or arrow keys.

We'll start by learning how to manipulate an object's Transform component and then replicate the same control scheme using applied force, which produces a more realistic movement effect. When we move the player, the camera will follow along from a position slightly behind and above, making aiming easier when we implement the shooting mechanic. Finally, we'll explore how collisions and physical interactions are handled by Unity's physics system by working with our item pickup prefab.

The following topics will be tied together in this chapter:

- Transform movement and rotation
- Managing player inputs
- Scripting camera behavior
- Unity physics and applied force
- Basic colliders and collision detection

Moving the player

When you're deciding how best to move your player character around your virtual world, consider what's going to look the most realistic and not run your game into the ground with expensive computations. This is somewhat of a trade-off in most cases, and Unity is no different.

The three most common ways of moving GameObjects and their results are as follows:

- **Option A**: Use a GameObjects **Transform** component for movement and rotation. This is the easiest solution, and the one we'll be working with first.
- **Option B**: Attach a **Rigidbody** component to a GameObject and apply force in code. This solution relies on Unity's physics system to do the heavy lifting, delivering a much more realistic effect. We'll update our code to use this approach later on in this chapter to get a feel for both methods.

Unity suggests sticking to a consistent approach when moving or rotating a GameObject; either manipulate an object's **Transform** or **Rigidbody** component, but never both at the same time.

- **Option C**: Attach a ready-made Unity component or prefab like a **Character Controller** or **FirstPersonController**. This cuts out the boilerplate code and still delivers a realistic effect, while speeding up prototyping time.

You can find more information on the **Character Controller** component and its uses here: https://docs.unity3d.com/ScriptReference/ CharacterController.html.

The **FirstPersonController** prefab is available from the Standard Assets Package, which you can download here: https://assetstore.unity. com/packages/essentials/asset-packs/standard-assets-32351.

Player setup

We want a third-person adventure setup for *Hero Born*, so we'll start with a capsule that can be controlled with keyboard input and a camera to follow the capsule as it moves. Even though these two GameObjects will work together in the game, we'll keep them and their scripts separate for better control.

Time for action – creating the player capsule

We can create a nice player capsule in just a few steps:

1. Click **Create** | **3D Object** | **Capsule** from the Hierarchy panel and name it `Player`.
2. Select the `Player` GameObject and click **Add Component** at the bottom of the **Inspector**. Search for **Rigidbody** and hit *Enter* to add it.
3. Expand the **Constraints** property at the bottom of the **Rigidbody** and check the boxes for **Freeze Rotation** on the **x** and **y** axes.
4. Select the `Materials` folder and click **Create** | **Material**. Name it `Player_Mat`.
5. Change the **Albedo** property to a bright **green** and drag the material onto the **Player** object in the Hierarchy:

What just happened?

We've created our **Player** out of a capsule primitive, a **Rigidbody** component, and a new bright green material. Don't worry about what the **Rigidbody** component is – all you need to know right now is that it allows our capsule to interact with the physics system. We'll go into more detail at the end of this chapter when we discuss how Unity's physics system works.

Understanding vectors

Now that we have a player capsule and camera set up, we can start talking about how to move and rotate a GameObject using its **Transform** component. The `Translate` and `Rotate` methods are part of the `Transform` class that Unity provides, and each needs a vector parameter to perform its given function.

In Unity, vectors are used to hold position and direction data in 2D and 3D spaces, which is why they come in two varieties—`Vector2` and `Vector3`. These can be used like any other variable type we've seen; they just hold different information. Since our game is in 3D, we'll be using `Vector3` objects, which means we'll need to construct them using x, y, and z values. For 2D vectors, only the x and y positions are needed. Remember, the most up-to-date orientation in your 3D scene will be displayed in the upper right graphic we discussed in the last chapter:

 If you want more information on vectors in Unity, check out the documentation and scripting reference here: `https://docs.unity3d.com/ScriptReference/Vector3.html`.

For instance, if we wanted to create a new vector to hold the origin position of our scene, we could use the following code:

```
Vector3 origin = new Vector(0f, 0f, 0f);
```

All we've done here is create a new `Vector3` variable and initialized it with a `0` for the x, `0` for the y, and `0` for the z positions, in that order. `Float` values can be written with or without a decimal, but they always need to end with a lowercase `f`.

We can also create directional vectors by using the `Vector2` or `Vector3` class properties:

```
Vector3 forwardDirection = Vector3.forward;
```

Instead of holding a position, `forwardDirection` references the forward direction in our scene along the z-axis in the 3D space. We'll go into using vectors later in this chapter, but for now just get used to thinking about 3D movement in terms of x, y, and z positions and directions.

 Don't worry if the concept of vectors is new to you – it's a complicated topic. Unity's vector cookbook is a great place to start: `https://docs.unity3d.com/Manual/VectorCookbook.html`.

Getting player input

Positions and directions are useful in themselves, but they can't generate movement without input from the player. This is where the `Input` class comes in, which handles everything from keystrokes and mouse position to acceleration and gyroscopic data.

We're going to be using the *W, A, S,* and *D* and arrow keys for movement in *Hero Born*, coupled with a script that lets the camera follow where the player points the mouse. To do that, we'll need to understand how input axes work.

First, go to **Edit** | **Project Settings** | **Input** to open up the **Input Manager**, which is shown in the following screenshot:

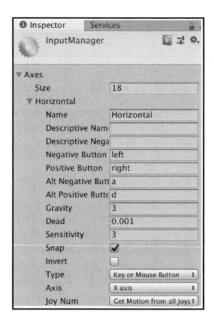

You'll see a long list of Unity's default inputs already configured, but let's take the **Horizontal** axis as an example. You can see that the **Horizontal** input axis has the **Positive** and **Negative** buttons set to left and right, as well as the **Alt Negative** and **Alt Positive** buttons set to the a and d keys.

Whenever an input axis is queried from the code, its value will be between -1 and 1. For example, when the left arrow or keys are pushed down, the horizontal axis registers a -1 value. When those keys are released, the value returns to 0. Likewise, when the right arrow or *D* keys are used, the horizontal axis registers a value of 1. This allows us to capture four different inputs for a single axis with only one line of code, as opposed to writing out a long if/else statement chain for each.

Capturing input axes is as simple as calling `Input.GetAxis()` and specifying the axis we want by name, which is what we'll do with the **Horizontal** and **Vertical** inputs in the following sections.

 Default inputs can be modified in any way you need, but you can also create custom axes by increasing the **Size** property in the **Input Manager** by 1 and renaming the copy that's been created for you.

Time for action – player locomotion

Before we get the player moving, we'll need to attach a script to our capsule:

1. Create a new C# script in the Scripts folder, name it PlayerBehavior, and drag it onto the **Player** capsule.

2. Add the following code and save:

```
public class PlayerBehavior : MonoBehaviour
{
    // 1
    public float moveSpeed = 10f;
    public float rotateSpeed = 75f;

    // 2
    private float vInput;
    private float hInput;

    void Update()
    {
        // 3
        vInput = Input.GetAxis("Vertical") * moveSpeed;

        // 4
        hInput = Input.GetAxis("Horizontal") * rotateSpeed;

        // 5
        this.transform.Translate(Vector3.forward * vInput *
        Time.deltaTime);

        // 6
        this.transform.Rotate(Vector3.up * hInput * Time.deltaTime);
    }
}
```

When you have empty methods, like Start in this case, it's common to delete them for clarity. However, if you prefer to have them in your script, that's fine too. It's really up to your preference.

Here's a breakdown of the preceding code:

1. Declares two public variables to be used as multipliers:
    - `movespeed` for how fast we want the **Player** to go forward and backwards
    - `rotateSpeed` for how fast we want the **Player** to rotate left and right

2. Declares two private variables to hold inputs from the player, initially set with no value:
    - `vInput` will store the vertical axis input
    - `hInput` will store the horizontal axis input

3. `Input.GetAxis("Vertical")` detects when the Up, Down, *W*, or *S* keys are pressed and multiplies that value by `moveSpeed`:
    - The Up and *W* keys return a value of 1, which will move the player in the forward (positive) direction
    - The Down and *S* keys return -1, which moves the player backwards in the negative direction

4. `Input.GetAxis("Horizontal")` detects when the Left, Right, *A* and *D* keys are pressed and multiplies that value by `rotateSpeed`:
    - The Right arrow and *D* keys return a value of 1, which will rotate the capsule to the right
    - The Left arrow and *A* keys return a -1, rotating the capsule to the left

If you're wondering if it's possible to do all the movement calculations on one line, the simple answer is yes. However, it's better to have your code broken down, even if you're the only one reading it.

5. Uses the `Translate` method, which takes in a `Vector3` parameter, to move the capsule's **Transform** component:
    - Remember that the `this` keyword specifies the GameObject the current script is attached to, which in this case is the player capsule.
    - `Vector3.forward` multiplied by `vInput` and `Time.deltaTime` supplies the direction and speed the capsule needs to move forward or back along the z axis at the speed we've calculated.
    - `Time.deltaTime` will always return the value in seconds since the last frame of the game was executed. It's commonly used to smooth values that are captured or run in the `Update` method instead of letting it be determined by a device's frame rate.

6. Uses the `Rotate` method to rotate the capsule's **Transform** relative to the vector we pass in as a parameter:

- `Vector3.up` multiplied by `hInput` and `Time.deltaTime` gives us the left/right rotation axis we want
- We use the `this` keyword and `Time.deltaTime` here for the same reasons

As we discussed previously, using direction vectors in the `Translate` and `Rotate` functions is only one way to go about this. We could have created new `Vector3` variables from our axis inputs and used them as parameters just as easily.

What just happened?

When you hit **Play**, you'll be able to move the capsule forward and back using the Up/Down Arrow and *W/S* keys, while rotating or turning with the Left/Right Arrow and *A/D* keys. With these few lines of code ,you've set up two separate controls that are frame rate independent and easily modified. However, our camera doesn't follow the capsule as it moves around, so let's fix that.

Camera follow

The easiest way to get one GameObject to follow another is to make one of them a child of the other. However, this approach means that any kind of movement or rotation that happens to the player capsule also affects the camera, which is something we don't necessarily want. Luckily, we can easily set the position and rotation of the camera relative to the capsule with methods from the `Transform` class.

Time for action – Scripting camera behavior

Since we want the camera behavior to be entirely separate from how the player moves, we'll be controlling where the camera is positioned relative to a target we can set from the **Inspector**:

1. Create a new C# script in the `Scripts` folder, name it `CameraBehavior`, and drag it onto the **Main Camera.**

2. Add the following code and save it:

```
public class CameraBehavior : MonoBehaviour
{
    // 1
    public Vector3 camOffset = new Vector3(0, 1.2, -2.6);

    // 2
    private Transform target;

    void Start()
    {
        // 3
        target = GameObject.Find("Player").transform;
    }

    // 4
    void LateUpdate()
    {
        // 5
        this.transform.position = target.TransformPoint(camOffset);

        // 6
        this.transform.LookAt(target);
    }
}
```

Here's a breakdown of the preceding code:

1. Declares a `Vector3` variable to store the distance we want between the **Main Camera** and the **Player**:
   - We'll be able to manually set the x, y, and z position of the camera offset in the **Inspector** because it's `public`
   - These default values are what I think looks best, but feel free to experiment

2. Creates a variable to hold the player capsule's **Transform** information:
   - This will give us access to its **position**, **rotation**, and **scale**
   - We don't want this data to be accessible outside of the `CameraBehavior` script, which is why it's `private`

3. Uses `GameObject.Find` to locate the capsule by name and retrieve its **Transform** property from the scene:
   - This means the capsule's x, y, and z positions are updated and stored in `target` every frame

4. `LateUpdate` is a `MonoBehavior` method, like `Start` or `Update`, that executes after `Update`:
   - Since our `PlayerBehavior` script moves the capsule in its `Update` method, we want the code in `CameraBehavior` to run after the movement happens; this guarantees that `target` has the most up-to-date position to reference

5. Sets the camera's position to `target.TransformPoint(camOffset)` every frame, which creates the following effect:
   - The `TransformPoint` method calculates and returns a relative position in the world space
   - In this case, it returns the position of the `target` (our capsule) offset by `0` in the x-axis, `1.2` in the y-axis (putting the camera above the capsule), and `-2.6` in the z-axis (putting the camera slightly behind the capsule)

6. The `LookAt` method updates the capsules rotation every frame, focusing on the **Transform** parameter we pass in, which in this case is `target`:

What just happened?

This was a lot to take in, but it's easier to process if you break it down into its chronological steps:

1. We created an offset position for the camera.
2. We found and stored the player capsule's position.
3. We manually updated its position and rotation every frame so that's it's always following at a set distance and looking at the player.

When using class methods that deliver platform-specific functionality, always remember to break things down to their most basic steps. This will help you stay above water in new programming environments.

Working with Unity physics

Up to this point. we haven't talked about how the Unity engine actually works, or how it manages to create lifelike interactions and movement in a virtual space. We'll spend the rest of this chapter on the basics of Unity's physics system:

Version 2019.2.0a7

Gonzalez, Andres Rafael Diez, Andrew Alcott, Andrew Bowell, Andrew Carlston, Andrew Dennison, Andrew Donnell, Andrew Gross, Andrew Horobin, Andrew Innes, Andrew Jenkins, Andrew Kasbari, Andrew Konecny, Andrew Luke, Andrew Maneri, Andrew Milsom, Andrew Montgomery, Andrew Peynado, Andrew Selby, Andrew Slater, Andrew Spiering, Andrew Tang, Andrey Shvets, Andrius Keidonas, Andrius Kuznecovas, Andrius Mitkus, Andy Bauerle, Andy Brammall, Andy Jepkes, Andy Keener, Andy Stark, Andy Stein, Andy Touch, Andy Wood, Angel Colberg, Angela Marian, Angela Park, Angela Pellegrino, Angela Wu, Angelo Ferro, Angie Cantwell, Angus Mackay, Ani Golovko, Anildas Haridas, Aniqa Kamal, Ankit Dubey, Anna Cho, Anna Lachowicz

Anna Szeto, Anne Duggan, Anne Evans, Anne Xie, Annie Liu, Anouska Smith, Ans Beaulieu, Anssi

Scripting powered by The Mono Project.

(c) 2011 Novell, Inc.

Physics powered by PhysX.

(c) 2011 NVIDIA Corporation.

Microsoft Visual Studio Tools for Unity 1.4.0.3 enabled

(c) 2019 Unity Technologies ApS. All rights reserved.

License type: Unity Pro, Team License, iOS Pro, Android Pro, Windows Store Pro

Serial number: SB-2UZS-7DTV-SF5X-ADTZ-XXXX

The two main components that power Unity's NVIDIA PhysX engine are as follows:

- **Rigidbody** components, which allow GameObjects to be affected by gravity and add properties like **Mass** and **Drag**. **Rigidbody** components can also be affected by applied force, generating a more realistic movement:

- **Collider** components, which determine how and when GameObjects enter and exit each other's physical space or simply collide and bounce away. While there should only be one **Rigidbody** attached to a given GameObject, there can be several **Collider** components. This is commonly referred to as a compound collider setup:

When two GameObjects collide with each other, the **Rigidbody** properties determine the resulting interaction. For example, if one GameObject's mass is higher than the other, the lighter GameObject will bounce away with more force, just like in real life. These two components are responsible for all physical interactions and simulated movement in Unity.

There are some caveats to using these components, which are best understood in terms of the types of movement Unity allows:

- *Kinematic* movement happens when a **Rigidbody** component is attached to a GameObject, but it doesn't register to the physics system in the scene:
    - This is only used in certain cases and can be enabled by checking the **isKinematic** property of a **Rigidbody**. Since we want our capsule to interact with the physics system, we won't be using this kind of motion.
- *Non-Kinematic* movement is when a **Rigidbody** is moved or rotated by applying force rather than manually changing a GameObject's **Transform** properties. Our goal for this section is to update the `PlayerBehavior` script to implement this type of motion.

The setup we have now , that is, manipulating the capsules' **Transform** component while using a **Rigidbody** to interact with the physics system, was meant to get you thinking about movement and rotation in a 3D space. However, it's not meant for production and Unity suggests avoiding a mix of kinematic and non-kinematic movement in your code.

Rigidbodies in motion

Since our player has a **Rigidbody** attached, we should let the physics engine control our movement instead of manually translating and rotating the **Transform**. There are two options when it comes to applying force:

- You can do it directly by using **Rigidbody** class methods like `AddForce` and `AddTorque` to move and rotate an object, respectively. This approach has it's drawbacks and often requires additional code to compensate for unexpected physics behavior.

  OR

- You can use other **Rigidbody** class methods like `MovePosition` and `MoveRotation`, which still use applied force but take care of edge cases behind the scenes.

We'll take the second route in the next section, but if you're curious about manually applying force and torque to your GameObjects, then start here: `https://docs.unity3d.com/ScriptReference/Rigidbody. AddForce.html`.

Either of these will give the player a more life-like feel and allow us to add in jumping and dashing mechanics in `Chapter 8`, *Scripting Game Mechanics*.

If you're curious about what happens when a moving object without a **Rigidbody** interacts with pieces of the environment that have them equipped, remove the component from the **Player** and run around the arena. Congratulations – you're a ghost and can walk through walls! Don't forget to add the **Rigidbody** back though!

Time for action – accessing the Rigidbody

We'll need to access and store the Rigidbody component on our player capsule before modifying it:

1. Update `PlayerBehavior` with the following changes:

```
public class PlayerBehavior : MonoBehaviour
{
  public float moveSpeed = 10f;
  public float rotateSpeed = 75f;

  private float vInput;
  private float hInput;

  // 1
      private Rigidbody _rb;

  // 2
      void Start()
      {
          // 3
          _rb = GetComponent<Rigidbody>();
      }

  void Update()
  {
    vInput = Input.GetAxis("Vertical") * moveSpeed;
    hInput = Input.GetAxis("Horizontal") * rotateSpeed;

    /* 4
```

```
        this.transform.Translate(Vector3.forward * vInput *
        Time.deltaTime);
        this.transform.Rotate(Vector3.up * hInput * Time.deltaTime);
        */
    }
}
```

Here's a breakdown of the preceding code:

1. Adds a `private Rigidbody` type variable that will contain the capsules' **Rigidbody** component information.
2. The `Start` method fires when a script is initialized in a scene, which happens when you hit play, and should be used any time variables need to be set at the beginning of a class.
3. The `GetComponent` method checks to see if the component type we're looking for, in this case, **Rigidbody**, exists on the GameObject the script is attached to and returns it:
   - If the component isn't attached to the GameObject, the method will return `null`, but since we know there's one on the player, we won't worry about error checking right now
4. Comments the `Transform` and `Rotate` method calls in the `Update` function so that we won't be running two different kinds of player controls
   - We want to keep our code that captures player input so that we can still use it later on

What just happened?

We've initialized and stored the **Rigidbody** component on our **Player** capsule and commented out our obsolete `Transform` code to set the stage for physics-based movement.

Time for action – moving the Rigidbody

We'll use the following steps to move and rotate the **Rigidbody**:

1. Add in the following code to `PlayerBehavior` underneath the `Update` method and save the file:

```
// 1
void FixedUpdate()
{
    // 2
    Vector3 rotation = Vector3.up * hInput;
```

```
        // 3
        Quaternion angleRot = Quaternion.Euler(rotation *
    Time.fixedDeltaTime);

        // 4
        _rb.MovePosition(this.transform.position +
    this.transform.forward * vInput * Time.fixedDeltaTime);

        // 5
        _rb.MoveRotation(_rb.rotation * angleRot);
    }
```

Here's a breakdown of the preceding code:

1. Any physics or **Rigidbody**-related code always goes inside `FixedUpdate`, rather than `Update` or other `MonoBehavior` methods
2. Creates a new `Vector3` variable to store our left and right rotation:
    - `Vector3.up * hInput` is the same rotation vector we used with the `Rotate` method in the previous example
3. `Quaternion.Euler` takes a `Vector3` and returns a rotation value in Euler angles:
    - We need a `Quaternion` value instead of a `Vector3` to use the `MoveRotation` method. This is just a conversion to the rotation type that Unity prefers.
    - We multiply by `Time.fixedDeltaTime` for the same reason we used `Time.deltaTime in Update`.

4. Calls `MovePosition` on our `_rb` component, which takes in a `Vector3` parameter and applies force accordingly:
    - The vector that's used can be broken down as follows: the capsules' transform position in the forward direction, multiplied by the vertical inputs and `Time.fixedDeltaTime`
    - The **Rigidbody** takes care of applying movement force to satisfy our vector parameter
5. Calls the `MoveRotate` method on the `_rb` component, which also takes in a `Vector3` parameter and applies the corresponding forces under the hood:
    - `angleRot` already has the horizontal inputs from the keyboard, so all we need to do is multiply the current Rigidbody rotation by `angleRot` to get the same left and right rotation

What just happened?

If you hit **Play** now, you'll be able to move forward and back in the direction your looking, as well as rotate around the y-axis. Applied force produces stronger effects than translating and rotating a **Transform**, so you may need to fine-tune the `moveSpeed` and `rotateSpeed` variables in the **Inspector**. We've now recreated the same type of movement scheme we had before, just with more realistic physics.

If you run up a ramp or drop off the central platform, you might see the player launch into the air, or slowly drop to the ground. Even though the **Rigidbody** is set to use gravity, it's fairly weak. We'll tackle applying our own gravity to the player in the next chapter when we implement the jump mechanic.

Colliders and collisions

Collider components not only allow GameObjects to be recognized by Unity's physics system, but they also make interactions and collisions possible. Think of Colliders as invisible force fields that surround GameObjects; they can be passed through or bumped into depending on their settings and come with a host of methods that fire during different interactions.

Unity's physics system works differently for 2D and 3D games, so we will only be covering the 3D topics in this book. If you're interested in making 2D games, check out the **Rigidbody2D** component and the list of available 2D Colliders.

Take a look at the following screenshot of the **Capsule** in the **Pickup_Prefab** object hierarchy:

The green shape around the object is its **Capsule Collider**, which can be moved and scaled using the **Center**, **Radius**, and **Height** properties. When a primitive is created, the **Collider** matches the primitives shape by default; since we created a **Capsule** primitive, it comes with a **Capsule Collider**.

Colliders also come in **Box**, **Sphere**, and **Mesh** shapes and can be manually added from the **Component** | **Physics** menu or from the **Add Component** button in the **Inspector**.

When a **Collider** come into contact in certain ways, they send out what's called a message, or broadcast. Any script that adds one or more of those methods will receive a notification when the **Collider** sends out a message. This is called an *Event*, which is a topic we'll cover in Chapter 12, *The Journey Continues*.

For example, when two GameObjects with Colliders come into contact, they both send out the OnCollisionEnter message, complete with a reference to the object they ran into. This information can be used for a variety of interactive events, but the simplest one is picking up an item, which we'll tackle next.

A complete list of **Collider** notifications can be found here under the Messages header: https://docs.unity3d.com/ScriptReference/Collider.html.

Collision and trigger events are only sent out when the colliding objects belong to a specific combination of Collider, Trigger and RigidBody components and Kinematic or non-Kinematic motion. You can find details under the Collision action matrix section at https://docs.unity3d.com/Manual/CollidersOverview.html.

Time for action – picking up an item

To update the **Pickup_Item** with collision logic, we need to follow these steps:

1. Create a new C# script in the Scripts folder, name it ItemBehavior and drag it onto the **Capsule** object under the **Pickup_Item** prefab in the scene:
   - Any script that uses collision detection MUST be attached to a GameObject with a **Collider** component, even if it's a child of a prefab

2. Hit apply with **Pickup_Item** selected to update the root prefab:

3. Add the following code to `ItemBehavior` and save it:

```
public class ItemBehavior : MonoBehaviour
{
    // 1
    void OnCollisionEnter(Collision collision)
    {
        // 2
        if(collision.gameObject.name == "Player")
        {
            // 3
            Destroy(this.transform.parent.gameObject);

            // 4
            Debug.Log("Item collected!");
        }
    }
}
```

4. Hit `Play` and move the player over the capsule to pick it up!

Here's a breakdown of the preceding code:

1. When another object runs into the **Pickup_Item** with its **isTrigger** turned off, Unity automatically calls the `OnCollisionEnter` method:
   - `OnCollisionEnter` comes with a parameter that stores a reference to the **Collider** that ran into it
   - Notice that the collision is of type `Collision`, not `Collider`

2. The `Collision` class has a property called `gameObject`, which holds a reference to the colliding GameObjects **Collider:**
   - We can use this property to get the GameObject's name and use an `if` statement to check if the colliding object is the `Player`

3. If the colliding object is the `Player`, we'll call the `Destroy()` method, which takes in a GameObject parameter:
   - We want the entire **Pickup_Item** object to be destroyed, not just the **Capsule**
   - Since `ItemBehavior` is attached to the **Capsule**, which is a child object of **Pickup_Item**, we use `this.transform.parent.gameObject` to set the **Pickup_Item** to be destroyed

4. Prints out a simple log to the console that we have collected an item:

What just happened?

We've set up `ItemBehavior` to essentially listen for any collisions with the **Capsule** object inside the **Pickup_Item** prefab. Whenever a collision occurs, `ItemBehavior` uses `OnCollisionEnter()` and checks if the colliding object is the **Player**, and if so destroys (or collects) the item. If you're feeling lost, think of the collision code we wrote as a receiver for notifications from the **Pickup_Item** Capsule; any time it's hit, the code fires.

It's also important to understand that we could have created a similar script with an `OnCollisionEnter()` method and attached it to the **Player**, then checked whether the colliding object was a **Pickup_Item**. Collision logic depends on the perspective of the object being collided with.

Using Collider triggers

By default, Colliders are set with the **isTrigger** property unchecked, meaning that the physics system treats them as solid objects. However, in some cases, you'll want to be able to pass through a **Collider** without it stopping your GameObject. This is where triggers come in. With **isTrigger** checked, a GameObject can pass through it, but the **Collider** will send out the `OnTriggerEnter`, `OnTriggerExit`, and `OnTriggerStay` notifications.

Triggers are most useful when you need to detect when a GameObject enters a certain area or passes a certain point. We'll use this to set up the areas around our enemies; if the player walks into the trigger zone, the enemies will be alerted, and later on attack the player.

Time for action – creating an enemy

To create an enemy, follow these steps:

1. Create a new primitive using **Create | 3D Object | Capsule** in the Hierarchy panel and name it `Enemy`.
2. Inside the `Materials` folder, use **Create | Material**, name it `Enemy_Mat`, and set its **Albedo** property to a bright **red:**
   - Drag and drop **Enemy_Mat** onto the **Enemy** GameObject
3. With **Enemy** selected, click **Add Component** and search for **Sphere Collider**. Then, hit *Enter* to add it:
   - Check the **isTrigger** property box and change the **Radius** to **8:**

What just happened?

Our new **Enemy** is now surrounded by an 8 unit trigger radius shaped like a sphere. Any time another object enters, stays, or exits that area, Unity will send out notifications that we can capture, just like we did with collisions.

Time for action – capturing trigger events

Now, we will see how to capture trigger events:

1. Create a new C# script in the `Scripts` folder, name it `EnemyBehavior`, and drag it onto **Enemy.**
2. Add the following code and save the file:

```csharp
public class EnemyBehavior : MonoBehaviour
{
    // 1
    void OnTriggerEnter(Collider other)
    {
        //2
        if(other.name == "Player")
        {
            Debug.Log("Player detected - attack!");
        }
    }

    // 3
    void OnTriggerExit(Collider other)
    {
        // 4
        if(other.name == "Player")
        {
            Debug.Log("Player out of range, resume patrol");
        }
    }

}
```

3. Hit **Play** and walk over to the **Enemy** to set off the first notification.
   • Walk away from the **Enemy** to set off the second notification

Here's a breakdown of the preceding code:

1. `OnTriggerEnter()` is fired whenever an object enters the **Enemy Sphere Collider** radius:
   - Similar to `OnCollisionEnter()`, `OnTriggerEnter()` stores a reference to the trespassing object's **Collider** component
   - Note that other is of type `Collider`, not `Collision`

2. We can use `other` to access the name of the colliding GameObject, and check if it's the `Player` with an `if` statement:
   - If it is, the console prints out a log that the `Player` is in the danger zone

3. `OnTriggerExit()` is fired when an object leaves the **Enemy Sphere Collider** radius:
   - This method also has a reference to the colliding object's **Collider** component:

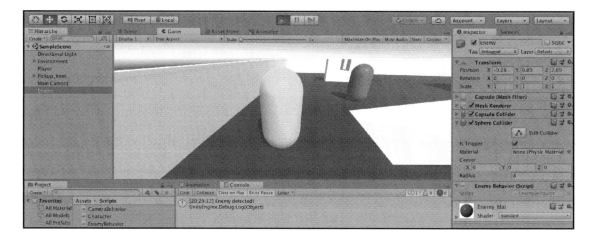

4. We check the object leaving the **Sphere Collider** radius by name using another `if` statement:

- If it's the `Player`, we print out another log to the console saying that they're safe:

What just happened?

The **Sphere Collider** on our **Enemy** sends out notifications when its area is invaded, and the `EnemyBehavior` script captures two of those events. Whenever the **Player** enters or exits the collision radius, a debug log appears in the console to let us know that the code is working. We'll continue to build on this in `Chapter 9`, *Basic AI and Enemy Behavior*.

Unity makes use of something called the *Component* design pattern. Without getting into too much detail, that's a fancy way of saying objects (and by extension, their classes) should be responsible for their own behavior. This is why we put separate collision scripts onto the pickup item and enemy instead of having a single class handle everything. More on this later on in `Chapter 12`, *The Journey Continues*.

Hero's trial – all the prefabs!

To get the project ready for the next chapter, go ahead and drag the **Player** and **Enemy** objects into the **Prefabs** folder. Remember that from now on, you always need to hit **Apply** in the **Inspector** to solidify any changes you make to these GameObjects.

Physics roundup

Before we wrap up the chapter, here are a few high-level concepts to really cement what we've learned:

- **Rigidbody** components add simulated real-world physics to GameObjects they are attached to
- **Collider** components interact with each other, as well as objects with **Rigidbody** components:
    - If a **Collider** is not a trigger, it acts like a solid object
    - If a **Collider** is a trigger, it can be walked through
- An object is *Kinematic* if it uses a **Rigidbody** but has **isKinematic** unchecked, telling the physics system to ignore it
- An object is *Non-Kinematic* if it uses a **Rigidbody** and applied force or torque to power its movement and rotation
- Colliders send out notifications based on their interactions:
    - These notifications depend on whether the **Collider** is set to be triggered or not
    - Notifications can be received from either colliding party, and come with reference variables that hold an object's collision information

Pop quiz – player controls and physics

1. What data type would you use to store 3D movement and rotation information?
2. What built-in Unity component allows you to track and modify player controls?
3. Which component adds real-world physics to a GameObject?
4. What method does Unity suggest using to execute physics-related code on GameObjects?

Summary

This wraps up your first experience creating independent gameplay behaviors and tying them all together into a cohesive, albeit simple, game. You've used vectors and basic vector math to determine positions and angles in a 3D space, and you're familiar with player input and the two main methods of moving and rotating GameObjects. You've even gone down into the bowels of the Unity physics system to get comfortable with **Rigidbody** physics, collisions, triggers, and event notifications. All in all, *Hero Born* is off to a great start.

In the next chapter, we'll start tackling more game mechanics, including jumping, dashing, shooting projectiles, and interacting with parts of the environment.

8
Scripting Game Mechanics

the last chapter, we focused on moving our player and camera in code, with another trip into Unity physics on the side. However, controlling a playable character isn't enough to make a compelling game; in fact, it's probably the one area that remains constant across different titles.

A game's unique spark comes from its core mechanics and the feeling of power and agency those mechanics give to players. Without fun and engrossing ways to affect the virtual environment you've created, your game doesn't stand a chance of repeat play, to say nothing of fun. As we venture into implementing the game's mechanics, we'll also be upgrading our knowledge of C# and its intermediate-level features.

This chapter will round out the *Hero Born* prototype with the following topics:

- Adding jumps with applied force
- Understanding layer masks
- Instantiating objects and prefabs
- Understanding game manager classes
- Getter and setter properties
- Keeping score
- Scripting user interfaces

Adding jumps

One great thing about using a **Rigidbody** component to control player movement is that we can easily add in different mechanics that rely on applied force, such as jumping. In this section, we'll get our player jumping, work with a new data type called enumerations, and write our first utility function.

 A utility function is a class method that performs some kind of grunt work so we don't clutter up gameplay code. For instance, wanting to check whether the player capsule is touching the ground in order to jump (hint).

Enter enumerations

By definition, an enumeration type is a set, or collection, of named constants that belong to the same variable. These are useful when you want a collection of different values, but with the added benefit of them all being of the same parent type.

It's easier to show rather than tell with enumerations, so let's take a look at their syntax:

```
enum PlayerAction { Attack, Defend, Flee };
```

Let's break down how this works:

- The enum keyword declares the type followed by the variable name/
- The different values an enum can have are written inside curly brackets, separated by a comma (except for the last item).
- The enum has to end with a semicolon, just like all other data types we've worked with.

To declare an enumeration variable we use the following syntax:

```
PlayerAction currentAction = PlayerAction.Defend;
```

Again, we can break this down as follows:

- The type is set as `PlayerAction`.
- The variable is named and set equal to a `PlayerAction` value.
- Each enum constant can be accessed using a dot notation.

Underlying types

Enums also come with an *underlying type*, meaning that each constant inside the curly brackets has an associated value. The default underlying type is `int` and starts at 0, just like arrays, with each sequential constant getting the next highest number.

Not all types are created equal – underlying types for enumerations are limited to `byte`, `sbyte`, `short`, `ushort`, `int`, `uint`, `long`, and `ulong`. These are called integral types, which are used to specify the size of numeric values that a variable can store.

This is a bit advanced for this book, but you'll be using `int` for most cases. More information on these types can be found here: `https://docs.microsoft.com/en-us/dotnet/csharp/language-reference/keywords/enum`.

For example, our `PlayerAction` enum values right now are listed as follows, even though they aren't explicitly written out:

```
enum PlayerAction { Attack = 0, Defend = 1, Flee = 2 };
```

There's no rule that says underlying values need to start at zero; in fact, all you have to do is specify the first value and then C# increments the rest of the values for us:

```
enumPlayerAction { Attack = 5, Defend, Flee };
```

In the preceding example, `Defend = 6` and `Flee = 7` automatically. However, if we wanted the `PlayerAction` enum to hold non-sequential values, we could explicitly add them in:

```
enum PlayerAction { Attack = 10, Defend = 5, Flee = 0};
```

We can even change the underlying type of `PlayerAction` to any of the approved types by adding a colon after the enum name:

```
enum PlayerAction : byte { Attack, Defend, Flee };
```

Retrieving an enum's underlying type takes an explicit conversion, but we've already covered those, so this syntax shouldn't be a surprise:

```
enum PlayerAction { Attack = 10, Defend = 5, Flee = 0};

PlayerAction currentAction = PlayerAction.Attack;
int actionCost = (int)currentAction;
```

Enumerations are extremely powerful tools in your programming arsenal, so keep them in mind for later.

Time for action – pressing the spacebar to jump!

Now that we have a basic grasp on enumeration types, we can capture keyboard input using the KeyCode enum:

1. Update **PlayerBehavior** with the following code, save, and hit play:

```
public class PlayerBehavior : MonoBehaviour
 {
     public float moveSpeed = 10f;
     public float rotateSpeed = 75f;

     // 1
     public float jumpVelocity = 5f;

     private float vInput;
     private float hInput;

     private Rigidbody _rb;

     void Start()
     {
         _rb = GetComponent<Rigidbody>();
     }

     void Update()
     {
         vInput = Input.GetAxis("Vertical") * moveSpeed;
         hInput = Input.GetAxis("Horizontal") * rotateSpeed;

         // 2
         if(Input.GetKeyDown(KeyCode.Space))
          {
            // 3
            _rb.AddForce(Vector3.up * jumpVelocity,
```

```
          ForceMode.Impulse);
       }

       //this.transform.Translate(Vector3.forward * vInput *
Time.deltaTime);
       //this.transform.Rotate(Vector3.up * hInput *
Time.deltaTime);
    }

    void FixedUpdate()
    {
       // ... No changes needed ...
    }
}
```

Let's break down this code:

1. Creates a new variable to hold the amount of applied jump force we want, which can adjust in the Inspector.
2. The `Input.GetKeyDown()` method returns a `bool` value depending on whether a specified key is pressed.
    - The method accepts a key parameter as either a `string` or a `KeyCode`, which is an enumeration type. We specify that we want to check for `KeyCode.Space`.
    - We use an **if** statement to check the method's return value; if it's `true`, we execute the body of the **if** statement.
3. Since we already have the **Rigidbody** component stored, we can pass the `Vector3` and `ForceMode` parameters to `RigidBody.AddForce()` and make the player jump.
    - We specify that the vector (or applied force) should be in the **up** direction multiplied by `jumpVelocity`.
    - The `ForceMode` parameter determines how the force is applied and is also an enumeration type. `Impulse` delivers an instant force to an object while taking its mass into account, which is perfect for a jump mechanic.

Other **ForceMode** choices can be useful in different situations, all of which are detailed here: `https://docs.unity3d.com/ScriptReference/ForceMode.html`.

What just happened?

If you play the game now, you'll be able to move around and jump when you hit the spacebar. However, the mechanic allows you to keep jumping indefinitely, which isn't what we want. We'll work on limiting our jump mechanic to one at a time in the next section, using something called a layer mask.

Working with layer masks

Think of layer masks as invisible groups that a GameObject can belong to0, used by the physics system to determine anything from navigation to intersecting collider components. While more advanced uses of layer masks are outside the scope of this book, we'll create and use one to perform a simple check – whether the player capsule is touching the ground.

Time for action – setting object layers

Before we can check that the player capsule is touching the ground we need to add all the objects in our level to a custom layer mask. This will let us perform the actual collision calculation with the **Capsule Collider** that's already attached to the player:

1. Select any GameObject in the **Hierarchy** and click on **Layer** | **Add Layer**:

2. Add a new layer called **Ground** by typing the name into the first available slot:

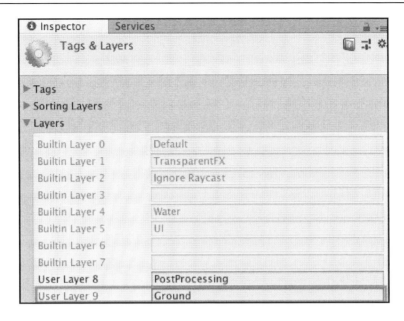

3. Select the **Environment** parent GameObject in the **Hierarchy**, click on the **Layer** dropdown, and select **Ground**.

   - Click **Yes** when a dialog appears asking you if you want to change all child objects:

What just happened?

By default, layers **0** - **7** are taken up by the Unity engine, which leaves us 24 slots for custom interactions. Here, we've defined a new layer called **Ground** and assigned every child object of **Environment** to that layer. Going forward, we can now all the objects on the **Ground** layer to check whether they intersect with a specific object.

Time for action – one jump at a time

Since we don't want code cluttering up the `Update()` method, we'll do our layer mask calculations in a utility function and return a `true` or `false` value based on the outcome:

1. Add the following code to **PlayerBehavior** and play the scene again:

```
public class PlayerBehavior : MonoBehaviour
  {
     public float moveSpeed = 10f;
     public float rotateSpeed = 75f;
     public float jumpVelocity = 5f;

     // 1
     public float distanceToGround = 0.1f;

     // 2
     public LayerMask groundLayer;

     private float _vInput;
     private float _hInput;
     private Rigidbody _rb;

     // 3
     private CapsuleCollider _col;

     void Start()
     {
         _rb = GetComponent<Rigidbody>();

         // 4
         _col = GetComponent<CapsuleCollider>();
     }

     void Update()
     {
         _vInput = Input.GetAxis("Vertical") * moveSpeed;
         _hInput = Input.GetAxis("Horizontal") * rotateSpeed;

         // 5
         if(IsGrounded() && Input.GetKeyDown(KeyCode.Space))
         {
             _rb.AddForce(Vector3.up * jumpVelocity,
   ForceMode.Impulse);
         }
     }
```

```
void FixedUpdate()
{
    // ... No changes needed ...
}

// 6
    private bool IsGrounded()
    {
        // 7
        Vector3 capsuleBottom = new
        Vector3(_col.bounds.center.x, _col.bounds.min.y,
        _col.bounds.center.z);
        // 8
        Bool grounded =
        Physics.CheckCapsule(_col.bounds.center, capsuleBottom,
        distanceToGround, groundLayer,
        QueryTriggerInteraction.Ignore);
        // 9
        return grounded;
    }
}
```

2. Set **Ground Layer** in the **Inspector** to **Ground** from the dropdown:

Let's break down this code:

1. Creates a new **float** variable for the distance we'll check between the player **CapsuleCollider** and any **Ground** layer object.
2. Creates a **LayerMask** variable that we can set in the **Inspector** and use for the collider detection.
3. Creates a **private** variable to store the players' **CapsuleCollider** component.
4. Uses `GetComponent()` to find and return the **CapsuleCollider** attached to the player.
5. Updates the **if** statement to check whether `IsGrounded` returns `true` and the spacebar is pressed before executing the jump code.
6. Declares the `IsGrounded()` method with a **bool** return type.
7. Creates a local `Vector3` variable to store the position at the bottom of the player's **CapsuleCollider**, which we'll use to check for collisions with any objects on the **Ground** layer.
   - All **Collider** components have a **bounds** property, which gives us access to the **min**, **max**, and **center** positions of its **x**, **y**, and z axes.
   - The bottom of the collider is the 3D point at **center x**, **min y**, and **center z.**
8. Creates a local **bool** to store the result of the `CheckCapsule()` method that we call from the `Physics` class, which takes in the following five arguments:
   - The start of the capsule, which we set to the middle of the **CapsuleCollider** since we only care about checking whether the bottom touches the ground.
   - The end of the capsule, which is the **capsuleBottom** position we've already calculated.
   - The radius of the capsule, which is the **distanceToGround** we've already set.
   - The layer mask we want to check collisions on, set to **groundLayer** in the Inspector.
   - The query trigger interaction, which determines whether the method should ignore colliders that are set as triggers. Since we don't want that, we used the **QueryTriggerInteraction.Ignore** enum.
9. Returns the value stored in **grounded** at the end of the calculation.

 We could have done the collision calculation manually, but that would require more complex 3D math than we have time to cover here. However, it's always a good idea to use built-in methods when available.

What just happened?

That was an involved piece of code that we just added into our PlayerBehavior, but when you break it down, the only new thing we did was use a method from the `Physics` class. In plain English, we supplied `CheckCapsule()` with a start and end point, a collision radius, and a layer mask. If the endpoint gets closer than the collision radius to an object on the layer mask, the method returns `true` – meaning the player is touching the ground. If the player is in mid-jump, `CheckCapsule()` returns `false`. Since we're checking `IsGround` in the `if` statement every frame in `Update()`, our player's jump skills are only allowed when touching the ground.

Shooting projectiles

Shooting mechanics are so common that it's hard to think of a first-person game without some variation present, and *Hero Born* is no different. In this section, we'll talk about how to instantiate GameObjects from prefabs while the game is running, and use the skills we've learned to propel them forward using Unity physics.

Instantiating objects

The concept of instantiating a GameObject in the game is the same as instantiating an instance of a class—both require starting values so C# knows what kind of object we want to create and where it needs to be created. However, when we instantiate a GameObject in the scene, we can streamline the process by using the `Instantiate()` method and providing a prefab object, a starting position, and starting rotation. Essentially, we can tell Unity to create a given object with all its components and scripts at this spot, looking in this direction, and then manipulate it as needed once it's born in 3D space!

Time for action – creating a projectile prefab

Before we can shoot any projectiles, we'll need a prefab reference, so let's create that now:

1. Select **Create** | **3D Object** | **Sphere** in the Hierarchy panel and name it **Bullet**.
   - Change its **Scale** to **0.15** in the **x**, **y**, and **z** axes in the **Transform** component.

2. Use the **Add Component** button to search and add a **Rigidbody** component, leaving all default properties as they are.

3. Create a new material in the **Materials** folder using **Create** | **Material**, and name it `Orb_Mat`.
   - Change the **Albedo** property to a deep yellow.
   - Drag and drop the material onto the **Bullet** GameObject.
4. Drag the **Bullet** into the `Prefabs` folder and delete it from the **Hierarchy**:

What just happened?

We created and configured a **Bullet** prefab GameObject that can be instantiated as many times as we need in the game and updated as needed.

Time for action – adding the shooting mechanic

Now that we have a prefab object to work with, we can instantiate and move copies of the prefab whenever we hit the spacebar to create a shooting mechanic:

1. Update **PlayerBehavior** with the following code:

```
public class PlayerBehavior : MonoBehaviour
{
    public float moveSpeed = 10f;
    public float rotateSpeed = 75f;
    public float jumpVelocity = 5f;
    public float distanceToGround = 0.1f;
    public LayerMask groundLayer;
```

```
// 1
public GameObject bullet;
public float bulletSpeed = 100f;

private float _vInput;
private float _hInput;
private Rigidbody _rb;
private CapsuleCollider _col;

void Start()
{
    // ... No changes needed ...
}

void Update()
{
    // ... No changes needed ...
}

void FixedUpdate()
{
    Vector3 rotation = Vector3.up * _hInput * Time.fixedDeltaTime;
    Quaternion deltaRotation = Quaternion.Euler(rotation);

    _rb.MovePosition(this.transform.position +
this.transform.forward * _vInput * Time.fixedDeltaTime);
    _rb.MoveRotation(_rb.rotation * deltaRotation);

    // 2
    if (Input.GetMouseButtonDown(0))
    {
        // 3
        GameObject newBullet = Instantiate(bullet,
        this.transform.position,
        this.transform.rotation) as GameObject;

        // 4
        Rigidbody bulletRB = newBullet.GetComponent<Rigidbody>
        ();

        // 5
        bulletRB.velocity = this.transform.forward *
        bulletSpeed;
    }
}

private bool IsGrounded()
{
```

```
            // ... No changes needed ...
        }
    }
```

2. Drag the **Bullet** prefab into the bullet property of **PlayerBehavior** in the **Inspector**:

3. Play the game and use the left mouse button to fire projectiles in the direction the player is facing!

Let's break down the code:

1. Creates two **public** variables: one to store the **Bullet** prefab, the other to hold the bullet's speed.
2. Uses an `if` statement to check that `Input.GetMouseButtonDown()` returns `true`, just like with `Input.GetKeyDown()`.
    - `GetMouseButtonDown()` takes an `int` parameter to determine which mouse button we want to check for; 0 is the **left button**, 1 is the **right button**, and 2 is the **middle button** or **scroll wheel**.

3. Creates a local GameObject variable every time the left mouse button is pressed.
   - We use the `Instantiate()` method to assign a GameObject to **newBullet** by passing in the **Bullet** prefab and using the capsule's position and rotation as its starting values.
   - We append **as GameObject** at the end to explicitly cast the returned object to the same type as **newBullet**.

4. Calls **GetComponent()** to return and store the **Rigidbody** on **newBullet**.
5. Sets the **velocity** property of the **Rigidbody** to the player's **transform.forward** direction multiplied by **bulletSpeed**:
   - Changing the **velocity** instead of using `AddForce()` ensures that gravity doesn't pull our bullets down in an arc when fired.

Managing GameObject buildup

Whether you're writing a completely code-based application or a 3D game, it's important to make sure that unused objects are regularly deleted to avoid overloading the program. Our bullets don't exactly play an important role after they are shot, they sort of just keep existing on the floor near whatever wall or object they collided with. With a mechanic such as shooting, this could result in hundreds, if not thousands, of bullets down the line, which is something we don't want.

Time for action – destroying bullets

For this task, we can take the skills we've already learned and make the bullets responsible for their own self-destructive behavior:

1. Create a new C# script in the `Scripts` folder and name it **BulletBehavior**.
2. Drag and drop the **BulletBehavior** script onto the **Bullet** prefab in the `Prefabs` folder.
3. Add the following code to **BulletBehavior**:

```
public class BulletBehavior : MonoBehaviour
{
    // 1
    public float onscreenDelay = 3f;

    void Update ()
    {
        // 2
```

```
            Destroy(this.gameObject, onscreenDelay);
        }
    }
```

Let's break down this code:

1. Declares a `float` variable to store how long we want the **Bullet** prefabs to remain in the scene after they are instantiated.

2. Uses the `Destroy()` method to delete the GameObject.
   - `Destroy()` always needs an object as a parameter, in this case, we use the **this** keyword to specify the object that the script is attached to.
   - `Destroy()` can optionally take an additional **float** parameter as a delay, which we use to keep the bullets onscreen for a short amount of time.

What just happened?

Now our **Bullet** prefab takes care of destroying itself from the scene after a specific delay. This means that the bullet executes its own defined behavior, without another script having to tell it what to do, which is an ideal application of the *Component* design pattern. We'll talk more about that in `Chapter 12`, *The Journey Continues*.

The game manager

A common misconception when learning to program is that all variables should automatically be made public, but in general, this is not a good idea. In my experience, variables should be thought of as protected and private from the start, and only made public if necessary. One way you'll see experienced programmers protect their data is through manager classes, and since we want to build good habits, we'll be following suit. Think of manager classes as a funnel where important variables and methods can be accessed safely.

When I say safely, I mean just that, which might seem unfamiliar in a programming context. However, when you have different classes communicating and updating data with each other, things can get messy. That's why having a single contact point, such as a manager class, can keep this to a minimum.

Tracking player properties

Hero Born is a simple game, so the only two data points we need to keep track of are how many items the player has collected and how much health they have left. We want these variables to be private so that they can only be modified from the manager class, giving us control and safety.

Time for action – creating a game manager

Game manager classes will be a constant facet of any project you develop in the future, so let's learn how to properly create one:

1. Create a new C# script in the **Scripts** folder and name it **GameBehavior**.

> Usually, this script would be named GameManager, but Unity reserves that name for its own uses. If you ever create a script and a cog wheel icon shows up next to its name instead of the C# file icon, that tells you it's restricted.

2. Create a new empty game object in the Hierarchy by using **Create | Create Empty** and name it **GameManager**.
   - Attach the **GameBehavior** script to the **GameManger** object.

> Manager scripts, and other non-game files, are set up on empty objects to put them in the scene, even though they don't interact with the actual 3D space.

3. Add the following code to **GameBehavior**:

```
public class GameBehavior : MonoBehaviour
{
    private int _itemsCollected = 0;
    private int _playerHP = 10;
}
```

Let's break down this code:

We added two new **private** variables to hold the number of items picked up and how many lives the player has left; these are **private** because they should only be modifiable in this class. If they were made **public**, other classes could change them at will, which can lead to the variables storing incorrect or concurrent data.

The Get and Set properties

We've got our manager script and private variables set up, but how do we access them from other classes if they're private? While we could write separate public methods in GameBehavior to handle passing new values to the private variables, let's see whether there is a better way of doing things.

In this case, C# provides all variables with `get` and `set` properties, which are perfectly suited to our task. Think of these as methods that are automatically fired by the C# compiler whether we explicitly call them or not, similar to how `Start()` and `Update()` are executed by Unity when a scene starts.

Get and set properties can be added to any variable, with or without an initial value:

```
public string firstName { get; set; };

OR

public string lastName { get; set; } = "Smith";
```

However, using them like this doesn't add any additional benefits; for that, you need to include a code block for each property:

```
public string FirstName
{
    get {
        // Code block executes when variable is accessed
    }

    set {
        // Code block executes when variable is updated
    }
}
```

Now, the get and set properties are set up to execute additional logic depending on where it's needed. We're not done yet though, we still need to handle the new logic.

Every get code block needs to return a value, while every set block needs to assign a value; this is where having a combination of a private variable, called a backing variable, and a public variable with get and set properties comes into play. The private variable remains protected, while the public variable allows controlled access from other classes:

```
private string _firstName
public string FirstName {
    get {
        return _firstName;
    }

    set {
        _firstName = value;
    }
}
```

Let's break this down:

- We can **return** the value stored in the private variable from the get property anytime another class needs it, without actually giving that outside class direct access.
- We can update the private variable any time an outside class assigns a new value to the public variable, keeping them in sync.
  - The **value** keyword is a stand-in for whatever new value is assigned.

This can seem a little esoteric without an actual application, so let's update **GameBehavior** with public variables with getter and setter properties to go along with our existing private variables.

Time for action – adding backing variables

Now that we understand the syntax of the get and set property accessors, we can implement them in our manager class for greater efficiency and code readability:

1. Update the code in **GameBehavior** as follows:

```
public class GameBehavior : MonoBehaviour
{
    private int _itemsCollected = 0;

    // 1
    public int Items
    {
        // 2
        get { return _itemsCollected; }

        // 3
        set {
            _itemsCollected = value;
            Debug.LogFormat("Items: {0}",
            _itemsCollected);
        }
    }

    private int _playerHP = 3;

    // 4
    public int HP
    {
        get { return _playerHP; }
        set {
            _playerHP = value;
            Debug.LogFormat("Lives: {0}",
            _playerHP);
        }
    }
}
```

Let's break down the code:

1. Declares a new `public` variable called `Items` with `get` and `set` properties
2. Uses the `get` property to `return` the value stored in `_itemsCollected` whenever `Items` is accessed from an outside class
3. Uses the `set` property to assign `_itemsCollected` to the new `value` of `Items` whenever it's updated, with an added `Debug.LogFormat()` call to print out the modified value of `_itemsCollected`
4. Sets up a `public` variable called `HP` with `get` and `set` properties to complement the private `_playerHP` backing variable

What just happened?

Both private variables in **GameBehavior** are now accessible, but only through their public counterparts. With this setup, we ensure that our private data can only be accessed and modified from specific contact points; this makes it easier to communicate with **GameBehavior** from our other mechanic scripts, as well as display the real-time data in the simple user interface we'll create at the end of the chapter.

Time for action – updating item collection

Now that we have our variables set up in **GameBehavior**, we can update **Items** every time we collect a **Pickup_Item** in the scene:

1. Add the following code to **ItemBehavior**:

```
public class ItemBehavior : MonoBehaviour
{
    // 1
    public GameBehavior gameManager;

    void Start()
    {
        // 2
        gameManager = GameObject.Find("Game
        Manager").GetComponent<GameBehavior>();
    }

    void OnCollisionEnter(Collision collision)
    {
        if (collision.gameObject.name == "Player")
        {
            Destroy(this.transform.parent.gameObject);
```

```
                    Debug.Log("Item collected!");

                    // 3
                    gameManager.Items += 1;
                }
            }
        }
```

2. Hit play and collect the pickup item to see the new console log print out from the manager script:

Let's break down the code:

1. Creates a new variable of the **GameBehavior** type to store a reference to the attached script.
2. Uses `Start()` to initialize **gameManager** by looking it up in the scene with **Find()** and adding a call to `GetComponent()`.

> You'll see this kind of code done in a single line quite often in Unity documentation and community projects. This is done for simplicity, but if you feel more comfortable writing out the `Find()` and `GetComponent()` calls separately, go right ahead; there's nothing wrong with clear, explicit formatting.

3. Increments the **Items** property in the **gameManager** class in `OnCollisionEnter()` after the **Pickup_Item** prefab is destroyed.

What just happened?

Since we already set up the ItemBehavior class to take care of collision logic, it's easy to modify `OnCollisionEnter()` to communicate with our manager class when an item is picked up by the player. Keep in mind that separating functionality out like this is what makes the code more flexible and less likely to break as you make changes during development.

Player Polish

At this point, we have several scripts working together to give players access to movement, jumping, collecting, and shooting mechanics. However, we're still missing any kind of display or visual cue that shows our player's stats, as well as a way to win and lose the game. We'll focus on these two topics as we close out this last section.

Graphical User Interfaces

User interfaces, commonly referred to as UI, are the visual components of any computer system. The mouse cursor, folder icons, and programs on your laptop are all UI elements. For our game, we want a simple display to let our players know how many items they've collected, their current health, and a text box to give them updates when certain events happen.

UI elements in Unity can be added in two ways:

- Directly from the **Create** menu in the Hierarchy panel like any other GameObject.
- Using the built-in **GUI** class in code.

We want to stick to the code version for this project and add in our three UI elements in the **GameBehavior** class. This isn't to say that one approach is better than the other, but since we are learning to program, it's a good idea to stay consistent.

The **GUI** class provides several methods to create and position components; all **GUI** method calls go in a *MonoBehavior* method called `OnGUI()`. Think of `OnGUI()` as the `Update()` method for all things UI; it runs anywhere from once to several times per frame, and is the main contact point for programmatic interfaces.

We'll only be covering a small percentage of the GUI class in our next example, but it has so much to offer it would be a waste not to take a quick look at the documentation yourself: `https://docs.unity3d.com/ScriptReference/GUI.html`.

If you're curious about non-programmatic UI, take a tour of Unity's own video tutorial series: `https://unity3d.com/learn/tutorials/s/user-interface-ui`.

Time for action – adding UI elements

We don't have that much information to display to the player at this point, but what we do have should be put onscreen in a pleasing, noticeable way:

1. Update **GameBehavior** with the following code and collect an item:

```
public class GameBehavior : MonoBehaviour
{
    // 1
    public string labelText = "Collect all 4 items and win
    your freedom!";
            public int maxItems = 4;

    private int _itemsCollected = 0;
    public int Items
    {
        get { return _itemsCollected; }
        set {
            _itemsCollected = value;

            // 2
            if(_itemsCollected >= maxItems)
                {
                    labelText = "You've found all the
                    items!";
                        }
                        else
                        {
            labelText = "Item found, only " + (maxItems -
            _itemsCollected) + " more to go!";
                        }
        }
    }

    private int _playerLives = 3;
```

```
public int Lives
{
    get { return _playerLives; }
    set {
        _playerLives = value;
        Debug.LogFormat("Lives: {0}", _playerLives);
    }
}

// 3
    void OnGUI()
    {
// 4
GUI.Box(new Rect(20, 20, 150, 25), "Player
Health:" + _playerLives);

// 5
GUI.Box(new Rect(20, 50, 150, 25), "Items
Collected: " + _itemsCollected);

// 6
GUI.Label(new Rect(Screen.width / 2 - 100,
Screen.height - 50, 300, 50), labelText);
    }
}
```

2. Run the game and take a look at our new onscreen GUI boxes:

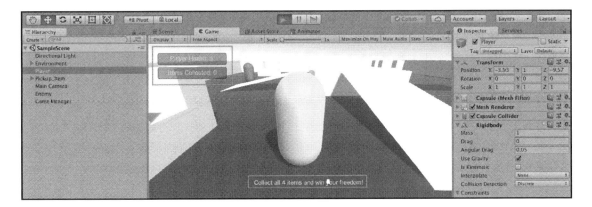

Let's break down the code:

1. Creates two new **public** variables: one for the text we want to show at the bottom of the screen, the other for the max number of items in the level.
2. Declares an **if** statement in the set property of **_itemsCollected**.
   - If the player has gathered more than or equal to **maxItems**, they've won and the **labelText** is updated.
   - Otherwise, the **labelText** shows how many items are still left to collect.
3. Declares the **OnGUI()** method to house the UI code.
4. Creates a **GUI.Box()** with specified dimensions and a string message:
   - The **Rect** class constructor takes in **x, y, width**, and **height** values.
   - A **Rect** position always starts in the upper-left side of the screen.
   - **new Rect(20, 20, 150, 25)** translates to a 2D box in the upper-left corner, 20 units from the left edge, 20 units from the top, with a width of 150 and a height of 25.
5. Creates another GUI.Box() underneath the health box to display the current item count.
6. Creates a GUI.Label() centered at the bottom of the screen to display the **labelText**.
   - Because OnGUI() fires at least once per frame, whenever the value of **labelText** changes it will be updated immediately onscreen.
   - Instead of manually calculating the middle of the screen, we use the Screen class **width** and **height** properties to give us the absolute values.

What just happened?

When we play the game now, our three UI elements show up with the correct values; when a **Pickup_Item** is collected, the **labelText** and **_itemsCollected** count update:

Win and Loss Conditions

We've implemented our core game mechanics and a simple UI, but *Hero Born* is still missing an important game design element: its win and loss conditions. These conditions will manage how the player wins or loses the game, and execute different code depending on the situation.

Back in the game document from `Chapter 5`, *Getting Your Hands Dirty with Unity*, we set out our win and loss conditions as follows:

- Collecting all items in the level with at least 1 health point remaining to win
- Taking damage from enemies until health points are at 0 to lose

These conditions are going to affect both our UI and game mechanics, but we've already set up up **GameBehavior** to handle this efficiently. Our `get` and `set` properties will handle any game-related logic, while `OnGUI()` will handle changes to the UI when a player wins or loses.

> We're going to implement the win condition in this section because we have the pickup system already in place. When we get to the enemy AI behavior in the next chapter, we'll add in the loss condition logic.

Time for action – winning the game

We always want to give players clear and immediate feedback, so we'll start by adding in logic for a win condition:

1. Update **GameBehavior** to match the following code:

```
public class GameBehavior : MonoBehaviour
{
    public string labelText = "Collect all 4 items and win your
freedom!";
    public int maxItems = 4;

    // 1
    public bool showWinScreen = false;

    private int _itemsCollected = 0;
    public int Items
    {
        get { return _itemsCollected; }
        set {
            _itemsCollected = value;

            if (_itemsCollected >= maxItems)
            {
                labelText = "You've found all the items!";

                // 2
                showWinScreen = true;
            }
            else
            {
                labelText = "Item found, only " + (maxItems -
_itemsCollected) + " more to go!";
            }
        }
    }

    // ... No changes needed ...

    void OnGUI()
    {
        GUI.Box(new Rect(20, 20, 150, 25), "Player Health: " +
        _playerLives);
        GUI.Box(new Rect(20, 50, 150, 25), "Items Collected: " +
        _itemsCollected);
        GUI.Label(new Rect(Screen.width / 2 - 100, Screen.height -
        50, 300, 50), labelText);
```

```
// 3
if (showWinScreen)
{
    // 4
    if (GUI.Button(new Rect(Screen.width/2 - 100,
    Screen.height/2 - 50, 200, 100), "YOU WON!"))
    {

    }
    }
    }
}
```

2. Change **maxItems** to 1 in the **Inspector** to test out the new screen:

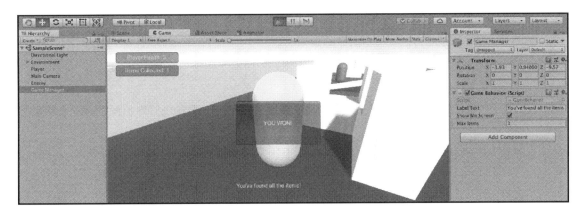

Let's break down the code:

1. Creates a new **bool** variable to track when the win screen should appear.
2. Sets **showWinScreen** to `true` in the **set** property of **Items** when the player has collected all pickups.
3. Uses an **if** statement inside `OnGUI()` to check whether the win screen should be displayed.
4. Creates a clickable `GUI.Button()` in the middle of the screen with a message for the player:
   - The `GUI.Button()` method returns a `bool` value, `true` when the button is clicked, `false` when it's not.
   - Embedding the `GUI.Button()` call inside an **if** statement executes the body of the **if** statement when the button is clicked.

What just happened?

With **maxItems** set to 1, the win button will show up on collecting the only `Pickup_Item` in the scene. Clicking the button doesn't do anything right now, but we'll address that in the next section.

Using directives and namespaces

Right now, our win condition works as expected, but the player still has control over the capsule and doesn't have a way of restarting the game once it's over. Unity provides a property in the `Time` class called **timeScale**, which when set to 0 freezes the game scene. However, in order to restart the game, we need access to a *namespace* called **SceneManagement** that isn't accessible from our classes by default.

A namespace collects and groups a set of classes under a specific name in order to organize large projects and avoid conflicts between scripts that may share the same names. A `using` directive needs to be added to a class in order to access a namespaces' classes.

All C# scripts created from Unity come with three default `using` directives:

```
using System.Collections;
using System.Collections.Generic;
using UnityEngine;
```

These allow access to common namespaces, but Unity and C# offer plenty more that can be added with the `using` keyword followed by the name of the namespace.

Time for action – pausing and restarting

Since our game will need to be paused and restarted when a player wins or loses, this is a good time to use a namespace that isn't included in new C# scripts by default:

1. Add the following code to **GameBehavior** and play:

```
using System.Collections;
using System.Collections.Generic;
using UnityEngine;

// 1
using UnityEngine.SceneManagement;

public class GameBehavior : MonoBehaviour
{
```

```
    // ... No changes needed ...

    private int _itemsCollected = 0;
    public int Items
    {
        get { return _itemsCollected; }
        set {
            _itemsCollected = value;

            if (_itemsCollected >= maxItems)
            {
                labelText = "You've found all the items!";
                showWinScreen = true;

                // 2
                Time.timeScale = 0f;
            }
            else
            {
                labelText = "Item found, only " + (maxItems -
_itemsCollected) + " more to go!";
            }
        }
    }

    // ... No other changes needed ...

    void OnGUI()
    {
        // ... No changes to GUI layout needed ...

        if (showWinScreen)
        {
            if (GUI.Button(new Rect(Screen.width/2 - 100,
Screen.height/2 - 50, 200, 100), "YOU WON!"))
            {
                // 3
                SceneManager.LoadScene(0);

                // 4
                Time.timeScale = 1.0f;
            }
        }
    }
}
```

Let's break down the code:

1. Adds the **SceneManagement** namespace with the **using** keyword, which handles all scene-related logic that Unity offers.
2. Sets **Time.timeScale** to 0 to pause the game when the win screen is displayed, which disables any input or movement.
3. Calls `LoadScene()` when the win screen button is clicked.
   - `LoadScene()` takes in a scene index as an `int` parameter.
   - Because there is only one scene in our project, we use index 0 to restart the game from the beginning.
4. Resets the **Time.timeScale** to the default value of 1 so that when the scene restarts, all controls and behaviors will be able to execute again.

What just happened?

Now when you collect an item and click on the win screen button, the level restarts, with all scripts and components restored to their original values and set up for another round.

Pop quiz – working with mechanics

1. What type of data do enumerations store?
2. How would you create a copy of a Prefab GameObject in an active scene?
3. Which variable properties allow you to add functionality when its value is referenced or modified?
4. What Unity method displays all user interface objects in the scene?

Summary

Congratulations! *Hero Born* is now in a playable state from the gamer's perspective. We implemented jumping and shooting mechanics, managed physics collisions and spawning objects, and added in a few basic UI elements to display feedback. We even got as far as resetting the level when the player wins!

A lot of new topics were introduced in this chapter, and it's important to go back and really make sure you understand what went into the code we wrote. Pay special attention to our discussions on enumerations, `get` and `set` properties, and namespaces. From here on in, the code is only going to get more complex as we dive further into the possibilities of the C# language.

In the next chapter, we'll start working on getting our enemy GameObjects to take notice of our player when we get too close, resulting in a follow-and-shoot protocol that will up the stakes for our player.

Basic AI and Enemy Behavior

Virtual scenarios need conflicts, consequences, and potential rewards to feel real to players. Without these three things, there's no incentive for the player to care what happens to their in-game character, much less continue to play the game after a cursory attempt. And while there are plenty of game mechanics that deliver on one or more of these conditions, nothing beats an enemy that will seek you out and try to end your session.

Programming an intelligent enemy is no easy task, and often goes hand in hand with long hours and frustration. However, Unity has built-in features, components, and classes we can use to design and implement AI systems in a more user-friendly way. These tools will push the first playable iteration of *Hero Born* over the finish line and provide a springboard for more advanced C# topics.

In this chapter, we'll focus on the following topics:

- The Unity navigation system
- Static objects and navigation meshes
- Navigation agents
- Procedural programming and logic
- Taking and dealing damage
- Adding a loss condition
- Refactoring techniques

Navigating in Unity

When we talk about navigation in real life, it's usually a conversation about how to get from point A to point B. Navigating around virtual 3D space is largely the same, but how do we account for the experiential knowledge we humans have accumulated since the day we first started crawling? Everything from walking on a flat surface to climbing stairs and jumping off of curbs is a skill we learned by doing; how can we possibly program all that into a game without going insane?

Navigation components

The short answer is that Unity has spent a lot of time perfecting their navigation system and delivering components that we can use to govern how playable and non-playable characters can get around. Each of the following components comes standard with Unity and has complex features already built-in:

- A **NavMesh** is essentially a map of the walkable surfaces in a given level; the **NavMesh** itself is created from the level geometry in a process called baking. Baking a **NavMesh** into your level creates a unique project asset that holds the navigation data.
- If **NavMesh** is the level map, then a **NavMeshAgent** is the moving piece on the board. Any object with a **NavMeshAgent** component attached will automatically avoid other agents or obstacles it comes into contact with.
- The navigation system needs to be aware of any moving or stationary objects in the level that could cause a **NavMeshAgent** to alter their route. Adding **NavMeshObstacle** components to those objects lets the system know that they need to be avoided.

While this description of the Unity navigation system is far from complete, it's enough for us to move forward with our enemy behavior. For this chapter, we'll be focusing on adding a **NavMesh** to our level, setting up the **Enemy** as a **NavMeshAgent**, and getting the **Enemy** to move along a predefined route in a seemingly intelligent way.

We'll only be using a **NavMesh** and **NavMeshAgent** in this chapter, but if you want to spice up your level, take a look at how to create obstacles: `https://docs.unity3d.com/Manual/nav-CreateNavMeshObstacle.html`.

Time for action – setting up the NavMesh

Let's set up and configure our level's **NavMesh**:

1. Select the **Environment** GameObject, click on the arrow icon next to **Static** in the **Inspector** and choose **Navigation Static**:

2. Click **Yes, change children** when the dialogue window pops up to set all the **Environment** child objects as **Navigation Static.**

3. Go to **Window** | **AI** | **Navigation** and select the **Bake** tab. Leave everything set to their default values and click **Bake**:

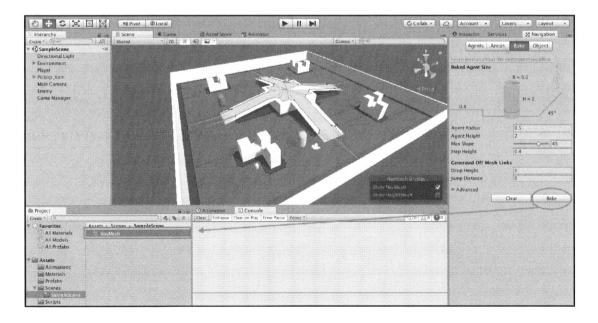

What just happened?

Every object in our level is now marked as **Navigation Static**, which means that our newly-baked **NavMesh** has evaluated their accessibility based on its default **NavMeshAgent** settings. Now everywhere you see a light blue overlay in the preceding screenshot is a perfectly walkable surface for any object with a **NavMeshAgent** component attached.

Time for action – setting up enemy agents

Let's register the **Enemy** as a **NavMeshAgent**:

1. Select the **Enemy** GameObject, click **Add Component** in the **Inspector** and search for **NavMesh Agent**:

2. Click **Create | Create Empty** from the Hierarchy and name the GameObject `Patrol Route`. With **Patrol Route** selected, click **Create | Create Empty** again to add a child GameObject and name it `Location 1`. Position **Location 1** in one of the corners of the level:

3. Create three more empty child objects in **Patrol Route**, name them `Location 2`, `3`, and `4`, and position them in the remaining corners of the level to form a square:

What just happened?

Adding a **NavMeshAgent** component to our **Enemy** tells the **NavMesh** to take notice and register it as an object that has access to its autonomous navigation features. Creating the four empty game objects in each corner of the level lays out the simple route we want our enemies to eventually patrol; grouping them in an empty parent object makes it easier to reference them in code and makes for a more organized Hierarchy.

Moving enemy agents

Our patrol locations are set and the **Enemy** has a **NavMeshAgent** component, but now we need to figure out how to reference those locations and get the enemy moving on its own. In order to do that, we'll first need to talk about an important concept in the world of software development: procedural programming.

Procedural programming

Even though it's in the name, the idea behind procedural programming can be elusive until you get your head around it; once you do, you'll never see a code challenge the same way.

Any task that executes the same logic on one or more sequential objects is the perfect candidate for procedural programming. In fact, you already did a little procedural programming when you debugged arrays, lists, and dictionaries with for and `foreach` loops. Each time those looping statements executed, you performed the same call to `Debug.Log()`, iterating over each item sequentially. The idea now is to use that skill to get a more useful outcome.

One of the most common uses for procedural programming is adding items from one collection to another, often modifying them along the way. This works great for our purposes since we want to reference each child object in the empty `patrolRoute` parent and store them in a list.

Time for action – referencing the patrol locations

Now that we understand the basics of procedural programming, it's time to get a reference to our patrol locations and assign them to a usable list:

1. Add the following code to **EnemyBehavior**:

```
public class EnemyBehavior : MonoBehaviour
{
    // 1
    public Transform patrolRoute;

    // 2
    public List<Transform> locations;

    void Start()
    {
        // 3
```

```
            InitializePatrolRoute();
        }

        // 4
            void InitializePatrolRoute()
        {
            // 5
            foreach(Transform child in patrolRoute)
            {
                // 6
                locations.Add(child);
            }
        }

        void OnTriggerEnter(Collider other)
        {
            // ... No changes needed ...
        }

        void OnTriggerExit(Collider other)
        {
            // ... No changes needed ...
        }
    }
```

2. Drag the **Patrol Route** object from the Hierarchy and drop it onto the **Patrol Route** variable in **EnemyBehavior**:

3. Hit the arrow icon next to the **Locations** variable in the **Inspector** and run the game to see the list populate:

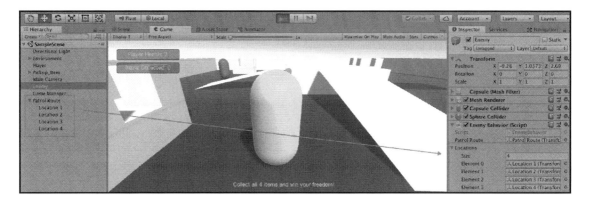

Let's break down the code:

1. Declares a variable for storing the `patrolRoute` empty parent GameObject.
2. Declares a `List` variable to hold all the child **Transform** components in `patrolRoute`.
3. Uses `Start()` to call the `InitializePatrolRoute()` method when the game begins.
4. Creates `InitializePatrolRoute()` as a private utility method to procedurally fill `locations` with `Transform` values.
   - Remember that not including an access modifier makes variables and methods `private` by default.
5. We use a `foreach` statement to loop through each child GameObject in `patrolRoute` and reference its **Transform** component.
   - Each `Transform` is captured in the local `child` variable declared in the `foreach` loop.

6. We add each sequential `child Transform` to the list of `locations` using the `Add()` method as we loop through the child objects in `patrolRoute`.
   - This way, no matter what changes we make in the Hierarchy panel, `locations` will always fill with all the `child` objects under the `patrolRoute` parent

What just happened?

While we could have assigned each location GameObject to **locations** by dragging and dropping them directly from the Hierarchy into the **Inspector**, it's easy to lose or break these connections; changes to the location object names, object additions or deletions, or project updates can all throw a wrench into a classes initialization. It's much safer, and more readable, to procedurally fill GameObject lists or arrays in the Start() method.

 Following that reasoning, I also tend to use GetComponent() in the Start() method to find and store component references attached to a given class instead of assigning them in the **Inspector**.

Time for action – moving the enemy

With a list of patrol locations initialized on Start(), we can grab the enemy **NavMeshAgent** component and set its first destination.

1. Update **EnemyBehavior** with the following code and hit **Play**:

```
// 1
using UnityEngine.AI;

public class EnemyBehavior : MonoBehaviour
{
    public Transform patrolRoute;
    public List<Transform> locations;

    // 2
    private int locationIndex = 0;

    // 3
    private NavMeshAgent agent;

    void Start()
    {
        // 4
        agent = GetComponent<NavMeshAgent>();

        InitializePatrolRoute();

        // 5
        MoveToNextPatrolLocation();
    }
```

```
void InitializePatrolRoute()
{
    // ... No changes needed ...
}

void MoveToNextPatrolLocation()
{
    // 6
    agent.destination = locations[locationIndex].position;
}

void OnTriggerEnter(Collider other)
{
    // ... No changes needed ...
}

void OnTriggerExit(Collider other)
{
    // ... No changes needed ...
}
}
```

Let's break down the code:

1. Adds the `UnityEngine.AI` using directive so that `EnemyBehavior` has access to Unity's navigation classes, in this case, `NavMeshAgent`.
2. Declares a variable to keep track of which patrol location the enemy is currently walking towards. Since `List` items are zero-indexed, we can have the **Enemy** move between patrol points in the order they are stored in `locations`.
3. Declares a variable to store the **NavMeshAgent** component attached to the **Enemy** GameObject. This is `private` because no other classes should be able to access or modify it.
4. Uses `GetComponent()` to find and return the attached **NavMeshAgent** component to `agent`.
5. Calls the `MoveToNextPatrolLocation()` method on `Start()`.
6. Declares `MoveToNextPatrolLocation()` as a private method and sets the `agent.destination`:
   - `destination` is a `Vector3` position in 3D space.
   - `locations[locationIndex]` grabs the **Transform** item in `locations` at a given index.
   - Adding `.position` references the **Transform** component's `Vector3` position.

What just happened?

Now when our scene starts, **locations** are procedurally filled with patrol points and `MoveToNextPatrolLocation()` is called to set the **destination** of the **NavMeshAgent** to the item at `locationIndex` 0 in the list of **locations**.

Time for action – patrolling continuously between locations

Our enemy moves to the first patrol point just fine, but then it stops. What we want is for it to continually move between each sequential location, which will require additional logic in `Update()` and `MoveToNextPatrolLocation()`. Let's create that behavior:

1. Add the following code to **EnemyBehavior** and hit **Play**:

```
public class EnemyBehavior : MonoBehaviour
{
    // ... No changes needed ...

    void Start()
    {
        // ... No changes needed ...
    }

    void Update()
    {
        // 1
        if(agent.remainingDistance < 0.2f && !agent.pathPending)
        {
            // 2
            MoveToNextPatrolLocation();
        }
    }

    void MoveToNextPatrolLocation()
    {
        // 3
        if (locations.Count == 0)
            return;

        agent.destination = locations[locationIndex].position;

        // 4
        locationIndex = (locationIndex + 1) % locations.Count;
    }
```

```
        void OnTriggerEnter(Collider other)
        {
            // ... No changes needed ...
        }

        void OnTriggerExit(Collider other)
        {
            // ... No changes needed ...
        }
    }
```

Let's break down the code:

1. Declares the `Update()` method and adds an `if` statement to check whether two different conditions are true.
   - `remainingDistance` returns how far the **NavMeshAgent** currently is from its set `destination`.
   - `pathPending` returns a `true` or `false` Boolean depending on whether Unity is computing a path for the NavMeshAgent.

2. If the `agent` is very close to its destination, and no other path is being computed, the `if` statement returns `true` and calls `MoveToNextPatrolLocation()`.

3. Here, we added an `if` statement to make sure that `locations` isn't empty before the rest of the code in `MoveToNextPatrolLocation()` is executed.
   - If `locations` is empty, we use the `return` keyword to exit the method without continuing.

 This is referred to as defensive programming, and, coupled with refactoring, it is an essential skill to have in your arsenal as you move toward more intermediate C# topics.

4. We set `locationIndex` to its current value `+1` followed by the modulo (%) of `locations.Count`.
   - This will increment the index from 0 to 4, then restart it at 0 so our **Enemy** moves in a continuous path.
   - The modulo operator returns the remainder of two values being divided – 2 divided by 4 has a remainder of 2, so 2 % 4 = 2. Likewise, 4 divided by 4 has no remainder, so 4 % 4 = 0.

Dividing an index by the maximum number of items in a collection is a quick way to always find the next item. If you're rusty on the modulo operator, revisit `Chapter 2`, *The Building Blocks of Programming*.

What just happened?

We now check that the **Enemy** is moving toward its set patrol location every frame in `Update()`; when it gets close, `MoveToNextPatrolLocation()` is fired, which increments `locationIndex` and sets the next patrol point as the destination. If you drag the **Scene** view down next to the **Console** window, as I've done in the following screenshot, and hit play, you can watch the **Enemy** walk around the corners of the level on a continuous loop:

Enemy game mechanics

Now that our **Enemy** is on a continuous patrol circuit, it's time to give it some interaction mechanics of its own; there wouldn't be much risk or reward if we left it walking around with no way to act against us.

Seek and destroy

In this section, we'll be focusing on switching the target of the enemies NavMeshAgent component when the player gets too close and dealing damage if a collision occurs. When the enemy successfully lowers the player's health, it will return to its patrol route until its next run-in with the player. However, we're not going to leave our player helpless; we'll also add in code to track enemy health, detect when an enemy is successfully hit with one of the player's bullets, and when an enemy needs to be destroyed.

Time for action – changing the agent's destination

Now that the **Enemy** is moving around on patrol, we need to get a reference to the player's position and change the **NavMeshAgent** destination:

1. Add the following code to **EnemyBehavior** and hit **Play**:

```
public class EnemyBehavior : MonoBehaviour
{
    // 1
    public Transform player;

    public Transform patrolRoute;
    public List<Transform> locations;

    private int locationIndex = 0;
    private NavMeshAgent agent;

    void Start()
    {
        agent = GetComponent<NavMeshAgent>();

        // 2
        player = GameObject.Find("Player").transform;
    }

    /* ... No changes to Update,
           InitializePatrolRoute, or
           MoveToNextPatrolLocation ... */

    void OnTriggerEnter(Collider other)
    {
        if(other.name == "Player")
        {
            // 3
            agent.destination = player.position;
```

```
                Debug.Log("Enemy detected!");
            }
        }

        void OnTriggerExit(Collider other)
        {
            // .... No changes needed ...
        }
    }
}
```

Let's break down the code:

1. Declares a `public` variable to hold the `Player` capsule's `Transform` value.
2. We use `GameObject.Find("Player")` to return a reference to the player object in the scene.
   - Adding the `.transform` directly references the objects `Transform` value in the same line.
3. We set `agent.destination` to the player's `Vector3` position in `OnTriggerEnter()` whenever the player enters the enemies attack zone.

What just happened?

If you play the game now and get too close to the patrolling **Enemy**, you'll see that it breaks from its path and comes straight for you. Once it reaches the player, the code in the `Update()` method takes over again the **Enemy** resumes its patrol.

Time for action – lowering player health

While our enemy mechanic has come a long way, it's still anti-climactic to have nothing happen when the **Enemy** collides with the **Player**. To fix this, we'll tie in the new enemy mechanics with the game manager by following these steps:

1. Update **PlayerBehavior** with the following code and hit **Play**:

```
public class PlayerBehavior : MonoBehaviour
{
    // ... No changes to public variables needed ...

    private float _vInput;
    private float _hInput;
    private Rigidbody _rb;
    private CapsuleCollider _col;

    // 1
```

```
private GameBehavior _gameManager;

void Start()
{
    _rb = GetComponent<Rigidbody>();
    _col = GetComponent<CapsuleCollider>();

    // 2
    _gameManager = GameObject.Find("Game
    Manager").GetComponent<GameBehavior>();
}

/* ... No changes to Update,
       FixedUpdate, or
       IsGrounded ... */

// 3
void OnCollisionEnter(Collision collision)
{
    // 4
    if(collision.gameObject.name == "Enemy")
    {
        // 5
        _gameManager.Lives -= 1;
    }
}
}
```

Let's break down the code:

1. Declares a `private` variable to hold the reference to the instance of `GameBehavior` we have in the scene.
2. Finds and returns the `GameBehavior` script attached to the `Game Manager` object in the scene.
   - Using `GetComponent()` on the same line as `GameObject.Find()` is a common way to cut down on unnecessary lines of code.
3. Since our **Player** is the object being collided with, it makes sense to declare `OnCollisionEnter()` in `PlayerBehavior`.
4. We check for the name of the colliding object; if it's the **Enemy**, we execute the body of the `if` statement.
5. We subtract 1 from the public `Lives` variable using the `_gameManager` instance.

What just happened?

Whenever the **Enemy** tracks and collides with the player now, the game manager will fire the **set** property on **Lives**. This means that we the UI will update with a new value for player health, and we have an opportunity to put in some additional logic for the loss condition later on.

Time for action – detecting bullet collisions

Now that we have our loss condition, it's time to add in a way for our player to fight back and survive enemy attacks:

1. Open up **EnemyBehavior** and modify it with the following code:

```
public class EnemyBehavior : MonoBehaviour
{
    public Transform player;
    public Transform patrolRoute;
    public List<Transform> locations;

    private int locationIndex = 0;
    private NavMeshAgent agent;

    // 1
    private int _lives = 3;
    public int EnemyLives
    {
                  // 2
        get { return _lives; }

        // 3
        private set
        {
            _lives = value;

            // 4
            if (_lives <= 0)
            {
                Destroy(this.gameObject);
                Debug.Log("Enemy down.");
            }
        }
    }

    /* ... No changes to Start,
            Update,
```

```
                    InitializePatrolRoute,
                    MoveToNextPatrolLocation,
                    OnTriggerEnter, or
                    OnTriggerExit ... */

        void OnCollisionEnter(Collision collision)
        {
            // 5
            if(collision.gameObject.name == "Bullet(Clone)")
            {
                // 6
                EnemyLives -= 1;
                Debug.Log("Critical hit!");
            }
        }
    }
```

Let's break down the code:

1. Declares a `private int` variable called `_lives` with a `public` backing variable called `EnemyLives`. This will let us control how `EnemyLives` is referenced and set, just like in `GameBehavior`.

2. We set the `get` property to always return `_lives`.

3. We use the `private set` to assign the new value of `EnemyLives` to `_lives` to keep them both in sync.

 We haven't seen a `private get` or `set` before, but they can have their own access modifiers just like any other executable code. Declaring a `get` or `set` as `private` means that only the parent class has access to their functionality.

4. We add an `if` statement to check whether `_lives` is less than or equal to 0, meaning the `Enemy` should be dead.
    - When that's the case, we destroy the `Enemy` GameObject and print out a message to the console.

5. Because `Enemy` is the object getting hit with bullets, it's sensible to put a check for those collisions in `EnemyBehavior` with `OnCollisionEnter()`.

6. If the name of the colliding object matches a bullet clone object, we decrement `EnemyLives` by 1 and print out another message.

Notice that the name we're checking for is `"Bullet(Clone)"` even though our bullet prefab is named `Bullet`. This is because Unity adds the (Clone) suffix to any object created with the `Instantiate()` method, which is how we made them in our shooting logic.

What just happened?

Now the player can fight back when the Enemy tries to take one of its lives by shooting it three times and destroying it. Again, our use of `get` and `set` properties to handle additional logic proves to be a flexible and scalable solution.

Time for action – updating the game manager

In order to fully implement the loss condition, we need to update the manager class:

1. Open up **GameBehavior** and add the following code, then get the **Enemy** to collide with you three times:

```
public class GameBehavior : MonoBehaviour
{
    public string labelText = "Collect all 4 items and win your
    freedom!";
    public int maxItems = 4;
    public bool showWinScreen = false;

    // 1
    public bool showLossScreen = false;

    private int _itemsCollected = 0;
    public int Items
    {
        // ... No changes needed ...
    }

    private int _playerLives = 3;
    public int Lives
    {
        get { return _playerLives; }
        set {
            _playerLives = value;

            // 2
            if(_playerLives <= 0)
            {
                labelText = "You want another life with that?";
```

```
                    showLossScreen = true;
                    Time.timeScale = 0;
                }
                else
                {
                    labelText = "Ouch... that's got hurt.";
                }
            }
        }

    void OnGUI()
    {
        GUI.Box(new Rect(20, 20, 150, 25), "Player Health: " +
        _playerLives);
        GUI.Box(new Rect(20, 50, 150, 25), "Items Collected: " +
        _itemsCollected);
        GUI.Label(new Rect(Screen.width / 2 - 100, Screen.height -
        50, 300, 50), labelText);

        if (showWinScreen)
        {
            if (GUI.Button(new Rect(Screen.width/2 - 100,
            Screen.height/2 - 50, 200, 100), "YOU WON!"))
            {
                SceneManager.LoadScene(0);
                Time.timeScale = 1.0f;
            }
        }

        // 3
        if(showLossScreen)
        {
            if (GUI.Button(new Rect(Screen.width / 2 - 100,
            Screen.height / 2 - 50, 200, 100), "You lose..."))
            {
                SceneManager.LoadScene(0);
                Time.timeScale = 1.0f;
            }
        }
    }
}
```

Let's break down the code:

1. Declares a `public bool` to keep track of when the GUI needs to display the loss screen button.
2. Adds in an `if` statement to check when `_playerLives` drops below `0`.
   - If it's `true`, the `labelText`, `showLossScreen`, and `Time.timeScale` are all updated.
   - If the player is still alive after an **Enemy** collision, the `labelText` shows a different message.
3. We continually check whether `showLossScreen` is `true`, at which point we create and display a button that matches the dimensions of the win condition button but with different text.
   - When the user clicks the loss button, the level is restarted and `timeScale` is reset to `1` so that input and motion are re-enabled.

Refactoring and keeping it DRY

The **Don't Repeat Yourself** (**DRY**) acronym is the software developer's conscience: it tells you when you're in danger of making a bad or questionable decision, and gives you a feeling of satisfaction after a job well done.

In practice, repeated code is part of programming life. Trying to avoid it by constantly thinking ahead will put up so many roadblocks in your project that it won't seem worth it to continue. A more efficient—and sane—approach to dealing with repeating code is to quickly identify it when and where it occurs and then look for the best way to remove it. This task is called refactoring, and our `GameBehavior` class could use a little of its magic right now.

Time for action – creating a restart method

To refactor the existing level restart code, you'll need to update **GameBehavior** as follows:

```
public class GameBehavior : MonoBehaviour
{
    // ... No changes needed ...

    // 1
    void RestartLevel()
    {
```

```
        SceneManager.LoadScene(0);
        Time.timeScale = 1.0f;
    }

    void OnGUI()
    {
        GUI.Box(new Rect(20, 20, 150, 25), "Player Health: " +
        _playerLives);
        GUI.Box(new Rect(20, 50, 150, 25), "Items Collected: " +
        _itemsCollected);
        GUI.Label(new Rect(Screen.width / 2 - 100, Screen.height - 50,
        300, 50), labelText);

        if (showWinScreen)
        {
            if (GUI.Button(new Rect(Screen.width/2 - 100,
            Screen.height/2 - 50, 200, 100), "YOU WON!"))
            {
                // 2
                RestartLevel();
            }
        }

        if(showLossScreen)
        {
            if (GUI.Button(new Rect(Screen.width / 2 - 100,
            Screen.height / 2 - 50, 200, 100), "You lose..."))
            {
                RestartLevel();
            }
        }
    }
}
```

Let's break down the code:

1. Declares a `private` method named `RestartLevel()` that executes the same code as the win/loss buttons in `OnGUI()`.
2. Replaces both instances of the repeated restart code in `OnGUI()` with a call to `RestartLevel()`.

Hero's trial – refactoring win/lose logic

While you've got your refactoring brain in gear, you might have noticed that the code that updates `labelText`, `showWinScreen/showLossScreen`, and `Time.timeScale` is repeated in the set block of both **Lives** and **Items**. Your mission is to write a `private` utility function that takes parameters for each of the updated variables mentioned and assign them accordingly. Then replace the repeated code in **Lives** and **Items** with a call to the new method. Happy coding!

Pop quiz – AI and navigation

1. How is a **NavMesh** created in a Unity scene?
2. What component identifies a **GameObject** to a **NavMesh**?
3. Executing the same logic on one or more sequential objects is an example of which programming technique?
4. What does the DRY acronym stand for?

Summary

With that, our **Enemy** and **Player** interactions are complete. We can deal damage as well as take it, lose lives and fight back, all while updating the onscreen GUI. Each GameObject is responsible for its own behavior, internal logic, and object collisions, while the game manager keeps track of the variables that govern the games state.

You should feel a sense of accomplishment at this point, especially if you started the book as a total beginner. Getting up to speed with a new programming language while building a working game is no easy trick. In the next chapter, you'll be introduced to some intermediate topics in C#.

Section 3: Leveling Up Your C# Code

Our final section will dive into more intermediate C# concepts, such as interfaces, generics, and design patterns, while also leaving you with resources and further reading for taking your programming journey forward.

The following chapters will be covered in this section:

- Chapter 10, *Revisiting Types, Methods, and Classes*
- Chapter 11, *Exploring Generics, Delegates, and Beyond*
- Chapter 12, *The Journey Continues*

By the end of the book, you will have a working knowledge of Unity, C#, and many of the soft skills it takes to be a programmer or game developer, setting you up to go out into the community and make your mark!

Revisiting Types, Methods, and Classes

10

Since we've programmed our game mechanics and interactions with Unity's built-in classes, now let's we expand on our core C# knowledge and focus on the intermediate applications of the foundation we've laid. We'll revisit old friends—variables, types, methods, and classes—but we'll target their deeper applications and relevant use cases. Many of the topics we'll be covering don't apply to *Hero Born* in its current state, so some examples will be theoretical rather than specific to our current game prototype.

I'll be throwing a lot of new information your way, so if you feel overwhelmed at any point, don't hesitate to revisit the first few chapters to really solidify those building blocks. We'll also be using this chapter to break away from gameplay mechanics and features specific to Unity by focusing on the following topics:

- Intermediate modifiers
- Method overloading
- Using the out and ref parameters
- Working with interfaces
- Abstract classes and overriding
- Extending class functionality
- Namespace conflicts
- Type aliasing

Access Modifier redux

While we've gotten into the habit of pairing the public and private access modifiers with our variable declarations, there remains a laundry list of modifier keywords that we haven't seen. We can't go into detail for each and every one of them in this chapter, but the five that we'll focus on will further your understanding of the C# language and give your programming skills a boost.

This section will cover the first three modifiers in the following list, while the remaining two will be discussed later on in the *OOP Redux* section:

- const
- readonly
- static
- abstract
- override

 You can find a full list of available modifiers at https://docs.microsoft. com/en-us/dotnet/csharp/language-reference/keywords/modifiers.

Constant and read-only properties

There will be times when you need to create variables that store constant, unchanging values. Adding the const keyword after a variable's access modifier will do just that, but only for built-in C# types. A good candidate for a constant value is our maxItems in the GameBehavior class:

```
public const int maxItems = 4;
```

The problem you'll run into with constant variables is that they can only be assigned a value in their declaration, meaning we couldn't leave maxItems without an initial value. However, using the readonly keyword to declare a variable will give us the same unmodifiable value as a constant, while still letting us assign its initial value at any time:

```
public readonly int maxItems;
```

Using the static keyword

We've already gone over how objects, or instances, are created from a class blueprint, and that all properties and methods belong to that particular instance. While this is great for object-oriented functionality, not all classes need to be instantiated and not all properties need to belong to a specific instance. However, static classes are sealed, meaning they cannot be used in class inheritance.

Utility methods are a good case for this situation, where we don't necessarily care about instantiating a particular Utility class instance because all its methods wouldn't be dependent on a particular object.

Time for action – creating a static class

Let's create a new class to hold some of our future methods that deal with raw computations or repeated logic that doesn't depend on the gameplay:

1. Create a new C# script in the `Scripts` folder and name it `Utilities`.
2. Open it up and add in the following code:

```
using System.Collections;
using System.Collections.Generic;
using UnityEngine;

// 1
using UnityEngine.SceneManagement;

// 2
public static class Utilities
{
    // 3
    public static int playerDeaths = 0;

    // 4
    public static void RestartLevel()
    {
        SceneManager.LoadScene(0);
        Time.timeScale = 1.0f;
    }
}
```

3. Delete `RestartLevel()` from `GameBehavior` and modify the `OnGUI()` method with the following code:

```
void OnGUI()
{
    // ... No other changes needed ...

    if (showWinScreen)
    {
        if (GUI.Button(new Rect(Screen.width/2 - 100,
        Screen.height/2 - 50, 200, 100), "YOU WON!"))
        {
            // 5
            Utilities.RestartLevel();
        }
    }

    if(showLossScreen)
    {
        if (GUI.Button(new Rect(Screen.width / 2 - 100,
        Screen.height / 2 - 50, 200, 100), "You lose..."))
        {
            Utilities.RestartLevel();
        }
    }
}
```

Let's break down the code:

1. Adds the **SceneManagement** using directive so we can access the `LoadScene()` method.
2. Declares `Utilities` as a public `static` class that does not inherit from MonoBehavior because we won't need it to be in the game scene.
3. Creates a public `static` variable to hold the number of times our player has died and restarted the game.
4. Declares a public `static` method to hold our level restart logic, which is currently hardcoded in `GameBehavior`.
5. Calls `RestartLevel()` from the static `Utilities` class when either the win or lose GUI button is pressed. Notice that we didn't need an instance of the Utilities class to call the method because it's static, just dot notation.

What just happened?

We've now extracted the restart logic out of `GameBehavior` and put it into its own static class, which makes it easier to reuse across our code base. Marking it as `static` will also ensure that we never have to create or manage instances of the `Utilities` class before we use its class members.

 Non-static classes can have properties and methods that are static and non-static. However, if an entire class is marked as static, all properties and methods must follow suit.

Methods Redux

Methods have been a big part of our code since we learned how to use them in `Chapter 3`, *Diving into Variables, Types, and Methods*, but there are two intermediate use cases we haven't covered yet: method overloading and using the `ref` and `out` parameter keywords.

Overloading methods

The term method overloading refers to creating multiple methods with the same name but with different signatures. A method's signature is made up of its name and parameters, which is how the C# compiler recognizes it. Take the following method as an example:

```
public bool AttackEnemy(int damage) {}
```

The method signature of `AttackEnemy` is written as:

```
AttackEnemy(int)
```

Now that we know the signature of `AttackEnemy`, it can be overloaded by changing the number of parameters or the parameter types themselves, while still keeping its name. This offers added flexibility when you need more than one option for a given operation.

The `RestartLevel()` method in `GameBehavior` is a great example of a situation where method overloading comes in handy. Right now, `RestartLevel()` only restarts the current level, but what happens if we expanded the game to include multiple scenes? We could refactor `RestartLevel()` to accept parameters, but that often leads to bloated and confusing code.

Time for action – overloading the level restart

Let's add an overloaded version of `RestartLevel()`:

1. Open up `Utilities` and add the following code:

```
public static class Utilities
{
    public static int playerDeaths = 0;

    public static void RestartLevel()
    {
        SceneManager.LoadScene(0);
        Time.timeScale = 1.0f;
    }

    // 1
    public static bool RestartLevel(int sceneIndex)
    {
        // 2
        SceneManager.LoadScene(sceneIndex);
        Time.timeScale = 1.0f;

        // 3
        return true;
    }
}
```

2. Open `GameBehavior` and update one of the calls to `Utilities.RestartLevel()` in the `OnGUI()` method to the following:

```
if (showWinScreen)
{
    if (GUI.Button(new Rect(Screen.width/2 - 100, Screen.height/2 -
    50, 200, 100), "YOU WON!"))
    {
        // 4
        Utilities.RestartLevel(0);
    }
}
```

Let's break down the code:

1. Declares an overloaded version of the `RestartLevel()` method that takes in an `int` parameter and returns a **bool**.
2. Calls `LoadScene()` and passes in the **sceneIndex** parameter instead manually hardcoding that value.

3. Returns **true** after the new scene is loaded and the **timeScale** property has been reset.

4. Calls the overloaded **RestartLevel()** method and passes in a **sceneIndex** of 0 when the win button is pressed. Overloaded methods are automatically detected by Visual Studio and are displayed by number, as shown here:

```
if (showWinScreen)
{
    if (GUI.Button(new Rect(Screen.width/2 - 100, Screen.height/2 - 50, 200, 100), "YOU WON!"))
    {
        Utilities.RestartLevel()
    }
                              bool Utilities.RestartLevel(int sceneIndex)    ▲ 2 of 2 ▼
}
```

What just happened?

The functionality in the `RestartLevel()` method is now much more customizable and can account for additional situations or use cases we may need later.

> Method overloading is not limited to static methods, this was just in line with the previous example. Any method can be overloaded as long as its signature differs from the original.

Ref parameters

When we talked about classes and structs back in `Chapter 5`, *Working with Classes, Structs, and OOP*, we discovered that not all objects are passed the same way: value types are passed by copy, while reference types are passed by reference. However, we didn't go over how objects, or values, are used when they're passed into methods as parameter arguments.

By default, all arguments are passed by value, meaning that a variable passed into a method will not be affected by any changes to its value inside the method body. While this works for most cases, there are situations where you'll want to pass in a method argument by reference; prefixing a parameter declaration with either the `ref` or `out` keyword will mark the argument as a reference.

Here are a few key points to keen in mind about using the `ref` keyword:

- Arguments have to be initialized before being passed into a method.
- You don't need to initialize or assign the reference parameter value before ending the method .
- Properties with get or set accessors can't be used as `ref` or `out` arguments.

Time for action – tracking player restarts

Let's create a method to update `playerDeaths` to see method arguments being passed by reference in action:

1. Open up `Utilities` and add in the following code:

```
public static class Utilities
{
    public static int playerDeaths = 0;

    // 1
    public static string UpdateDeathCount(ref int countReference)
    {
        // 2
        countReference += 1;
        return "Next time you'll be at number " + countReference;
    }

    public static void RestartLevel()
    {
        SceneManager.LoadScene(0);
        Time.timeScale = 1.0f;

        // 3
        Debug.Log("Player deaths: " + playerDeaths);
        string message = UpdateDeathCount(ref playerDeaths);
        Debug.Log("Player deaths: " + playerDeaths);
    }

    public static bool RestartLevel(int sceneIndex)
    {
        // ... No changes needed ...
    }
}
```

Let's break down the code:

1. Declares a new `static` method that returns a `string` and takes in an **int** passed by reference.
2. Updates the reference parameter directly, incrementing its value by `1` and returning a string that contains the new value.
3. Debugs the **playerDeaths** variable in `RestartLevel()` before and after it is passed by reference to `UpdateDeathCount()`.

What just happened?

The debug log shows that **playerDeaths** is increased by 1 inside `UpdateDeathCount()` because it was passed by reference and not by value:

 We're using the `ref` keyword in this situation for the sake of the example, but we could have also updated **playerDeaths** directly inside `UpdateDeathCount()`, or added logic inside `RestartLevel()` to only fire `UpdateDeathCount()` when the restart was due to a loss.

Out parameters

The **out** keyword does the same job as `ref` but with different rules:

- Arguments do not need to be initialized before being passed into a method.
- The referenced parameter value does need to be initialized or assigned in the calling method before returning.

For instance, we could replace `ref` with `out` in `UpdateDeathCount()` as long as we initialized or assigned the `countReference` parameter before returning from the method:

```
public static string UpdateDeathCount(out int countReference)
{
    countReference = 1;
    return "Next time you'll be at number " + countReference;
}
```

Methods that use the `out` keyword are better suited to situations where you need to return multiple values from a single function, while the `ref` keyword works best when a reference value only needs to be modified.

OOP redux

An object-oriented mindset is crucial to creating meaningful applications and understanding how the C# language works behind the scenes. The tricky part is that classes and structs by themselves aren't the end of the line when it comes to OOP and designing your own objects. They'll always be the building blocks of your code, but classes are limited to single inheritance, meaning they can only ever have one parent or superclass, and structs can't inherit at all. So the question you should be asking yourself right about now is simple: "How can I create objects from the same blueprint but with different implementations?"

Interfaces

One of the ways to gather groups of functionality together is through interfaces. Like classes, interfaces are blueprints for data and behaviors, but with one important difference: they can't have any actual implementation logic or stored values. Instead, it's up to the adopting class or struct to fill in the values and methods outlined in the interface. The great part about interfaces is that both classes and structs can use them, and there's no upper limit on how many can be adopted by a single object.

For example, what if we wanted our enemies to be able to shoot back at our player when they're in close range? We could create a parent class that both the player and enemy could derive from, which would base them both on the same blueprint. The problem with that approach is that enemies and players won't necessarily share the same behaviors and data. The more efficient way to handle this would be to define an interface with a blueprint for what shootable objects need to do, then have both the enemy and player adopt it. That way, they still have the freedom to be separate, but share common functionality.

Time for action – creating a manager interface

Refactoring the shooting mechanic into an interface is a challenge I'll leave to you, but we still need to know how to create and adopt interfaces in code. For this example, we'll create an interface that all manager scripts would hypothetically need to implement in order to share a common structure:

1. Create a new C# script in the **Scripts** folder, name it `IManager`, and update its code as follows:

```
using System.Collections;
using System.Collections.Generic;
using UnityEngine;

// 1
public interface IManager
{
    // 2
    string State { get; set; }

    // 3
    void Initialize();
}
```

Let's break down the code

1. Declares a **public** interface called `IManager` using the `interface` keyword.
2. Adds a `string` variable to `IManager` named `State` with `get` and `set` accessors to hold the current state of the adopting class.

 All interface properties need at least a `get` accessor to compile, but can have both a `get` and `set` if necessary.

3. Defines a method named `Initialize()` with no return type for the adopting class to implement.

Time for action – adopting an interface

To keep things simple, let's have the game manager adopt our new interface and implement its blueprint:

1. Update GameBehavior with the following code:

```
// 1
public class GameBehavior : MonoBehaviour, IManager
{
    // 2
    private string _state;

    // 3
    public string State
    {
    get { return _state; }
    set { _state = value; }
    }

    // ... No other changes needed ...

    // 4
    void Start()
    {
        Initialize();
    }

    // 5
    public void Initialize()
    {
        _state = "Manager initialized..";
        Debug.Log(_state);
    }

    void OnGUI()
    {
        // ... No changes needed ...
    }
}
```

Let's break down the code:

1. Declares that GameBehavior adopts the IManager interface using a comma and its name, just like with subclassing.
2. Adds a private variable that we'll use to back the public State value we have to implement from IManager.

3. Adds the public `State` variable declared in `IManager` and uses `_state` as its private backing variable.
4. Declares the `Start()` method and calls the `Initialize()` method.
5. Declares the `Initialize()` method declared in `IManager` with an implementation that sets and prints out the public `State` variable.

What just happened?

We specified that `GameBehavior` adopts the `IManager` interface and implemented its `State` and `Initialize()` members. The great part is that the implementation is specific to `GameBehavior`; if we had another manager class we could do the same thing but with different logic:

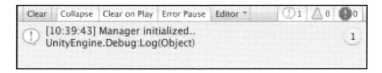

Abstract classes

Another approach to separating out common blueprints and sharing them between objects is the abstract class. Like interfaces, abstract classes cannot include any implementation logic for their methods; they can, however, store variable values. Any class that subclasses from an abstract class must fully implement all variables and methods marked with the `abstract` keyword. They can be particularly useful in situations where you want to class inheritance without having to write out a base class' default implementation.

For example, let's take the `IManager` interface functionality we just wrote and turn it into an abstract base class instead:

```
// 1
public abstract class BaseManager
{
    // 2
    protected string _state;
    public abstract string state { get; set; }

    // 3
    public abstract void Initialize();
}
```

The code breaks down as follows:

1. Declares a new class named `BaseManager` using the `abstract` keyword.
2. Creates two variables:
   - A `protected` string named `_state` that can only be accessed by classes that inherit from `BaseManager`
   - An `abstract string` named `state` with `get` and `set` accessors to be implemented by the subclass
3. Adds `Initialize()` as an `abstract` method, also to be implemented in the subclass.

With this setup, `BaseManager` has the same blueprint as `IManager`, allowing any subclasses to define their own implementations of `state` and `Initialize()` using the `override` keyword:

```
// 1
public class CombatManager: BaseManager
{
    // 2
    public override string state
    {
        get { return _state; }
        set { _state = value; }
    }

    // 3
    public override void Initialize()
    {
        _state = "Manager initialized..";
        Debug.Log(_state);
    }
}
```

Breaking down the code we get:

1. Declares a new class called `CombatManager` that inherits from the `BaseManager` abstract class.
2. Adds the `state` variable implementation from `BaseManager` using the `override` keyword.
3. Adds the `Initialize()` method implementation from `BaseManager` using the override keyword again and sets the protected `_state` variable.

Even though this is only the tip of the iceberg of interfaces and abstract classes, their possibilities should be jumping around in your programming brain. Interfaces will allow you to spread and share pieces of functionality between unrelated objects, leading to a Lego-like assembly when it comes to your code.

Abstract classes, on the other hand, will let you keep the single-inheritance structure of OOP while separating a class' implementation from its blueprint. These approaches can even be mixed and matched, as abstract classes can adopt interfaces just like non-abstract ones.

As always with complicated topics, your first stop should be the documentation. Check it out at `https://docs.microsoft.com/en-us/dotnet/csharp/language-reference/keywords/abstract` and `https://docs.microsoft.com/en-us/dotnet/csharp/language-reference/keywords/interface`.

Class extensions

Let's step away from custom objects and talk about how we can extend existing classes to fit our own needs. The idea behind class extensions is simple: take an existing built-in C# class and add on any functionality that you need it to have. Since we don't have access to the underlying code that C# is built on, this is the only way to get custom behavior out of objects the language already has.

Classes can only be modified with methods, no variables or other entities are allowed. However limiting this might be, it makes the syntax consistent:

```
public static returnType MethodName(this ExtendingClass localVal) {}
```

Extension methods are declared using the same syntax as normal methods, but with a few caveats:

- All extension methods need to be marked as static.
- The first parameter needs to be the `this` keyword followed the name of the class we want to extend and a local variable name.
  - This special parameter lets the compiler identify the method as an extension, and gives us a local reference for the existing class.
  - Any class methods and properties can then be accessed through the local variable.

- It's common to store extension methods inside a static class, which in turn is stored inside its own namespace. This allows you to control what other scripts have access to your custom functionality.

Time for action – extending the string class

Let's take a look at extensions in practice by adding a custom method to the **string** class:

1. Create a new C# script in the `Scripts` folder, name it `CustomExtensions`, and add in the following code:

```
using System.Collections;
using System.Collections.Generic;
using UnityEngine;

// 1
namespace CustomExtensions
{
    // 2
    public static class StringExtensions
    {
        // 3
        public static void FancyDebug(this string str)
        {
            // 4
            Debug.LogFormat("This string contains {0} characters.",
            str.Length);
        }
    }
}
```

Let's break down the code:

1. Declares a namespace named **CustomExtensions** to hold all extension classes and methods.
2. Declares a `static` class named **StringExtensions** for organizational purposes; each individual group of class extensions should follow this setup.

3. Adds a `static` method named `FancyDebug` to the `StringExtensions` class:
   - The first parameter, `this string str`, marks the method as an extension.
   - The `str` parameter will hold a reference to the actual text value that `FancyDebug()` is called from; we can operate on `str` inside the method body as a stand-in for all string literals.
4. Prints out a debug message whenever `FancyDebug` is executed, using `str.Length` to reference the string variable that the method is called on.

Time for action – using an extension method

In order to use our new custom string method, we'll need to include it in whatever class we want to have access to it:

1. Open up `GameBehavior` and update the class with the following code:

```
using System.Collections;
using System.Collections.Generic;
using UnityEngine;

// 1
using CustomExtensions;

public class GameBehavior : MonoBehaviour, IManager
{
    // ... No changes needed ...

    void Start()
    {
        // ... No changes needed ...
    }

    public void Initialize()
    {
        _state = "Manager initialized..";

        // 2
        _state.FancyDebug();

        Debug.Log(_state);
    }

    void OnGUI()
    {
```

```
                    // ... No changes needed ...
            }
        }
```

Let's break down the code:

1. Adds the `CustomExtensions` namespace with a `using` directive at the top of the file.
2. Calls `FancyDebug` on the `_state` string variable with dot notation inside `Initialize()` to print out the number of individual characters its value has.

What just happened?

Extending the entire string class with `FancyDebug()` means that any string variable has access to it. Since the first extension method parameter has a reference to whatever `string` value that `FancyDebug()` is called on, its length will be printed out properly.

 A custom class can also be extended using the same syntax, but it's more common to just add in extra functionality directly into the class if it's one you control.

Namespace Redux

As your applications get more complicated, you'll start to section off your code into namespaces, ensuring that you have control over where and when it's accessed. You'll also use third-party software tools and plugins—to save on time implementing a feature from the ground up that someone else has already made available. Both of these scenarios show that you're progressing in your programming knowledge, but they can also cause namespace conflicts.

Namespace conflicts happen when there are two or more classes or types with the same name, which happens more than you'd think. Good naming habits tend to produce similar results, and before you know it, you're dealing with multiple classes named Error or Extension, and Visual Studio is throwing out errors. Luckily C# has a simple solution to these situations: type aliasing.

Type aliasing

Defining a type alias lets you explicitly choose which conflicting type you want to use in a given class, or create a more user-friendly name for a longwinded existing one. Type aliases are added at the top of the class file with a `using` directive, followed by the alias name and the assigned type:

```
using aliasName = type;
```

For instance, if we wanted to create a type alias to refer to the existing `Int64` type, we could say the following:

```
using CustomInt = System.Int64;
```

Now that `CustomInt` is a type alias for the `System.Int64` type, the compiler will treat it as an Int64, letting us use it like any other type:

```
public CustomInt playerHealth = 100;
```

 You can use type aliasing with your own custom types, or existing ones with the same syntax, as long as they're declared at the top of script files with the other `using` directives.

Pop quiz – leveling up

1. Which keyword would mark a variable as unmodifiable?
2. How would you create an overloaded version of a base method?
3. What is the main difference between classes and interfaces?
4. How would you solve a namespace conflict in one of your classes?

Summary

With new modifiers, method overloading, and object-oriented skills under our belts, we are only one step away from the end of our C# journey. Remember, these intermediate topics are intended to get you thinking about more complex applications of the knowledge you've been gathering throughout this book; don't think of what you've learned in this chapter as all that there is to know on these concepts. Take them as a starting point and continue from there.

In the next chapter, we'll discuss the basics of generic programming, get a little hands-on experience with delegates and events, and wrap up with an overview of exception handling.

11
Exploring Generics, Delegates, and Beyond

The more time you spend programming, the more you start thinking in systems. Structuring how classes and objects interact, communicate, and exchange data are all examples of systems we've worked with so far; the question now is how to make them safer and more efficient.

Since this will be the last practical chapter of the book, we'll be going over examples of generic programming concepts, delegation, event creation, and error handling. Each of these topics is a large area of study in its own right, so take what you learn here and expand on it in your own projects. After we complete our practical coding, we'll finish up with a brief overview of design patterns and how they'll play a part in your programming journey going forward.

We'll cover the following topics in this chapter:

- Generic programming
- Using delegates
- Creating events and subscriptions
- Throwing and handling errors
- Understanding design patterns

Introducing generics

All our code so far has been very specific in terms of defining and using types. However, there will be cases when you need a class or method to treat its entities in the same way, no matter their type, while still being type-safe. Generic programming allows us to create reusable classes, methods, and variables using a placeholder rather than a concrete type.

When a generic class instance is created or a method is used, a concrete type will be assigned, but the code itself treats it as a generic type. You'll see generic programming most often in custom collection types that need to be able to perform the same operations on elements regardless of type. While this might not conceptually make sense yet, it will once when we look at a concrete example in the next section.

 We've already seen this in action with `list`, which is a generic type itself. We can access all its addition, removal, and modification functions no matter whether it's storing integers, strings, or individual characters.

Generic objects

Creating a generic class is the same as a non-generic class with one important difference: its generic type parameter. Let's take a look at an example of a generic `list` class we might want to create to get a clearer picture of how this works:

```
public class SomeGenericCollection<T> {}
```

We've declared a generic collection class named `SomeGenericCollection` and specified that its type parameter will be named `T`. Now, `T` will stand in for the element type that the generic list will store and can be used inside the generic class just like any other type.

Whenever we create an instance of `SomeGenericCollection`, we'll need to specify the type of values it can store:

```
SomeGenericCollection<int> highScores = new SomeGenericCollection<int>();
```

In this case, `highScores` stores integer values and `T` stands in for the `int` type, but the `SomeGenericCollection` class will treat any element type the same.

 You have complete control over naming a generic type parameter, but the industry standard in many programming languages is a capital `T`. If you are going to name your type parameters differently, consider starting the name with a capital `T` for consistency and readability.

Time for action – creating a generic collection

Let's create a more complete generic `list` class to store some fictional inventory items with the following steps:

1. Create a new C# script in the `Scripts` folder, name it `InventoryList`, and update its code to the following:

```
using System.Collections;
using System.Collections.Generic;
using UnityEngine;

// 1
public class InventoryList<T>
{
    // 2
    public InventoryList()
    {
        Debug.Log("Generic list initalized...");
    }
}
```

2. Create a new instance of `InventoryList` in `GameBehavior`:

```
public class GameBehavior : MonoBehaviour, IManager
{
    // ... No changes needed ...

    void Start()
    {
        Initialize();

        // 3
        InventoryList<string> inventoryList = new
        InventoryList<string>();
    }

    // ... No changes to Initialize or OnGUI ...
}
```

Let's break down the code:

1. Declares a new generic class named `InventoryList` with a `T` type parameter.
2. Adds a `default` constructor with a simple debug log to print out whenever a new `InventoryList` instance is created.

3. Creates a new instance of `InventoryList` in `GameBehavior` to hold string values:

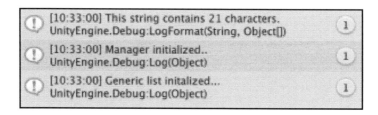

What just happened?

Nothing new has happened here yet in terms of functionality, but Visual Studio recognizes `InventoryList` as a generic class because of its generic type parameter, `T`. This sets us up to include additional generic operations in the `InventoryList` class itself.

Generic methods

A standalone generic method needs to have a placeholder type parameter just like a generic class, which allows it to be included inside either a generic or non-generic class as needed:

```
public void GenericMethod<T>(T genericParameter) {}
```

The `T` type can then be used inside the method body and defined when the method is actually called:

```
GenericMethod<string>("Hello World!");
```

However, if you want to declare a generic method inside a generic class you don't need to specify a new one:

```
public class SomeGenericCollection<T>
{
    public void NonGenericMethod(T genericParameter) {}
}
```

When you call a non-generic method that uses a generic type parameter, there's no issue because the generic class has already taken care of assigning a concrete type:

```
SomeGenericCollection<int> highScores = new SomeGenericCollection<int>();
highScores.NonGenericMethod(35);
```

Generic methods can be overloaded and marked as static, just like non-generic methods. If you want the specific syntax for those situations, check out https://docs.microsoft.com/en-us/dotnet/csharp/programming-guide/generics/generic-methods.

Time for action – adding a generic item

Since we already have a generic class with a defined type parameter, let's add a non-generic method to see them working together:

1. Open up **InventoryList** and update the code as follows:

```
public class InventoryList<T>
{
    // 1
    private T _item;
    public T item
    {
        get { return _item; }
        set { _item = value; }
    }

    public InventoryList()
    {
        Debug.Log("Generic list initialized...");
    }

    // 2
    public void SetItem(T newItem)
    {
        // 3
        _item = newItem;
        Debug.Log("New item added...");
    }
}
```

2. Go into **GameBehavior** and add and item to **inventoryList**:

```
public class GameBehavior : MonoBehaviour, IManager
{
    // ... No changes needed ...

    void Start()
    {
        Initialize();
        InventoryList<string> inventoryList = new
```

```
                    InventoryList<string>();

                    // 4
                    inventoryList.SetItem("Potion");
                    Debug.Log(inventoryList.item);
            }

            public void Initialize()
            {
                    // ... No changes needed ...
            }

            void OnGUI()
            {
                    // ... No changes needed ...
            }
    }
```

Let's break down the code

1. Adds a public `item` variable of the `T` type with a private backing variable of the same type.
2. Declares a new method inside `InventoryList`, named `SetItem`, that takes in a `T` type parameter.
3. Sets the value of `_item` to the generic parameter passed into `SetItem()` and debugs out a success message.
4. Assigns a string value to the `item` property on `inventoryList` using `SetItem()` and prints out a debug log:

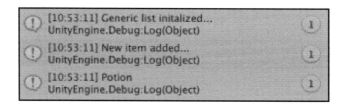

What just happened?

We wrote `SetItem()` to take in a parameter of whatever type our generic `InventoryList` is created with and assign it to a new class property using a public and private backing approach. Since `inventoryList` was created to hold string values, we assigned `"Potion"` to the item property without any issues. However, this method works equally well with any type that an `InventoryList` instance might hold.

Constraining type parameters

One of the great things about generics is that their type parameters can be limited. This might seem counterintuitive to what we've learned about generics so far, but just because a class can contain any type doesn't mean it should necessarily be allowed to.

To constrain a generic type parameter, we need a new keyword and a syntax we haven't seen before:

```
public class SomeGenericCollection<T> where T: ConstraintType {}
```

The `where` keyword defines the rules that `T` must pass before it can be used as a generic type parameter. It essentially says `SomeGenericClass` can take in any `T` type as long as it conforms to the constraining type. The constraining rules aren't anything mystical or scary, in fact they're concepts we've already covered:

- Adding the `class` keyword would constrain `T` to types that are classes.
- Adding the `struct` keyword would constrain `T` to types that are structs.
- Adding an interface, such as `IManager`, as the type would limit `T` to types that adopt the interface.
- Adding a custom class, such as `Character`, would constrain `T` to only that class type.

If you need a more flexible approach to account for classes that subclass, you can use `where T : U`, which specifies that the generic `T` type must be or derive from the `U` type. This is a little advanced for our needs, but you can find more details at `https://docs.microsoft.com/en-us/dotnet/csharp/programming-guide/generics/constraints-on-type-parameters`.

Time for action – limiting generic elements

Just for fun, let's constrain **InventoryList** to only be able to accept types that are classes:

1. Open up **InventoryList** and add in the following code:

```
// 1
public class InventoryList<T> where T: class
{
    // ... No changes needed ...
}
```

What just happened?

Since our `inventoryList` instance, example uses strings, and strings are classes, there's no problem with our code. However, if we were to change the type constraint to struct or an interface name, our generic class would throw an error. This kind of situation is especially useful when you need to safeguard your generic classes or methods against types that you don't want to support.

Delegating actions

There will be times when you need to pass off, or delegate, the actual execution of a method. In C#, this can be accomplished through delegate types, which store references to methods and can be treated like any other variable. The only caveat is that the delegate itself and any assigned method need to have the same signature—just like integer variables can only hold whole numbers and strings can only hold text.

Basic syntax

Creating a delegate is a mix between writing a function and declaring a variable:

```
public delegate returnType DelegateName(int param1, string param2);
```

You start with an access modifier followed the keyword `delegate`, which identifies it to the compiler as a `delegate` type. The `delegate` can have a return type and name like a regular function, as well as parameters if needed. However, this syntax only declares the delegate type itself; in order to use it you need to create an instance like we do with classes:

```
public DelegateName someDelegate;
```

With a delegate type variable declared, it's easy to assign a method that matches the delegate signature:

```
public DelegateName someDelegate = MatchingMethod;

public void MatchingMethod(int param1, string param2)
{
    // ... Executing code here ...
}
```

Notice that you don't have to include the parentheses when assigning MatchingMethod to the someDelegate variable, as it's not calling the method at this point. What it's actually doing is delegating the calling responsibility of MatchingMethod to someDelegate, which means we can call the function as follows:

```
someDelegate();
```

This might seem cumbersome at this point in your C# skills, but I promise you being able to store and execute methods as variables will come in handy down the road.

Time for action – creating a debug delegate

Let's create a simple delegate type to define a method that takes in a string and eventually prints it out using an assigned method:

1. Open up **GameBehavior** and add in the following code:

```
public class GameBehavior : MonoBehaviour, IManager
{
    // ... No other changes needed ...

    // 1
    public delegate void DebugDelegate(string newText);

    // 2
    public DebugDelegate debug = Print;

    // ... No other changes needed ...

    void Start()
    {
        // ... No changes needed ...
    }

    public void Initialize()
    {
        _state = "Manager initialized..";
        _state.FancyDebug();

        // 3
        debug(_state);
    }

    // 4
    public static void Print(string newText)
    {
```

```
            Debug.Log(newText);
    }

    void OnGUI()
    {
        // ... No changes needed ...
    }
}
```

Let's break down the code:

1. Declares a `public delegate` type named `DebugDelegate` to hold a method that takes in a `string` parameter and returns `void`
2. Creates a new `DebugDelegate` instance named `debug` and assigns it a method with a matching signature named `Print()`
3. Replaces the `Debug.Log(_state)` code inside `Initialize()` with a call to the `debug` delegate instance instead
4. Declares `Print()` as a `static` method that takes in a `string` parameter and logs it to the console:

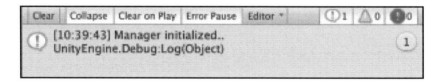

What just happened?

Nothing in the console has changed, but instead of directly calling `Debug.Log()` inside `Initialize()`, that operation has been delegated to the `debug` delegate instance. While this is a simplistic example, delegation is a powerful tool when you need to store, pass, and execute methods as their own types. We've already worked with a real-world example of delegation with the `OnCollisionEnter()` and `OnCollisionExit()` methods, which are Unity methods that are called through delegation.

Delegates as parameter types

Since we've seen how to create delegate types for storing methods, it makes sense that a delegate type could also be used as a method parameter itself. This really isn't that far removed from what we've already done, but it's a good idea to cover our bases.

Time for action – using a delegate argument

Let's see how a delegate type can be used as a method parameter:

1. Update **GameBehavior** with the following code:

```
public class GameBehavior : MonoBehaviour, IManager
{
    // ... No changes needed ...

    void Start()
    {
        // ... No changes needed ...
    }

    public void Initialize()
    {
        _state = "Manager initialized..";
        _state.FancyDebug();

        debug(_state);

        // 1
        LogWithDelegate(debug);
    }

    public static void Print(string newText)
    {
        // ... No changes needed ...
    }

    // 2
    public void LogWithDelegate(DebugDelegate delegate)
    {
        // 3
        delegate("Delegating the debug task...");
    }

    void OnGUI()
    {
        // ... No changes needed ...
    }
}
```

Let's break down the code:

1. Calls `LogWithDelegate()` and passes in our `debug` variable as its type parameter
2. Declares a new method that takes in a parameter of the `DebugDelegate` type
3. Calls the delegate parameter's function and passes in a string literal to be printed out:

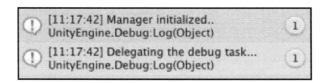

What just happened?

We've created a method that takes in a parameter of the `DebugDelegate` type, which means that the actual argument passed in will represent a method and can be treated as one. Think of this example as a delegation chain, where `LogWithDelegate()` is two steps removed from the actual method doing the debugging, which is `Print()`.

It's easy to get lost with delegation if you miss an important mental connection, so go back and review the code from the beginning of the section and check the docs at `https://docs.microsoft.com/en-us/dotnet/csharp/programming-guide/delegates/`.

Firing events

C# events allow you to essentially create a subscription system based on actions in your games or apps. For instance, if you wanted to send out an event whenever an item was collected, or a player pressed the spacebar, you could do that. However, when an event fires, it doesn't automatically have a subscriber, or receiver, to handle any code that needs to execute after the event action.

Any class can subscribe or unsubscribe to an event through the calling class the event is fired from; just like signing up to receive notifications on your phone when a new post is shared on Facebook, events form a kind of distributed-information superhighway for sharing actions and data across your application.

Basic syntax

Declaring events is similar to declaring delegates in that an event has a specific method signature. In fact, we'll use a delegate to specify the method signature we want the event to have, then create the event using the `delegate` type and the `event` keyword:

```
public delegate void EventDelegate(int param1, string param2);
public event EventDelegate eventInstance;
```

This setup allows us to treat `eventInstance` as a method because it's a delegate type, which means we can send it out at any time by calling it:

```
eventInstance(35, "John Doe");
```

After the event fires, it's up to its subscribers to process it and do any additional operations, which we'll see in the *Handling Event Subscriptions* section next.

Time for action – creating an event

Let's create an event to fire off any time our player jumps:

1. Open up **PlayerBehavior** and add in the following changes:

```
public class PlayerBehavior : MonoBehaviour
{
    // ... No other variable changes needed ...

    // 1
    public delegate void JumpingEvent();

    // 2
    public event JumpingEvent playerJump;

    void Start()
    {
        // ... No changes needed ...
    }

    void Update()
    {
        _vInput = Input.GetAxis("Vertical") * moveSpeed;
        _hInput = Input.GetAxis("Horizontal") * rotateSpeed;

        if(IsGrounded() && Input.GetKeyDown(KeyCode.Space))
        {
            _rb.AddForce(Vector3.up * jumpVelocity,
```

```
        ForceMode.Impulse);

            // 3
            playerJump();
        }
    }

    // ... No changes needed in FixedUpdate,
        IsGrounded, or
        OnCollisionEnter
}
```

Let's break down the code

1. Declares a new `delegate` type that returns `void` and takes in no parameters
2. Creates an `event` of the `JumpingEvent` type, named `playerJump`, that can be treated as a method that matches the delegate's void return and no parameter signature
3. Calls `playerJump` after force is applied in `Update()`

What just happened?

We successfully created a simple delegate type that takes in no parameters and returns nothing, as well as an event of that type to execute whenever the player jumps. Each time the player jumps, the `playerJump` event is sent out to any of its subscribers to notify them of the action.

Handling event subscriptions

Right now, our `playerJump` event has no subscribers, but changing that is simple and very similar to how we assigned method references to delegate types in the last section:

```
someClass.eventInstance += EventHandler;
```

Since events are variables that belong to the class they're declared in, and subscribers will be other classes, a reference to the events-containing class is necessary for subscriptions. The += operator is used to assign a method that will fire when an event executes, just like setting up an out-of-office email. Like assigning delegates, the method signature of the event handler method must match the events type. In our previous syntax example, that means `EventHandler` needs to be the following:

```
public void EventHandler(int param1, string param2) {}
```

In cases where you need to unsubscribe from an event, you simply do the reverse of the assignment using the `-=` operator:

```
someClass.eventInstance -= EventHandler;
```

Event subscriptions are generally handled when a class is initialized or destroyed, making it easy to manage multiple events without messy code implementations.

Time for action – subscribing to an event

Now that our event is firing every time the player jumps, we need a way to capture that action:

1. Go back to **GameBehavior** and update the following code:

```
public class GameBehavior : MonoBehaviour, IManager
{
    // ... No changes needed ...

    void Start()
    {
        // ... No changes needed ...
    }

    public void Initialize()
    {
        _state = "Manager initialized..";
        _state.FancyDebug();

        debug(_state);
        LogWithDelegate(debug);

        // 1
        GameObject player = GameObject.Find("Player");

                // 2
                PlayerBehavior playerBehavior =
    player.GetComponent<PlayerBehavior>();

        // 3
        playerBehavior.playerJump += HandlePlayerJump;
    }

    // 4
```

```
public void HandlePlayerJump()
{
                debug("Player has jumped...");
}

// ... No changes in Print,
        LogWithDelegate, or
        OnGUI ...
}
```

Let's break down the code:

1. Finds the `Player` object in the scene and stores its `GameObject` in a local variable
2. Uses `GetComponent()` to retrieve a reference to the `PlayerBehavior` class attached to the `Player` and stores it in a local variable
3. Subscribes to the `playerJump` event declared in `PlayerBehavior` with a method named `HandlePlayerJump`
4. Declares the `HandlePlayerJump()` method with a signature that matches the events type and logs a success message using the debug delegate each time the event is received:

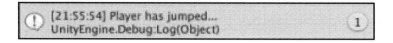

What just happened?

In order to correctly subscribe and receive events in `GameBehavior`, we had to grab a reference to the `PlayerBehavior` class attached to the **Player**. We could have done this all in one line, but it's much more readable when it's split up. We then assigned a method to the `playerJump` event that will execute whenever the event is received, completing the subscription process. Since the **Player** is never destroyed in our prototype, there's no need to unsubscribe to `playerJump`, but don't forget that step if the situation calls for it.

Handling exceptions

Efficiently incorporating errors and exceptions into your code is both a professional and personal benchmark in your programming journey. Before you start yelling, "Why would I add errors when I've spent all this time trying to avoid them!" you should know that I don't mean adding errors to break your existing code. It's quite the opposite—including errors or exceptions and handling them appropriately when pieces of functionality are used incorrectly makes your code base stronger and less prone to crashes, not weaker.

Throwing exceptions

When we talk about adding errors, we refer to the process as *exception throwing*, which is an apt visual analogy. Throwing exceptions is part of something called defensive programming, which essentially means that you actively and consciously guard against improper or unplanned operations in your code. To mark those situations, you literally throw out an exception from a method that is then handled by the calling code.

Let's take an example: say we have an if statement that checks whether a player's email address is valid before letting them sign up. If the email entered is not valid, we want our code to throw an exception:

```
public void ValidateEmail(string email)
{
    if(!email.Contains("@"))
    {
        throw new System.ArgumentException("Email is invalid");
    }
}
```

We use the `throw` keyword to send out the exception, which is created with the `new` keyword followed by the exception we specify. `System.ArgumentException()` will log the information about where and when the exception was executed by default, but can also accept a custom string if you want to be more specific.

`ArgumentException` is a subclass of the `Exception` class and accessed through the preceding `System` class shown. C# comes with many built-in exception types, but we're not going to dig too deeply into those as that's something you can do once you understand the basics of the overall system.

A full list of C# exceptions can be found under the *Choosing Standard Exceptions* heading at `https://docs.microsoft.com/en-us/dotnet/api/ system.exception?view=netframework-4.7.2#Standard`.

Time for action – checking negative scene indexes

Let's keep things simple on our first foray into exceptions and make sure that our level only restarts if we provide a positive scene index number:

1. Open up **Utilities** and add in the following code to the overloaded version of `RestartLevel()`:

```
public static class Utilities
{
    public static int playerDeaths = 0;

    public static string UpdateDeathCount(out int countReference)
    {
        // ... No changes needed ...
    }

    public static void RestartLevel()
    {
        // ... No changes needed ...
    }

    public static bool RestartLevel(int sceneIndex)
    {
        // 1
        if(sceneIndex < 0)
        {
            // 2
            throw new System.ArgumentException("Scene index cannot
            be negative");
        }

        SceneManager.LoadScene(sceneIndex);
        Time.timeScale = 1.0f;

        return true;
    }
}
```

2. Change `RestartLevel()` in the `OnGUI()` method of `GameBehavior` to take in a negative scene index and lose the game:

```
if(showLossScreen)
{
        if (GUI.Button(new Rect(Screen.width / 2 - 100, Screen.height
/ 2 - 50, 200, 100), "You lose..."))
        {
                // 3
                Utilities.RestartLevel(-1);
        }
}
```

Let's break down the code:

1. Declares an `if` statement to check that `sceneIndex` is not less than zero, or a negative number

2. Throws an `ArgumentException` with a custom message if a negative scene index is passed in as an argument

3. Calls `RestartLevel()` with a scene index of -1:

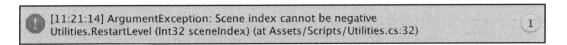

What just happened?

When we lose the game now, `RestartLevel()` is called, but since we're using -1 as the scene index argument, our exception is fired before any of the scene manager logic is executed. This will put a stop to our game as we don't have any other button options at this point, but the safeguard works as expected and doesn't let us take an action that might crash the game (Unity doesn't support negative indexes when loading scenes).

Using a try-catch

Now that we've thrown an error, it's our job to safely handle the possible outcomes that calling `RestartLevel()` might have, because at this point it's not addressed properly. The way to do this is with a new kind of statement, called a try-catch:

```
try
{
    // Call a method that might throw an exception
}
```

```
catch (ExceptionType localVariable)
{
    // Catch all exception cases individually
}
```

The `try-catch` statement is made up of consecutive code blocks that are executed on different conditions, it's like a specialized `if/else`. We call any methods that potentially throw exceptions in the `try` block—if no exceptions are thrown, the code keeps executing without interruption. If an exception is thrown, the code jumps to the `catch` statement that matches the thrown exception, just like `switch` statements do with their cases. `Catch` statements need to define what exception they are accounting for and specify a local variable name that will represent it inside the `catch` block.

 You can chain as many `catch` statements after the `try` block as you need to handle multiple exceptions that might be thrown from a single method.

There's also an optional `finally` block that can be declared after any `catch` statements that will execute at the very end of the `try-catch`, regardless of whether an exception was thrown:

```
finally
{
    // Executes at the end of the try-catch no matter what
}
```

Time for action – catching restart errors

Now that we have an exception being thrown when we lose the game, let's handle it safely:

1. Update **GameBehavior** with the following code and lose the game again:

```
public class GameBehavior : MonoBehaviour, IManager
{
    // ... No variable changes needed ...

    // ... No changes needed in Start
            Initialize,
            Print,
            or LogWithDelegate ...

    void OnGUI()
    {
        // ... No other changes to OnGUI needed ...
```

```
if(showLossScreen)
{
    if (GUI.Button(new Rect(Screen.width / 2 - 100,
    Screen.height / 2 - 50, 200, 100), "You lose..."))
    {
        // 1
        try
        {
            Utilities.RestartLevel(-1);
            debug("Level restarted successfully...");
        }
        // 2
        catch (System.ArgumentException e)
        {
            // 3
            Utilities.RestartLevel(0);
            debug("Reverting to scene 0: " +
e.ToString());
        }
        // 4
        finally
        {
            debug("Restart handled...");
        }
    }
}
}
```

Let's break down the code:

1. Declares the `try` block and moves the call to `RestartLevel()` inside with a `debug` command to print out if the restart is successfully completed without any exceptions
2. Declares the `catch` block and defines `System.ArgumentException` as the exception type it will handle and `e` as the local variable name
3. Restarts the game at the default scene index if the exception is thrown
   - Uses the `debug` delegate to print out a custom message plus the exception information, which can be accessed from `e` and converted to a string with the `ToString()` method

Since e is of the `ArgumentException` type, there are several properties and methods associated with the `Exception` class that you can access. These are often useful when you need detailed information about a particular exception.

4. Adds a `finally` block with a debug message to signal the end of the exception-handling code:

```
[19:07:26] Reverting to scene 0: System.ArgumentException: Scene index cannot be negative
    at Utilities.RestartLevel (Int32 sceneIndex) [0x0000e] in /Users/harrisonferrone/Documents/Gi

[19:07:26] Restart handled...
UnityEngine.Debug:Log(Object)
```

What just happened?

When `RestartLevel()` is called now, our `try` block safely allows it to execute, and if an error is thrown, it's caught inside the `catch` block. The `catch` block restarts the level at the default scene index and the code proceeds to the `finally` block, which simply logs a message for us.

 It's important to understand how to work with exceptions, but you shouldn't get in the habit of putting them in everywhere in your code. This will lead to bloated classes and might affect the game's processing time. Instead, you want to use exceptions where they are most needed—invalidation or data processing rather than game mechanics.

 C# allows you the freedom to create your own exception types to suit any specific needs your code might have, but that's outside the scope of this book. It's just a good thing to remember for the future: https://docs. microsoft.com/en-us/dotnet/standard/exceptions/how-to-create-user-defined-exceptions.

Design pattern primer

Before we wrap up the chapter, I want to talk about a concept that will play a huge part in your programming career if you choose to continue on: design patterns. Googling design patterns or software programming patterns will give you a host of definitions and examples, which can be overwhelming if you've never encountered them before. Let's simplify the term and define a design pattern as follows:

A template for solving programming problems or situations that you'll run into on a regular basis during any kind of application development. These are not hardcoded solutions—they're more like tested guidelines and best practices that can be adapted to fit a specific situation.

There's a lot of history behind how design patterns became an integral part of the programming lexicon, but that excavation is up to you. If this concept strikes a chord with your programming brain, start with *Design Patterns: Elements of Reusable Object-Oriented Software* and its authors, the *Gang of Four*.

 The design patterns we're talking about only apply to OOP languages and paradigms, so they're not universally applicable if you are working in non-OOP environments.

Common game patterns

While there are over 35 documented design patterns broken up over 4 subdomains of functionality, a few of them are uniquely suited to game development. We'll spend a little time here briefly introducing them so you get the hang of what we've been talking about so far:

- The **Singleton** pattern ensures that a given class only has one instance in a program, paired with one global access point (very useful for game manager classes).
- The **Observer** pattern lays out a blueprint for notification systems, alerting subscribers to changes in behavior through events. We've seen this in action on a small scale with our delegate/event examples, but it can be expanded to cover much more ground.

- The **State** pattern allows an object to change its behavior based on what state it's in. This is extremely useful in creating smart enemies who appear to change tactics based on player actions or environmental conditions.
- The **Object Pool** pattern recycles objects that aren't being used anymore, instead of having the program create new ones each time. This would be a great update to the shooting mechanic in *Hero Born* since there could potentially be a lag if too many bullets were spawned on a machine with low processing power.

If you're still unsure of how important design patterns are, know that Unity is built along the lines of the **Composite** (sometimes **Component**) pattern, which allows us to construct complex objects made up of separate functional pieces.

 Again, this barely scratches the surface of what design patterns can do in real-world programming situations. I highly encourage you to dig into their history and application as soon as you finish up the next chapter—they'll be one of your best resources going forward.

Pop quiz – intermediate C#

1. What is the difference between a generic and non-generic class?
2. What needs to match when assigning a value to a delegate type?
3. How would you unsubscribe to an event?
4. Which C# keyword would you use to send out an exception in your code?

Summary

While this chapter brings us to the end of our adventure into C# and Unity 2019, I hope that your journey into game programming and software development has just begun. The topics we've covered have been a level above what we dealt with for the majority of this book, and with good reason. You already know your programming brain is a muscle, which you need to exercise before you can advance to the next plateau. That's all generics, events, and design patterns are, just the next rung.

In the next chapter, I will leave you with resources, further reading, and lots of other helpful (and, dare I say, cool) opportunities and information about the Unity community and the software development industry at large.

Happy coding!

12
The Journey Continues

If you started this book as a complete newcomer to the world of programming, congratulations on your achievement! If you came in knowing a bit about Unity or another scripting language, guess what? Congratulations to you as well. If you began with all the topics and concepts we covered already firmly solidified in your head, you guessed it: congratulations. There is no such thing as an insignificant learning experience, no matter how much or little you may think you came away with. Revel in the time you spent learning something new, even if it only turned out to be a new keyword.

As you reach the end of this journey, it's important to look back at the skills you've acquired along the way. Like all instructional content, there's always more to learn and explore, so this chapter will focus on cementing the following topics and giving you resources for your next adventure:

- Programming fundamentals
- Putting C# into action
- Object-oriented programming and beyond
- Approaching Unity projects
- Unity certifications
- Next steps and future learning

Scratching the surface

While we've done a good amount of work with variables, types, methods, and classes throughout this book, there are still areas of C# that were left unexplored. Learning a new skill shouldn't be a simple bombardment of information without context; it should be a careful stack of bricks, one on top of the other, each building on the foundational knowledge already acquired.

Here are some of the concepts you'll want to look into as you progress in your programming journey with C#, regardless of whether it's with Unity:

- Optional and dynamic variables
- Data queues and stacks
- Debugging approaches
- Concurrent programming
- Networking and RESTful APIs
- Recursion and reflection
- LINQ expressions
- Intermediate and advanced design patterns

Putting the pieces together

As you revisit the code we've written over the course of this book, don't just think about what we accomplished, but also how our project works together. Our code is modular, meaning actions and logic are self-contained; our code is flexible, making it easy to improve and update; our code is clean, making it readable to anyone who looks at it down the line, even if that's us.

The takeaway here is that digesting basic concepts takes time, however clearly they're laid out. Things don't always sink in on the first try, and the "Aha!" moments don't always come when you expect. The key is to keep learning new things, but always with one eye on your foundation.

Remembering your OOP

Object-oriented programming is a vast field of expertise, and its mastery requires not only study but time spent applying its principles to real-life software development. With all the foundational information you learned in this book, it might seem like a mountain you're just better off not even attempting to climb. However, when you feel that way, take a step back and revisit these concepts:

- Classes are blueprints for objects you want to create in code:
  - Classes can contain properties, methods, and events
  - Classes use constructors to define how they are instantiated
  - Instantiating objects from a class blueprint creates a unique instance of that class

- Classes are reference types, while structs are value types
- Classes can use inheritance to share common behavior and data with subclasses
- Classes use access modifiers to encapsulate their data and behaviors
- Classes can be composed of other class or struct types
- Polymorphism allows subclasses to be treated the same as their parent class
  - Polymorphism also allows subclass behaviors to be changed without affecting the parent class

Approaching Unity projects

Even though Unity is a 3D game engine, it still has to follow the principles set down by the code it's built on. When you think of your game, remember that the GameObjects, components, and systems you see on screen are just visual representations of classes and data; they're not magical or unknown—they're the result of taking the programming foundations you've learned in this book to their advanced conclusion.

Everything in Unity is an object, but that doesn't mean all C# classes have to work within the engine's MonoBehavior framework. Don't be limited to thinking in game mechanics; branch out and define your own data or behavior the way your project needs.

Lastly, always ask yourself how you can best separate code out into pieces of functionality instead of creating huge, bloated, thousand-line classes. A related code should be responsible for its own behavior and stored together. That means creating separate MonoBehavior classes and attaching them to the GameObjects they effect. I said it at the beginning of this book and I'll say it again: programming is more a mindset or contextual framework than syntax memorization. Keep training your brain to think like a programmer and eventually, you won't be able to see the world any differently.

Unity features we didn't cover

We managed to shallowly cover many of Unity's core features in Chapter 6, *Getting Your Hands Dirty with Unity*, but there is still so much more the engine has to offer. These topics aren't in any particular order of importance, but if you're going forward with Unity development, you'll want to have at least a passing familiarity with the following:

- Shaders and effects
- Scriptable objects

- Editor extension scripting
- Non-programmatic UI
- ProBuilder and Terrain tools
- PlayerPrefs and saving data
- Model rigging
- Animator states and transitions

You should also go back and dive into the Lighting, Navigation, Particle Effects, and Animation features in the editor.

Next steps

Now that you have a basic literacy level in the C# language, you're ready to seek out additional skills and syntax. This most commonly takes the form of online communities, tutorial sites, and Youtube, but can also include textbooks, such as this one. Transitioning from a reader to an active member of the software-development community can be tough, especially with the abundance of options out there, so I've laid out some of my favorite C# and Unity resources to get you started.

C# resources

When I'm developing games or applications in C#, I always have the Microsoft documentation open in a window I can get to easily. If I can't find an answer to a specific question or problem, I'll start checking out the community sites I use most often:

- C# Corner: `https://www.c-sharpcorner.com`
- Dot Net Pearls: `http://www.dotnetperls.com`
- StackOverflow: `https://stackoverflow.com`

Since most of my C# questions relate to Unity, I tend to gravitate toward those kinds of resources, which I've laid out in the next section.

Unity resources

The best Unity learning resources are at the source; video tutorials, articles, free assets, and documentation are all available from `https://unity3d.com`. However, if you're looking for community answers or a specific solution to a programming problem, give the following sites a visit:

- Unity Answers: `https://answers.unity.com`
- StackOverflow: `https://stackoverflow.com`
- Unify Community wiki: `http://wiki.unity3d.com/index.php`
- Unity Gems: `http://unitygems.com`

There is also a huge video tutorial community on Youtube if that's more your speed; here are my top five:

- Brackeys: `https://www.youtube.com/user/Brackeys`
- quill18creates: `https://www.youtube.com/user/quill18creates`
- Sykoo: `https://www.youtube.com/user/SykooTV/videos`
- Renaissance Coders: `https://www.youtube.com/channel/UCkUIs-k38aDaImZq2Fgsyjw`
- BurgZerg Arcade: `https://www.youtube.com/user/BurgZergArcade`

The Packt library also has a wide variety of books and videos on Unity, Game Development, and C#, available at `https://search.packtpub.com/?query=Unity`.

Unity certifications

Unity now offers various levels of certification for programmers and artists, which will lend a certain amount of credibility and empirical skill ranking to your resume. These are great if you're trying to break into the game industry as a self-taught or non-Computer Science major, and come in the following flavors:

- Certified Programmer
- Certified Artist
- Certified Expert – Gameplay Programmer
- Certified Expert – Technical Artist: Rigging and Animation
- Certified Expert – Technical Artist: Shading and Effects

Unity also provides preparatory courses in-house and through third-party providers to help you get ready for the various certifications. You can find all the information at `https://certification.unity.com`.

Hero's trial – putting something out into the world

The last task I'll offer you in this book is probably the hardest, but also the most rewarding. Your assignment is to take your C# and Unity knowledge and create something to put out into the software- or game-development communities. Whether it's a small game prototype or a full-scale mobile game, get your code out there in the following way:

- Join Github (`https://github.com`)
- Contribute to the Unify Community wiki
- Get active on StackOverflow and Unity Answers
- Sign up to publish custom assets on the Unity Asset Store (`https://assetstore.unity.com`)

Whatever your passion project is, put it out into the world.

Summary

You might be tempted to think that this marks the end of your programming journey, but you couldn't be more wrong. There is no end to learning, only a beginning. We set out to understand the building blocks of programming, the basics of the C# language, and how to transfer that knowledge into meaningful behaviors inside Unity. If you've gotten to this last page, I'm confident we've achieved those goals, and you should be too.

One last word of advice that I wish someone had told me when I first started out: you're a programmer if you say you are. There will be plenty of people in the community that will tell you that you're a noob, that you lack the experience necessary to be considered a "real" programmer, or better yet, that you need some kind of intangible professional stamp of approval. That's absolutely false: you're a programmer if you practice thinking like one on a regular basis, aim to solve problems with efficiency and clean code, and love the act of learning new things. Own that identity; it'll make your journey one hell of a ride.

Completed Game Files

Bullet behavior

This is attached to the **Bullet** prefab, as follows:

```
using System.Collections;
using System.Collections.Generic;
using UnityEngine;

public class BulletBehavior : MonoBehaviour
{
    public float onscreenDelay = 5f;

    void Update ()
    {
        Destroy(this.gameObject, onscreenDelay);
    }
}
```

Camera behavior

This is attached to the **Main Camera** object, as follows:

```
using System.Collections;
using System.Collections.Generic;
using UnityEngine;

public class CameraBehavior : MonoBehaviour
{
    public Vector3 offset;

    private Transform playerPos;

    void Start()
    {
        playerPos = GameObject.Find("Player").transform;
    }

    void LateUpdate()
    {
```

```
            this.transform.position = playerPos.TransformPoint(offset);
            this.transform.LookAt(playerPos);
        }
    }
```

Enemy behavior

This is attached to the **Enemy** object and it requires a parent GameObject with patrol points, as follows:

```
using System.Collections;
using System.Collections.Generic;
using UnityEngine;
using UnityEngine.AI;

public class EnemyBehavior : MonoBehaviour
{
    public Transform player;
    public Transform patrolRoute;
    public List<Transform> locations;

    private int locationIndex = 0;
    private NavMeshAgent agent;
    private int _lives = 3;

    public int Lives
    {
        get { return _lives; }
        private set
        {
            _lives = value;

            if (_lives <= 0)
            {
                Destroy(this.gameObject);
                Debug.Log("Enemy down.");
            }
        }
    }

    void Start()
    {
        agent = GetComponent<NavMeshAgent>();
        player = GameObject.Find("Player").transform;

        InitializePatrolRoute();
```

```
        MoveToNextPatrolLocation();
    }

    void Update()
    {
        if (agent.remainingDistance < 0.2f && !agent.pathPending)
        {
            MoveToNextPatrolLocation();
        }
    }

    void InitializePatrolRoute()
    {
        foreach (Transform child in patrolRoute)
        {
            locations.Add(child);
        }
    }

    void MoveToNextPatrolLocation()
    {
        if (locations.Count == 0)
            return;
        agent.destination = locations[locationIndex].position;
        locationIndex = (locationIndex + 1) % locations.Count;
    }

    void OnTriggerEnter(Collider other)
    {
        if (other.name == "Player")
        {
            agent.destination = player.position;
            Debug.Log("Enemy detected!");
        }
    }

    void OnTriggerExit(Collider other)
    {
        if(other.name == "Player")
        {
            Debug.Log("Enemy out of range.");
        }
    }

    void OnCollisionEnter(Collision collision)
    {
        if(collision.gameObject.name == "Bullet(Clone)")
        {
```

```
                Lives -= 1;
                Debug.Log("Critical hit!");
            }
        }
    }
```

Game behavior

This is attached to an empty GameObject in the scene, as follows:

```
using System.Collections;
using System.Collections.Generic;
using UnityEngine;
using UnityEngine.SceneManagement;
using CustomExtensions;

public class GameBehavior : MonoBehaviour, IManager
{
    public string labelText = "Collect all 4 items and win your freedom!";
    public readonly int maxItems = 4;
    public bool showWinScreen = false;
    public bool showLossScreen = false;

    public delegate void DebugDelegate(string newText);
    public DebugDelegate debug = Print;

    private string _state;
    public string State
    {
        get { return _state; }
        set { _state = value; }
    }

    private int _itemsCollected = 0;
    public int Items
    {
        get { return _itemsCollected; }
        set {
            _itemsCollected = value;

            if (_itemsCollected >= maxItems)
            {
                labelText = "You've found all the items!";
                showWinScreen = true;
                Time.timeScale = 0;
            }
```

```
                else
                {
                    labelText = "Item found, only " + (maxItems -
_itemsCollected) + " more to go!";
                }
            }
        }

    private int _playerLives = 3;
    public int Lives
    {
        get { return _playerLives; }
        set {
            _playerLives = value;

            if(_playerLives <= 0)
            {
                labelText = "You want another life with that?";
                showLossScreen = true;
                Time.timeScale = 0;
            }
            else
            {
                labelText = "Ouch... that's got hurt.";
            }
        }
    }

    void Start()
    {
        Initialize();

        InventoryList<string> inventoryList = new InventoryList<string>();
        inventoryList.SetItem("Potion");
        Debug.Log(inventoryList.item);
    }

    public void Initialize()
    {
        _state = "Manager initialized..";
        _state.FancyDebug();

        debug(_state);
        LogWithDelegate(debug);

        PlayerBehavior playerBehavior =
GameObject.Find("Player").GetComponent<PlayerBehavior>();
        playerBehavior.playerJump += HandlePlayerJump;
```

```
    }

    public void HandlePlayerJump(bool isGrounded)
    {
        if(isGrounded)
        {
            debug("Player has jumped...");
        }
    }

    public static void Print(string newText)
    {
        Debug.Log(newText);
    }

    public void LogWithDelegate(DebugDelegate debug)
    {
        debug("Delegating the debug task...");
    }

    void OnGUI()
    {
        GUI.Box(new Rect(20, 20, 150, 25), "Player Health: " +
_playerLives);
        GUI.Box(new Rect(20, 50, 150, 25), "Items Collected: " +
_itemsCollected);
        GUI.Label(new Rect(Screen.width / 2 - 100, Screen.height - 50, 300,
50), labelText);

        if (showWinScreen)
        {
            if (GUI.Button(new Rect(Screen.width/2 - 100, Screen.height/2 -
50, 200, 100), "YOU WON!"))
            {
                Utilities.RestartLevel();
            }
        }

        if(showLossScreen)
        {
            if (GUI.Button(new Rect(Screen.width / 2 - 100, Screen.height /
2 - 50, 200, 100), "You lose..."))
            {
                try
                {
                    Utilities.RestartLevel(-1);
                    debug("Level restarted successfully...");
                }
```

```
                    catch (System.ArgumentException e)
                    {
                        Utilities.RestartLevel(0);
                        debug("Reverting to scene 0: " + e.ToString());
                    }
                    finally
                    {
                        Utilities.RestartLevel(0);
                        debug("Restart handled...");
                    }
                }
            }
        }
    }
}
```

Item behavior

This is attached to the **Pickup_Item** prefab, as follows:

```
using System.Collections;
using System.Collections.Generic;
using UnityEngine;

public class ItemBehavior : MonoBehaviour
{
    public GameBehavior gm;

    void Start()
    {
        gm = GameObject.Find("Game Manager").GetComponent<GameBehavior>();
    }

    void OnCollisionEnter(Collision collision)
    {
        if (collision.gameObject.name == "Player")
        {
            Destroy(this.transform.parent.gameObject);
            Debug.Log("Item collected!");

            gm.Items += 1;
        }
    }
}
```

Player behavior

This is attached to the **Player** object—it requires a **Rigidbody** and **CapsuleCollider** component, as follows:

```
using System.Collections;
using System.Collections.Generic;
using UnityEngine;

public class PlayerBehavior : MonoBehaviour
{
    public float moveSpeed = 10f;
    public float rotateSpeed = 75f;
    public float jumpVelocity = 5f;
    public float distanceToGround = 0.1f;
    public LayerMask groundLayer;
    public GameObject bullet;
    public float bulletSpeed = 100f;

    public delegate void JumpingEvent(bool isGrounded);
    public event JumpingEvent playerJump;

    private float _vInput;
    private float _hInput;
    private Rigidbody _rb;
    private CapsuleCollider _col;
    private GameBehavior _gameManager;

    void Start()
    {
        _rb = GetComponent<Rigidbody>();
        _col = GetComponent<CapsuleCollider>();
        _gameManager = GameObject.Find("Game
Manager").GetComponent<GameBehavior>();
    }

    void Update()
    {
        _vInput = Input.GetAxis("Vertical") * moveSpeed;
        _hInput = Input.GetAxis("Horizontal") * rotateSpeed;

        if(IsGrounded() && Input.GetKeyDown(KeyCode.Space))
        {
            _rb.AddForce(Vector3.up * jumpVelocity, ForceMode.Impulse);
            playerJump(IsGrounded());
        }
```

```
        //this.transform.Translate(Vector3.forward * vInput *
Time.deltaTime);
        //this.transform.Rotate(Vector3.up * hInput * Time.deltaTime);
    }

    void FixedUpdate()
    {
        Vector3 rotation = Vector3.up * _hInput * Time.fixedDeltaTime;
        Quaternion deltaRotation = Quaternion.Euler(rotation);

        _rb.MovePosition(this.transform.position + this.transform.forward *
_vInput * Time.fixedDeltaTime);
        _rb.MoveRotation(_rb.rotation * deltaRotation);

        if (Input.GetMouseButtonDown(0))
        {
            GameObject newBullet = Instantiate(bullet,
this.transform.position, this.transform.rotation) as GameObject;
            newBullet.transform.Translate(0f, 0.1f, 1.5f);

            Rigidbody bulletRB = newBullet.GetComponent<Rigidbody>();
            bulletRB.velocity = this.transform.forward * bulletSpeed;
        }
    }

    private bool IsGrounded()
    {
        Vector3 endPosition = new Vector3(_col.bounds.center.x,
_col.bounds.min.y, _col.bounds.center.z);
        return Physics.CheckCapsule(_col.bounds.center, endPosition,
distanceToGround, groundLayer, QueryTriggerInteraction.Ignore);
    }

    void OnCollisionEnter(Collision collision)
    {
        if(collision.gameObject.name == "Enemy")
        {
            _gameManager.Lives -= 1;
        }
    }
}
```

Supplementary Classes

Custom extensions

Extends the `string` class with a custom method, as follows:

```
using System.Collections;
using System.Collections.Generic;
using UnityEngine;

namespace CustomExtensions
{
    public static class StringExtensions
    {
        public static void FancyDebug(this string str)
        {
            Debug.LogFormat("This string contains {0} characters.",
str.Length);
        }
    }
}
```

IManager

Declares a common `interface` for all manager scripts to adopt, as follows:

```
using System.Collections;
using System.Collections.Generic;
using UnityEngine;

public interface IManager
{
    string State { get; set; }
    void Initialize();
}
```

Inventory list

Demonstrates a generic class and method implementations, as follows:

```
using System.Collections;
using System.Collections.Generic;
using UnityEngine;

public class InventoryList<T> where T: class
{
    private T _item;
    public T item
    {
        get { return _item; }
        set { _item = value; }
    }

    public InventoryList()
    {
        Debug.Log("Generic list initalized...");
    }

    public void SetItem(T newItem)
    {
        _item = newItem;
        Debug.Log("New item added...");
    }
}
```

Utilities

Demonstrates the uses of a `static` class, as follows:

```
using System.Collections;
using System.Collections.Generic;
using UnityEngine;
using UnityEngine.SceneManagement;

public static class Utilities
{
    public static int playerDeaths = 0;

    public static string UpdateDeathCount(out int countReference)
    {
        countReference = 1;
        return "Next time you'll be at number " + countReference;
```

```
    }

    public static void RestartLevel()
    {
        SceneManager.LoadScene(0);
        Time.timeScale = 1.0f;

        Debug.Log("Player deaths: " + playerDeaths);
        string message = UpdateDeathCount(out playerDeaths);
        Debug.Log("Player deaths: " + playerDeaths);
    }

    public static bool RestartLevel(int sceneIndex)
    {
        if(sceneIndex < 0)
        {
            throw new System.ArgumentException("Scene index cannot be
negative");
        }

        SceneManager.LoadScene(sceneIndex);
        Time.timeScale = 1.0f;

        return true;
    }
}
```

Pop Quiz Answers

Chapter 1 – Getting to Know Your Environment

Pop quiz – dealing with scripts

Q1	Unity and Visual Studio have a symbiotic relationship.
Q2	Unity's *Reference Manual*.
Q3	None, as it is a reference document not a test.
Q4	When the new file appears in the Project tab with the filename in edit mode, which will make the class name the same as the filename and avoid naming conflicts.

Chapter 2 – Introducing the Building Blocks of Programming

Pop quiz – C# building blocks

Q1	Storing a specific type of data for use elsewhere in a C# file.
Q2	Methods store executable lines of code for fast and efficient reuse.
Q3	By adopting `MonoBehavior` as its parent class and attaching it to a GameObject.
Q4	To access variables and methods of components or files attached to different GameObjects.

Chapter 3 – Diving into Variables, Types, and Methods

Pop quiz #1 – variables and types

Q1	Using camelCase.
Q2	Declare the variable as public.
Q3	`public`, `private`, `protected`, and `internal`.
Q4	When an implicit conversion doesn't already exist.

Pop quiz #2 – understanding methods

Q1	The type of data returned from the method, the name of the method with parenthesis, and a pair of curly brackets for the code block.
Q2	To allow parameter data to be passed into the code block.
Q3	The method will not return any data.
Q4	The `Update()` method is called every frame.

Chapter 4 – Using Collections and Controlling Your Code

Pop quiz #1 – If, and, or but

Q1	True or false
Q2	The NOT operator, written with the exclamation mark symbol (!)
Q3	The AND operator, written with double ampersand symbols (&&)
Q4	The OR operator, written with double bars (||)

Pop quiz #2 – all about collections

Q1	The location where data is stored.
Q2	The first element in an array or list is 0, as they are both zero-indexed.
Q3	No – when an array or a list is declared, the type of data it stores is defined, making it impossible for elements to be of different types.
Q4	An array cannot be dynamically expanded once it is initialized, which is why lists are a more flexible choice as they can be dynamically modified.

Chapter 5 – Working with Classes, Structs, and OOP

Pop quiz – all things OOP

Q1	The constructor
Q2	By copy, rather than by reference like classes
Q3	Encapsulation, inheritance, composition, and polymorphism
Q4	GetComponent

Chapter 6 – Getting Your Hands Dirty with Unity

Pop quiz – basic Unity features

Q1	Primitives
Q2	The z axis
Q3	Drag the GameObject into the Prefabs folder
Q4	Keyframes

Chapter 7 – Movement, Camera Controls, and Collisions

Pop quiz – player controls and physics

Q1	`Vector3`
Q2	InputManager
Q3	A `Rigidbody` component
Q4	`FixedUpdate`

Chapter 8 – Scripting Game Mechanics

Pop quiz – working with mechanics

Q1	set or collection, of named constants that belong to the same variable
Q2	Using the `Instantiate()` method with an existing Prefab
Q3	The `get` and `set` accessors
Q4	`OnGUI()`

Chapter 9 – Basic AI and Enemy Behavior

Pop quiz – AI and navigation

Q1	It's generated automatically from the level geometry.
Q2	`NavMeshAgent`
Q3	Procedural programming.
Q4	Don't repeat yourself.

Chapter 10 – Revisiting Types, Methods, and Classes

Pop quiz – leveling up

Q1	Readonly
Q2	Change the number of method parameters or their parameter types.
Q3	Interfaces cannot have method implementations or stored variables.
Q4	Create a type alias to differentiate conflicting namespaces.

Chapter 11 – Exploring Generics, Delegates, and Beyond

Pop quiz – intermediate C#

Q1	Generic classes need to have a defined type parameter.
Q2	The values method and the delegates method signature.
Q3	The -= operator.
Q4	The throw keyword.

Other Books You May Enjoy

If you enjoyed this book, you may be interested in these other books by Packt:

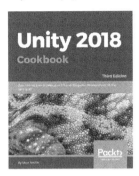

Unity 2018 Cookbook - Third Edition
Matt Smith

ISBN: 9781788471909

- Get creative with Unity's shaders and learn to build your own shaders with the new Shader Graph tool
- Create a text and image character dialog with the free Fungus Unity plugin
- Explore new features integrated into Unity 2018, including TextMesh Pro and ProBuilder
- Master Unity audio, including ducking, reverbing, and matching pitch to animation speeds
- Work with the new Cinemachine and timeline to intelligently control camera movements
- Improve ambiance through the use of lights and effects, including reflection and light probes
- Create stylish user interfaces with the UI system, including power bars and clock displays

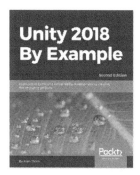

Unity 2018 By Example - Second Edition
Alan Thorn

ISBN: 9781788398701

- Understand core Unity concepts, such as game objects, components, and scenes
- Study level-design techniques for building immersive and interesting worlds
- Make functional games with C# scripting
- Use the toolset creatively to build games with different themes and styles
- Handle player controls and input functionality
- Work with terrains and world-creation tools
- Get to grips with making both 2D and 3D games

Leave a review - let other readers know what you think

Please share your thoughts on this book with others by leaving a review on the site that you bought it from. If you purchased the book from Amazon, please leave us an honest review on this book's Amazon page. This is vital so that other potential readers can see and use your unbiased opinion to make purchasing decisions, we can understand what our customers think about our products, and our authors can see your feedback on the title that they have worked with Packt to create. It will only take a few minutes of your time, but is valuable to other potential customers, our authors, and Packt. Thank you!

Index

3

3D space
  dealing with 132

A

abstract classes 255, 256
access modifiers
  about 45, 244
  constant 244
  private 45
  public 45
  read-only properties 244
  reference 244
  static 245
actions
  delegating 270
advanced modifiers
  internal 45
  protected 45
animating
  in Unity 145
Animation window 145
Animator window
  reference 145
arithmetic operators 54
arrays
  about 81
  indexing 83
  range exceptions 83
  subscripts 83
  syntax 82
assignment operators 55

B

backing variables
  adding 202

base constructors
  about 114
  calling 114, 115
Brackeys
  reference 291
built-in types, C#
  reference 47
BurgZerg Arcade
  reference 291

C

C# class
  looking up 22
C# Corner
  reference 290
C# exceptions
  reference 279
C# files
  broken sync, fixing 19
  opening 18
  syncing 19
C# resources
  locating 22
C# scripts
  creating 17
  naming mismatches 18
  working with 16
C#
  resources 290
  using, with Unity 16
  writing 42
camera 163
camera behavior
  scripting 163, 164, 165
character class
  creating 100
Character Controller component

reference 156
class fields
  adding 102
class methods
  declaring 105
class objects
  instantiating 101
classes
  about 33, 257
  Character class, creating 101
  defining 100
  example 34
  interaction, with components 39
  syntax 100
  versus struct 108
clips
  creating 146, 147
collections
  about 81
  arrays 81
  dictionary 86
  lists 84
Collider components 172
Collider triggers
  using 176
collision logic
  item, picking up with 173
collisions 172
comments
  about 35
  adding 36
  multiple-line comments 35
  single-line comments 35
Common Type System (CTS) 47
components, on GameObjects
  about 119
  current Transform component, accessing 120
  syntax 120
composition 115
constructors
  starting properties, specifying 104
  using 103
curves 150
custom types 50

D

debug delegate
  creating 271, 272
debugging
  simple debugging 43
delegate argument
  using 273, 274
delegates
  as parameter types 272
  syntax 270
design documentation, game
  Game Design Document (GDD) 128
  One-Page 129
  Technical Design Document 128
design patterns 285
dictionary pairs
  working with 88, 89
dictionary
  about 86
  inventory, setting up 87
  syntax 87
directional lights 144
directives
  using 212
documentation
  accessing 19
Don't Repeat Yourself (DRY) 105, 237
Dot Net Pearls
  reference 290
dot notation 39
drag and drop
  about 123
  variables, accessing in Unity 123

E

Editor tools
  Hand 137
  Move 137
  Rect Transform 137
  Rotate 137
  Scale 137
  Transform Gizmos 137
empty objects
  using 138

encapsulation
  about 112
  reset, adding 112
enemy agents
  moving 222
  setting up 220, 221
enemy game mechanics
  about 229
  agent's destination, modifying 230, 231
  bullet collisions, detecting 233, 234
  game manager, updating 235
  player health, lowering 231, 233
  seek and destroy 230
enemy
  creating 176
  moving 225, 226
enumeration
  about 184
  keyboard input, capturing with KeyCode enum
    186, 187
  types 185
event subscriptions
  handling 276, 277
events
  creating 275
  firing 274
  subscribing to 277, 278
  syntax 275
exceptions
  handling 279
  throwing 279
extension method
  about 257
  using 259, 260

F

FirstPersonController prefab
  reference 156
for loops
  about 90
  elements, finding 92
ForceMode
  reference 187
foreach loops 93
Frames Per Second (FPS) 66

functional variations 117

G

Game Design Document (GDD) 128
game design
  about 128
  art style 128
  concept 128
  control schemes 128
  core mechanics 128
  Hero Born One-Page 129
  story 128
  win and lose conditions 128
game levels
  building 130
  finishing 142
game manager
  about 198
  creating 199, 200
game patterns 285
game
  pausing 212
  restarting 214
  winning 210, 211
GameBehavior
  restart method, creating 237
GameObject buildup
  bullets, destroying 197
  managing 197
GameObjects
  about 118
  components, finding on objects 122
  finding 121
  moving, ways 156
generic collection
  creating 265
generic elements
  limiting 269
generic item
  adding 267, 268
generic methods
  about 266
  reference 266
generic objects 264
generic type parameter

constraining 269
generics 264
get properties 200
ground plane
  creating 131

H

health pickup
  creating 142
Hero Born One-Page 129

I

if-else statements
  about 70
  example 72, 73
  multiple conditions, evaluating 75
  nesting statements 74
  NOT operator, using 73, 74
  syntax 70, 71, 72
  treasure chest experiment 76
incorrect type operations
  executing 55, 56
inheritance 113
instance 101
instantiation 101
interface
  adopting 254
interfaces
  about 252
  adopting 254
interpolated strings
  creating 48
item collection
  updating 203, 204
item
  picking up, with collision logic 173
iteration statements
  about 90
  for loops 90
  foreach loops 93
  while loops 95

J

jumps
  adding 184

K

key-value pairs
  looping through 94
keyframes
  recording 147
keywords 44

L

layer mask calculations
  in utility function 190, 192
layer masks
  working with 188
level restart
  overloading 248
Light component
  properties 144
light probe groups
  reference 144
lighting
  basics 143
lightmap 143
lights
  creating 144
  directional lights 144
  point lights 144
  spotlights 144
lists
  about 84
  example 85
  methods 85, 86
  syntax 84
locations
  patrolling between 227, 228

M

manager interface
  creating 253
materials
  about 133
  ground color, modifying 134
method parameters
  adding 61, 62
methods driven actions 31
methods

about 30, 31, 247
access modifiers 57
as arguments 65
as placeholders 31
creating 32, 33
defining 56
logic detours 59
naming conventions 59
overloading methods 247
parameters 58
simple method, defining 58
syntax 56
modifiers
reference 45
MonoBehavior
about 38
in Scripting API 39
MonoBehaviour methods
reference 65

N

namespace 212, 260
navigation
components 218
in Unity 218
NavMesh
about 218
setting up 219, 220
NavMeshAgent 218
NavMeshObstacle 218
negative scene indexes
checking 280, 281
NVIDIA PhysX engine
Collider components 167
Rigidbody components 167

O

object layers
setting 188, 189
Object Pool pattern 286
object-oriented programming (OOP)
about 99, 111, 252, 288
abstract classes 255, 257
applying, in Unity 118
classes 257

composition 115
encapsulation 112
extension methods 257
inheritance 113
interfaces 252
key points 117
polymorphism 116
objects
as class 118
instantiating 193
Observer pattern 285
operators
about 54
arithmetic operators 54
assignment operators 55
out parameters 251
overloading methods 247

P

parameters
arguments, assigning 61
specifying 60
Particle System effects
about 152
reference 152
sparkle effects 152
patrol locations
referencing 222, 223, 225
player capsule
creating 157
player input
obtaining 159, 160
Player Polish
about 205
Graphical User Interfaces 205
UI elements, adding 206
player properties
tracking 199
player restarts
tracking 250
player
locomotion 161, 162, 163
moving 156
setting up 156
point lights 144

polymorphism 116
Precomputed Realtime Global Illumination
  reference 143
prefabs
  updating 141
  working with 139
primitives
  creating 130
procedural programming 222
project hierarchy
  organizing 138
projectile prefab
  creating 193, 194
protected keywords
  reference 44

Q

quill18creates
  reference 291

R

realtime lighting 143
ref keyword 250
ref parameters 249
reference types
  about 109
  example 109
reflection probes
  reference 144
Renaissance Coders
  reference 291
restart errors
  catching 282, 283, 284
return type
  adding 63
return values
  capturing 64
  specifying 62
  using 63
Rigidbody
  accessing 169, 170
  in motion 168, 169
  moving 170, 171

S

selection statements
  about 70
  if-else statements 70
  switch statement 77
set properties 200
shooting mechanic
  adding 194, 197
shooting projectiles 193
Singleton pattern 285
space
  local space 133
  world space 133
sparkle effects
  adding 152, 153
spin
  smoothing 151
spinning animation 148, 149
spotlights 144
StackOverflow
  reference 290, 291
State pattern 286
statements 42
static class
  creating 245, 246, 247
static keyword
  using 245
string class
  extending 258, 259
struct
  about 107
  limitations 107
  syntax 107
  versus classes 108
  weapon struct 107, 108
switch statement
  about 77
  fall-through cases 79, 80
  pattern matching 78
  syntax 77
Sykoo
  reference 291

T

tangents 150
Terrain Tool
 reference 130
Terrain Toolkit 2017
 reference 130
trigger events
 capturing 177, 178, 179
triggers 176
try-catch
 using 281
turrets
 creating 140
type aliasing 261
type conversions
 about 49
 explicit conversions 49
 implicit conversions 49
type-only declaration 44
types
 built-in types 47
 custom types 50
 inferred declarations 50
 key points 51
 working with 46, 48

U

Unity 2019
 about 12
 personal plan 13
Unity Answers
 reference 291
Unity Community wiki
 reference 291
Unity editor
 Console 15
 Game View 15
 Hierarchy Window 15
 Inspector Window 15
 navigating 14
 Project window 15
 Scene View 15
 Toolbar 15
Unity Gems

 reference 291
Unity physics
 working with 166
Unity projects
 approaching 289
Unity's documentation
 accessing 19
 Reference Manual, opening 20
 Scripting Reference, using 21
Unity, methods
 about 65
 start method 65
 update method 66
Unity
 C#, using with 16
 certifications 291
 features 289
 object-oriented programming (OOP), applying in 118
 objects, animating 145
 project, creating 14
 reference 12
 resources 291
 scripts, handling 36
utility function 184

V

value types
 about 110
 example 110
variable scope
 about 52, 53
 class 52
 global 52
 local 52
 member 52
variables
 as placeholders 27
 best practices 51, 52
 creating 28, 29
 defining 26
 in Inspector panel 37, 38
 naming 27, 51
 private, making 46
 syntax 43

type and value declarations 44
type-only declarations 44
value, modifying 30
vectors
  about 158, 159
  reference 158
Visual Studio 16
Visual Studio Editor 17

W

while loops
  about 95
  example 96
white-boxing 135
win and loss conditions 209
window's functionality, Unity docs
  reference 16

68151804R00187

Made in the USA
Columbia, SC
04 August 2019